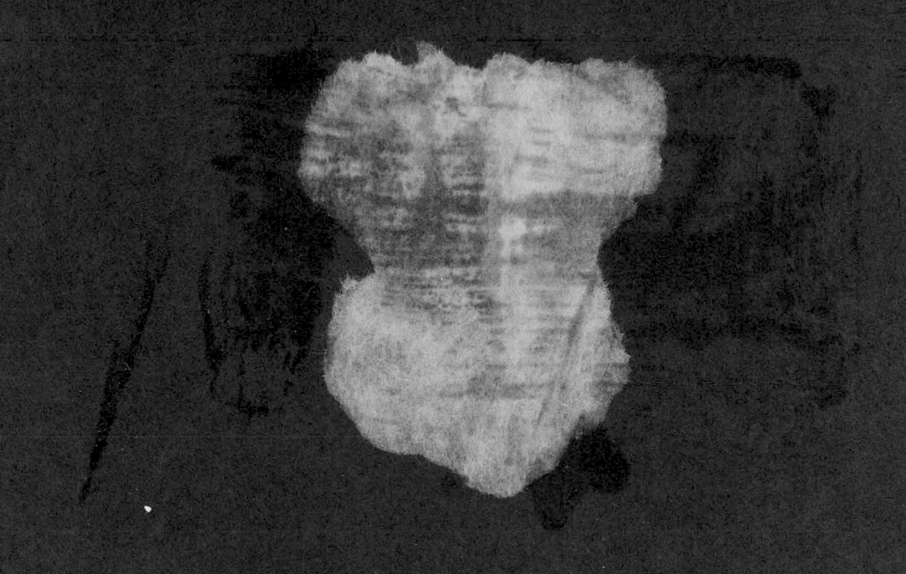

PEOPLE IN THE WAY

J.W. WILSON

THE HUMAN ASPECTS OF THE COLUMBIA RIVER PROJECT

People in the way

UNIVERSITY OF TORONTO PRESS

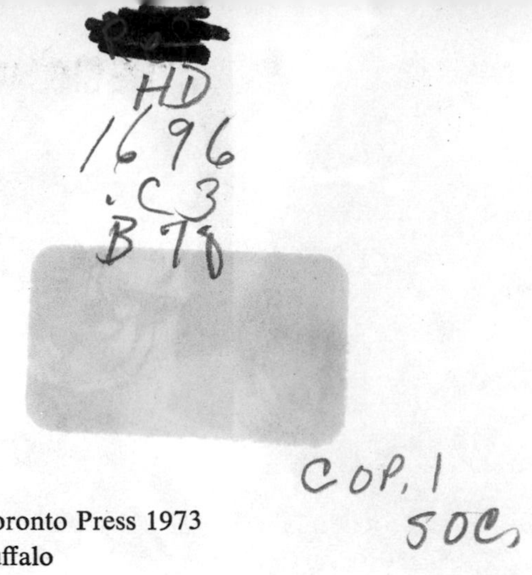

Toronto and Buffalo
Printed in Canada
ISBN 0-8020-5285-1
LC 72-95792

Photographs on title-page spread
courtesy of the National Film Board
Photographs between pp. 82 and 83
courtesy of the British Columbia Hydro
and Power Authority

To the people of the Arrow Lakes, who have taught me much:
may they live happily ever after.

Contents

Photographs

between pages 82 and 83

Diagrams

Preface

This is the story of the attempt to deal with the problems of human displacement and resettlement resulting from the Columbia River project. It is not a technical study, nor one which views its subjects through the lens of an academic discipline. Rather, it is intended to serve as a Canadian case study for students in fields such as engineering, planning, geography, and public administration. In it they will see how, in practice, all their fields have common ground in history, politics, and human behaviour, and how dependent they are on them. They will sense too how cloudy our crystal balls are and how frequently 'the best laid plans ... gang aft agley.'

This has been a difficult book to write, partly for the reason implicit in the old saying that human fashions have always been governed by two urges – the admitted urge to dress and the unadmitted urge to undress. Such impulses are hard enough for any writer to resist, but they were unusually strong in my case because the Arrow Lakes experience was not a clinical exercise for me. It brought me too close to the suffering of people I knew and liked. Nevertheless as an employee of the British Columbia Hydro and Power Authority (I was responsible for resettlement planning for the 20 months from May 1964 to February 1966), I knew Hydro's problems and frustrations too. As a result of these involvements I frequently had strong feelings on one side or the other. But my real task now is not to weep or laugh, or to judge, but to understand.

Much of my dilemma was resolved in the course of writing and rewriting certain chapters of this book, but strong feelings remained nevertheless. Parts of the book are somewhat critical of both BC Hydro and the Social Credit government of British Columbia. I hope that these criticisms are not unfair. Another dilemma was the use of the first person in writing. But there was no real choice. Not to use the first person in some places would have been artificial and flimsy. And besides, I have long inveighed against the depressing impersonality and sterility of so much writing in the public service, holding that personal judgment should not be obscured when it need not be. So 'I' it is.

I am grateful to the British Columbia Hydro and Power Authority for giving me unrestricted access to its files; to J.W. Milligan, W.D. Mitchell, and R.W. Gross for their generous assistance; to Dr Hugh Keenleyside for many enlightening comments arising from his long and intimate experience with the Columbia River project; to my Columbia colleague, Gerry Fitz patrick, for his usual sturdy comments; to the Canada Council for financing my field work in 1970; to Al Hildebrand of the University of Waterloo for the excellent maps and diagrams; to many others who helped in various significant ways; and most of all to the people of the Arrow Lakes, who not only opened their doors to this 'Hydro man' but even filled out his questionnaires.

This book has been published with the help of a grant from the Social Science Research Council of Canada, using funds provided by the Canada Council, and a grant from the Publications Fund of the University of Toronto Press.

J.W. WILSON
Waterloo, 1972

PEOPLE IN THE WAY

1
The setting

The Columbia River is a giant by any standards. An international river, it flows through Canada for 500 of its 1200 miles before spilling into the Pacific Ocean near Portland, Oregon (Diagram 1). It drains an area of more than 250,000 square miles, more than twice the area of the British Isles; from its head waters to the sea it fall through a height of half-a-mile; and at its peak it has produced flood flows at the mouth of more than a million cubic feet per second. In short, it is a river of awesome power; and before it was harnessed it wrought frightful destruction along its banks, as in 1948 when it drove 38,000 Americans from their homes and killed 41.

By 1950 a great deal of its potential power in the United States had already been captured by the construction of many dams, including the Grand Coulee Dam. But these could not realize their full potential until more of the run-off above them was captured by the construction of additional dams, and this was now possible only on the upper reaches of the river in Canada. How this was agreed by Canada and the United States after many years of study and negotiation is told in chapter 3. Suffice it to say here that in 1964 the Canadian Parliament ratified the Columbia River Treaty and thereby undertook to build three storage dams on the Columbia River. One of these is the Arrow dam (now known as the Hugh Keenleyside Dam) at the foot of the Arrow Lakes.

The Arrow Lakes area lies about 250 crow-miles from the coast, roughly halfway between Vancouver and Calgary (Diagram 1), and stretches from Castlegar, 20 miles north of the United States border, to Revelstoke, 150 miles further north (Diagram 2). It is very rugged country and the mountains climb as high as 8000 feet, often rising directly out of the lakes. It

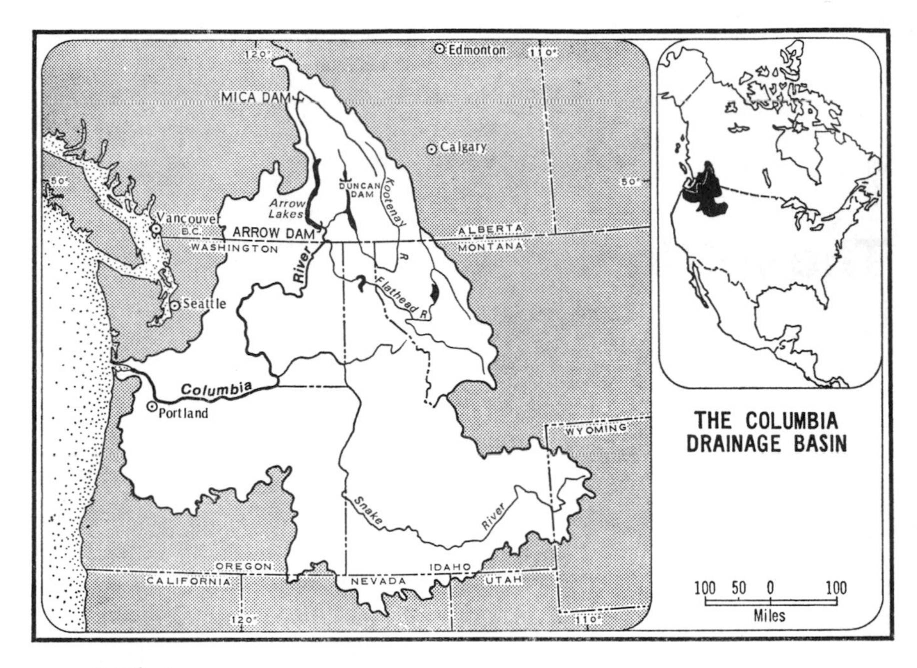

DIAGRAM 1

is also varied and beautiful country, with narrow green valleys setting off the massiveness of the mountains. To the north, snow-capped peaks stand aloof behind the lakeside hills, their snow and rock an exciting contrast against the soft green below. Sunset is a memorable time in the lake country, with golden sunlight on one shore and quiet shadow on the other followed by the most exquisite shadings of darkness on land and water. The evening view from Nakusp to the folded mountains at the Narrows is one whose softness I never recall without emotion.

Before the dam was built there were three main areas of settlement separated by long stretches of inhospitable shoreline: the northern area between Revelstoke and Arrowhead, the southern area between Castlegar and Renata, and between them the central area from Nakusp to Edgewood (Diagram 2). In 1954 these three areas, which for decades had been linked by boat service, were isolated from one another when the last of the sternwheelers, the *Minto*, was taken out of service. In terms of communications this left the north and south areas in reasonable shape, since they were conveniently linked by road to the main highway system of the province. The

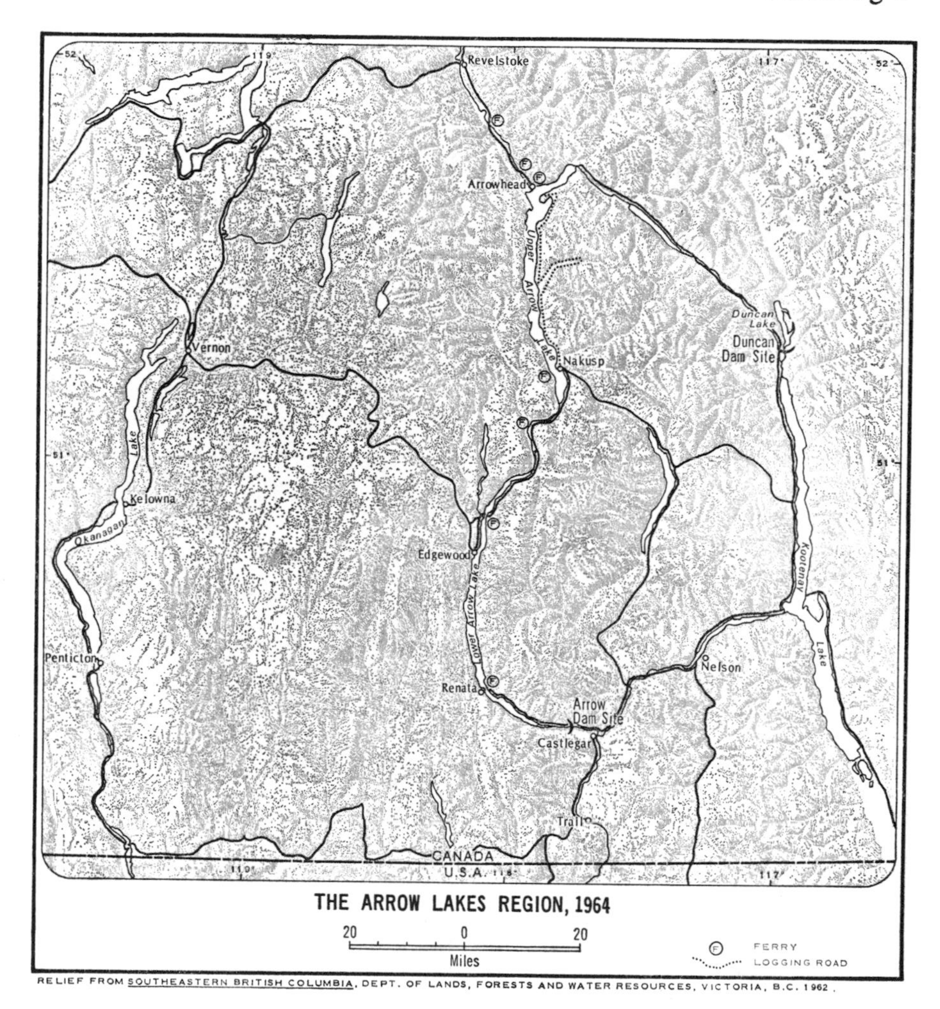

RELIEF FROM SOUTHEASTERN BRITISH COLUMBIA, DEPT. OF LANDS, FORESTS AND WATER RESOURCES, VICTORIA, B.C. 1962.

DIAGRAM 2

central area, however, was left ill served, being connected in the west to Vernon by a sinuous eighty-mile road across the Monashee Mountains, and in the south-east to Nelson and Castlegar by a tortuous road almost a hundred miles long.

The people displaced by the Columbia project in the northern section gravitated naturally to Revelstoke, and those in the southern section to the Castlegar area, for in neither section was there enough land to house a

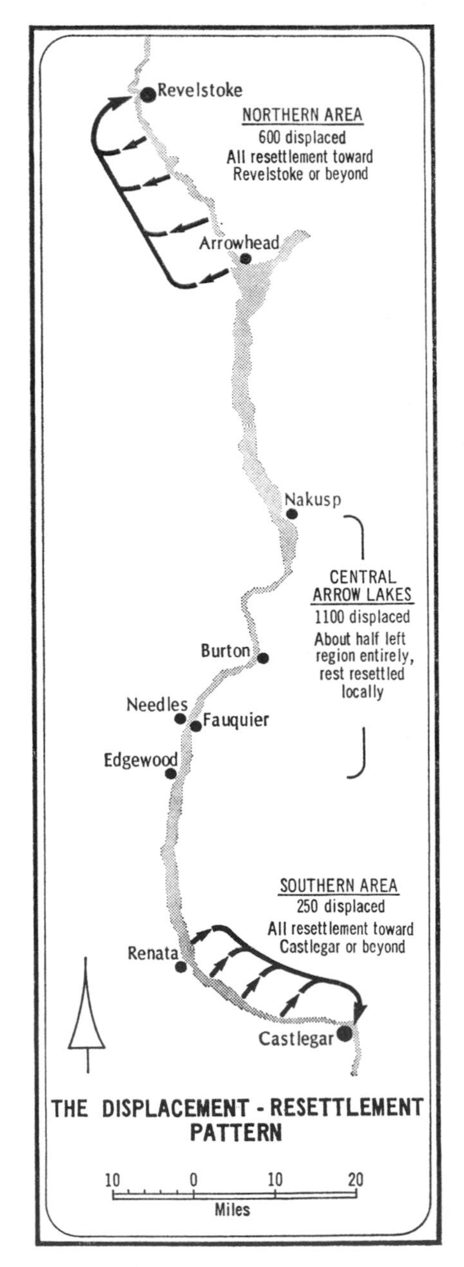

DIAGRAM 3

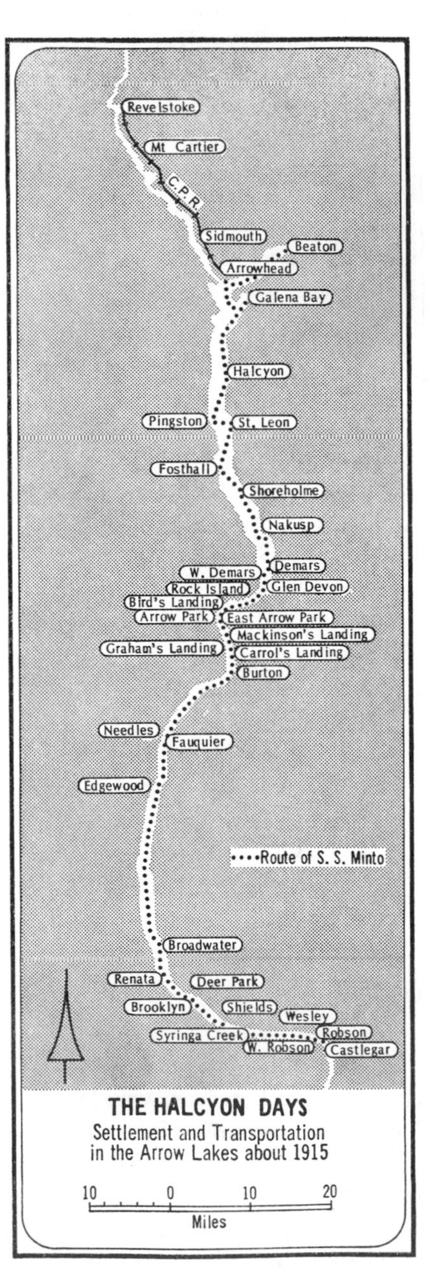

DIAGRAM 4

new community (Diagram 3). In consequence the task of resettlement arose only in the central area, and the main task of regional development lay in trying to improve the area's communications with 'the outside.' Thus this study concentrates on the area between Nakusp and Edgewood.

But this is not an abstract tale of areas, communications, and displacements; it tells of a valley and its people and their tribulations when British Columbia's 'progress' overtook them. By today's largely urban standards both were distinctive and deserve a chapter to themselves.

2
The way it was

The Arrow Lakes region in 1964 hid more than it revealed to the superficial eye. In the first place it had been stagnant for decades, the population between Edgewood and Revelstoke (inclusive) having increased, according to the census, only from 6150 to 6475 between 1921 and 1961. In fact its halcyon days were far behind it, having occurred before the First World War. In those days more than thirty small settlements adorned the shores of the lakes (Diagram 4). Many of these have since disappeared without trace; others still yield unexpected evidence such as fire hydrants and rotted timber sidewalks long overgrown by the long grass and bush.

The thread connecting these communities was the lake itself, on which sternwheelers plied busily, shuttling between railheads at Arrowhead in the north and Robson in the south, a distance of almost a hundred miles. In the heyday of the lakes more than half-a-dozen sternwheelers were in operation, not to mention ferries and barges.

Before the First World War the Arrow Lakes region lived primarily on lumbering and mining and contained, at Arrowhead, the largest sawmill of its day in the British Empire. The economy of the Lakes depended on the power of the horse, and to feed the teams hay was produced locally in considerable quantities. Tree fruits and milk were also produced. Farm lands were advertised and sold, not always accurately or ethically, in Winnipeg and London, and many immigrants settled from the United Kingdom. However, it became clear that for the production of fruit the Arrow Lakes climate was inferior to that of the adjacent Okanagan Valley and the crops were produced too late to be competitive on the market.

With the onset of war the English settlers 'joined up' in force and many did not return. Lumbering on the lakeshores declined in the twenties and the Canadian Pacific Railway reduced its lake services. During the thirties, despite total unemployment in a technical sense, hardship is said to have been tolerable, because the small holdings were able to provide a subsistence living.

In the forties the lumber-based economy revived following the granting of a tree farm licence to Celgar Limited, and many owners of small holdings joined the company's logging force. Many of their holdings were allowed to go wild, creating a misleading impression of general poverty.

In 1954 the last of the sternwheelers, the faithful *Minto*, was taken out of commission. The lake then ceased to be the main street of the region, and in effect the Arrow Lakes became not one region but three, focused on Revelstoke, Castlegar, and Nakusp respectively. The area also became totally dependent on the road 'system' (a euphemism of the first order), although traffic across the lakes continued to be accommodated by six ferries, a pleasant if somewhat archaic mode of travel in the 1960s.

The stock of usable land was limited to about fifty square miles, the only sizable area being that between Revelstoke and Arrowhead, most of it uncleared and of poor quality.[1] The lakeshore lands were either long, narrow strips or little shelves of land, and of the total only about ten square miles had been developed. From any but a purely local perspective it could scarcely be said that a significant amount of agricultural land was to be inundated by the Arrow Lakes reservoir, nor was much of that being farmed by any ordinary definition of the word.[2] This does not mean, however, that it was not valuable to its owners; it was frequently said that a small holding was worth 500 dollars per person per year, and recent studies in Newfoundland suggest that this is not an unreasonable estimate [12]. If home-raised milk, meat, vegetables, and fruit are added to bartered goods, lumber and fuel from the forests, a mortgage-free house, negligible taxes, and even a minimal cash income, the result may be a very satisfactory living, different though it is from the wage-based domestic economy of the typical city-dweller.

Overall, the impression given to the visitor in 1964 was that of a Rip van Winkle valley, much of it uncleared, uncultivated, unkempt, and dotted with weathered houses of yesterday. Much of the land had been allowed to

1 This excludes the Inonoaklin Valley and the Brouse area, neither of which was affected by the Columbia development.

2 Only five farms were recorded by the 1951 census, a farm by that definition being a holding of at least three acres, or of one to three acres yielding agricultural products valued in 1950 at 250 dollars or more.

go to seed even before the first alarm was given in 1954 by the Kaiser proposal.[3] Nevertheless it was a firmly held tenet of the inhabitants that the constant threat of the Columbia development had perpetuated the neglect of the valley thereafter, despite the stabilization of the local economy.

So much for the land. What of the people? To understand Hydro's task it is necessary to understand them at least a little, and the first thing to record is their diversity, especially in education and experience. While almost all were in some way closely bound up with the land through logging or farming, there were a few among them with, for example, university and English public school education, considerable experience of business and government far beyond the valley, and extensive foreign travel. On the other hand there were many people who had worked in or around the forests for fifty years in essentially manual jobs, and whose experience was much more limited. To ignore this diversity would be to court misunderstanding throughout this book. In 1964 there was no unemployment – among the employables, that is. Celgar's logging operations, centred in Nakusp and based on sustained yield management of 2.5 million acres of Crown land, saw to that. (The logging operation provided the raw material for Celgar's modern sawmill and pulpmill just south of the Arrow dam.)

There were many not employed, however – mostly older people, of whom the smaller communities had a high proportion. These were mainly people who had lived in the valley for decades and for whom the whole landscape, natural and human, was a comfortable tapestry of things familiar. Many of them were widows or widowers; many depended on old age or war service pensions; some lived on welfare payments; many bore the stigmata of age and neglect in the form of chronic illnesses; and many lived in solitude, being scarcely visible to the casual visitor. To them the valley was a kind place; though not developed in terms of commercial efficiency, the land still met many of their needs, many of their homes were free of mortgages, and neighbours were usually kind and helpful in matter-of-fact rural fashion.

For some at least the valley was more than a kind place: it was a chosen place. And to anyone who knew the lakes at all and who did not view them through urban-tinted glasses, that was understandable. For it was not only, in rugged Canadian terms, a lovely place, as no one seeing its velvet-shadowed summer evenings could possibly forget. It was also a place of casual ways and little pretence, where individuality could find expression

3 This was a proposal by the Kaiser Aluminum Company of the US to build a low dam across the lower end of the Arrow Lakes. It was vetoed by the government of the day in Ottawa, despite its acceptance by Premier Bennett.

largely untrammelled. As one resident put it: 'The good thing about this country is you can do as you damn well please. And that's the way the people feel about it. They're mighty independent.'

The Arrow Lakes are a man's world and the men are what the press likes to call 'two-fisted' (what else?). Nature is still their antagonist, and while they now have the diesel caterpillar as an ally (which merely enables them to do more, faster), they are still the handy, practical people they always were, moving rocks, trees, and dirt around in matter-of-fact fashion.[4] Theirs is a life still governed by the elements, by snow and ice, by rain and water, sometimes by fire and wind; and it is a life in which individual commonsense and alertness are the best guarantee that a man will return home in one piece. It is also a life with certain insistent demands which have no parallel in the city: when the forest ranger calls for fire-fighting crews, you may not refuse. And this spirit spills over into other situations less traumatic than forest fires.

The woman in this picture is somewhat the pioneer type. To survive at work a man must be well fed, well clothed, and of good cheer. It is the woman's job to see that he is, and in the not-so-old days of wood stoves and hand pumps this was a full-time job.

This is a world of staples which do not exist in the city – staples which are often used instead of money: land and lumber, animals, heavy machines, and human labour. In combination with a little cash income they were able to support an almost moneyless life for those who were industrious and imaginative. I knew one man who made snowshoes, cutting and bending the frames in summer, stringing them in winter; and another who made most of his cash needs from a few well-tended walnut trees. It follows that this is a land where the individual still counts, where a man is known and judged for his visible human qualities.

Yet another point of difference is that this is still a world which is run not so much by paper as by word-of-mouth. A scrawled notice on the door of the post office or the local store will suffice to brief a whole community. In the same way the communal needs of a village will be explored and met. Does the credit union (itself a more communal institution than a bank) need a new fence? Edgewood a new tennis court? Word circulates and out come the men, backed by their women, with the muscles, tools, machines, and

4 A friend in Nakusp delights to tell how one day as she sat chatting in the home of a friend whose husband is a logging contractor, a power saw poked through the end wall of the house and proceeded to cut out a bottle-shaped panel, for all the world like scissors and cardboard. The wife had apparently remarked that it would be nice if they had a fireplace; the husband was merely getting on with the job!

materials, and the job is on. This does not mean, of course, that the Arrow Lakes are the twentieth century paradise. Not everyone contributed, or did so equally, but enough did to make the communities function.

Along with this goes a strong sense of the essential. What does it matter if the ball park is overgrown with weeds? Come the twenty-fourth of May it will be cut, not before. And along with that went a tendency to make do. Build your shed or paint your garage when you can, and if you have to stop halfway because of money, so what? It can wait. And if the *Vancouver Sun* arrives two days later (as it always did) is that a disaster?

The social structure of the communities also seemed to reflect their inhabitants. In ordinary times they seemed to get along with a minimum of organization, none of the communities in the central area being incorporated in 1964. When organization was seen to be necessary it was often provided by the Women's Institute or church groups. (The men, it appeared, had to have much more compelling reasons to organize, such as memories of war years or simple aridity, both of which were ministered to at 'the Legion' or the Leland Hotel in Nakusp.) At least some of the communities were divided by internal conflicts based sometimes on politics, sometimes on personalities; and in most it was difficult to identify an acknowledged community leader. In this sense there was no existing 'power structure' for Hydro to grapple with. Consensus apparently arose out of common need or crisis, and spokesmen, if not leaders, with it. It should not be imagined that the people of the Arrow Lakes were in any sense homogeneous or united against even the Columbia project. People who would lose their homes, for example, were usually far more deeply concerned about the project than their more fortunate fellows. In fact many of those not personally affected regarded the Columbia development as simply an economic shot-in-the-arm for the region. But there were others who realized that a large part of their environment would be altered. And this environment was widely used and appreciated, for the lakes were intensively used in the local forest operations and to some extent by the residents for fishing. But beyond that the people and their communities had always looked to the water for transportation and were thoroughly lake-oriented. Thus any great changes in the condition of the lakes would be keenly felt by many people.

Even the older people showed great differences in reaction to displacement. For some the ties of place and memory took precedence over more mundane considerations. But for many others the comfort of urban facilities, especially medical services, was stronger and ultimately took them either to Nakusp or to the bigger communities beyond the Arrow Lakes. There were significant differences too between young and old. Anyone under twenty in 1964 had grown up in time of comparative affluence and mobility.

Many of them would have left their home communities in any event, mostly for education, for the day of the one-room school is long past.

The little communities reflected the people and their history. They were irregular, unkempt, and gap-toothed from the attrition of time. The houses, all timber, often reflected the age as well as the outlook of their owners. The epitome of these communities was Renata. Renata lay twenty miles north of Castlegar and was connected to the rest of the world by a cable ferry and a roller coaster road which was not for the faint of heart. Less than half-a-mile square and edged by sandy beaches, Renata was known for its magnificent cherries, the product of a benign combination of soil, setting, and micro-climate. In good years Renata marketed 7200 crates of cherries and 5000 of peaches, and in its biggest apple year it shipped 12,000 boxes; all this from about thirty growers. But Renata was much more than a climate and cherries; it was a way of life, idyllic and irreplaceable. Here could be felt most keenly the tragedy of those who were uprooted by the project. Every tree, every stone, every house was laden with memories, still alive, of eighty years of community as very few city-dwellers ever come to know it. (It was in Renata that I got a real sense of the significance for the remaining inhabitants of the burning of homes which could not be removed. This was apparently necessary to prevent vandalism and re-occupation by others; but it was a terrible, searing experience for long-time neighbours still living nearby.) It was therefore fitting that Hydro should publish *The Story of Renata* [26], a history written by two residents of the village recording something precious destroyed by technological progress.[5]

But even before 1964 there were signs of change in Arcadia. Even then it was no longer the undisputed domain of the self-reliant individual. Most of the land was now worked by Celgar, and most of the men were its employees. Far fewer men in the region were entirely responsible for their own decisions. Where once they managed and worked their own lands, bought their own equipment, hired their own help, marketed their own logs, they now worked for a pay cheque on lands for which they were not responsible, to a schedule produced in Vancouver, by a day which stopped at 4 p.m. regardless of the state of the job. As for the young, it was already decreed that very few would know the whole life or, in community terms, the organic life their fathers knew.

But the purpose of this chapter is not to lament the passing of an era and a race, though we might well do so. It is to portray and interpret the

5 Starting as a mass of unorganized notes and records, this history was whipped into shape by my wife Renate, a professional writer, who got roped in by a process best described as voluntary conscription.

scene into which Hydro was propelled in 1964. This was a scene of many faces. Its economy was of the twentieth century, as was its general technology; every home had power, and most had cars and television. It was a far cry from being 'the Ozarks of Canada,' as it had been described by ignorant and supercilious outsiders. At the same time it was, in the public sense, an area of neglect – its land and communities for reasons which we have discussed, its roads and communications for reasons which were probably connected with the imminence of the Columbia project. Most of all, it was a region which was permeated by social ways and standards which were not those of the urban majority of Vancouver or Victoria, where decisions were made.

This then was the stage setting for the Columbia River project in 1964, a stage across which a long and ominous shadow had just been cast.

3
The long shadow

In *The Tempest* Shakespeare speaks of a 'destiny to perform an act whereof what's past is prologue' – a glove-fitting description of BC Hydro's situation in the Arrow Lakes in 1964. For the past was indeed a prologue to the present. Thus the purpose of this chapter is to trace the evolution of the Columbia River scheme primarily as the people of the Arrow Lakes saw it. Only thus is it possible to understand their attitudes and reactions to Hydro when it first took up its task.

In looking over accounts of the evolution of the Columbia project one is struck by the extent to which the people affected by it lived for years in a fog of ignorance, purely technical information, and rumour. It is true that the *Arrow Lakes News* featured regular letters from the area's political representatives in Victoria and Ottawa, but it must be remembered that almost all the action took place at the administrative level within the confines of the federal and provincial governments of the day. Furthermore, the Arrow Lakes region was represented in those days by an opposition member at both the provincial and the federal levels so that access to current information was not easy. Thus one senses a feeling of impotence in the face of remote events which could scarcely be discerned, far less influenced, by those to whom they were of most immediate significance.

It started in 1944 when the governments of Canada and the United States requested the International Joint Commission to determine whether further development of the water resources of the Columbia basin would be practical and advantageous to both countries. For this purpose the Commission established the International Columbia River Engineering Board, which carried out technical studies for the next fifteen years.

These were fruitful years, for not only did they see the gradual emergence of the dimensions and possibilities of the Columbia River in Canada, but they witnessed the acceptance by the United States of two important principles: (1) that Canada was entitled to fifty per cent of the additional power which would be generated by existing American power plants as a result of Canadian storage schemes, and (2) that under the Boundary Waters Treaty of 1909 Canada was fully entitled to divert the Columbia or its tributaries as she might see fit. This acceptance, which evolved over several years of stormy negotiation, was due to the engineering skill, shrewdness, and toughness of General Andrew McNaughton, chairman of the Canadian Section of the International Joint Commission during these years [23]. However, the peculiar significance to this story of McNaughton's work lies not so much in these principles, fundamental as they were, as in the so-called McNaughton plan for the Columbia River. And this in turn stemmed from the unusual configuration of the river and some of its upper tributaries in relation to the Canada-US border (Diagram 5). The head waters of the Kootenay River rise in Canada 150 miles north of the border, and thence flow *south* into the US before returning to Canada. However, it would have been possible to dam the Kootenay at the border and divert it northwards into the headwaters of the Columbia. This McNaughton proposed to do, in order not only to increase the amount of water flowing down the Canadian stretch of the Columbia but also to make full use in Canada of the fall (head) available there. Given this, the McNaughton plan did not propose to dam the Arrow Lakes, although the Murphy dam it proposed downstream would have affected the lake levels to a minor extent.

In 1959 the Engineering Board produced its report [13] which Waterfield in *Continental Waterboy* [27, p. 19] describes as 'an esoteric document which none of us fully understood.' This outlined three possible schemes for the development of the Columbia – the McNaughton plan, the plan favoured by the United States, and a compromise between the two (Diagram 5). These were to be studied by special negotiating teams appointed by the two countries in order to decide which project should be undertaken and under what conditions.

Up to this time the people of the Arrow Lakes had apparently felt no threat, having been heartened both by McNaughton's opposition to an Arrow dam and by reservations which had been expressed by BC's Attorney General, Robert Bonner, regarding the loss of fertile land. It seems therefore to have shocked them to learn late in 1959 – through their participation in the work of a regional committee of Boards of Trade and Chambers of Commerce – that the provincial government now favoured a scheme incor-

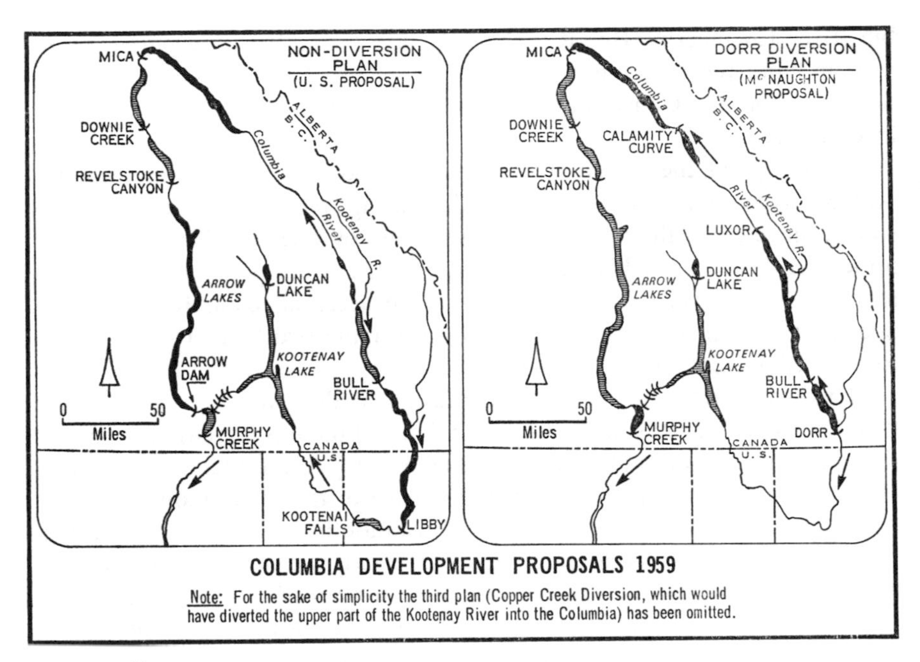

COLUMBIA DEVELOPMENT PROPOSALS 1959

Note: For the sake of simplicity the third plan (Copper Creek Diversion, which would have diverted the upper part of the Kootenay River into the Columbia) has been omitted.

DIAGRAM 5

porating the High Arrow Dam. It must have shocked them even more when the negotiating team announced by Prime Minister Diefenbaker in January 1960 did not include General McNaughton. From this point on their champion took no further part in the international aspects of the Columbia negotiations, although he participated in the Ottawa-Victoria discussions, spoke and wrote vigorously on behalf of his plan, and took part in the parliamentary hearings held in the spring of 1964.

The negotiations continued in places far from the Arrow Lakes until, as Waterfield records, in January 1961 'We began hearing rumours that an agreement between Canada and the United States was finalized ... and would be signed in Washington ... on 17 January 1961' [27, p. 35]. The Treaty was signed by President Eisenhower and Prime Minister Diefenbaker even though Premier Bennett had by this time notified the government of Canada of his reservations regarding the proposed financial arrangements.

Incidentally the information gap facing the residents about this time is well illustrated by a letter written by the Honourable R.G. Williston, BC minister of lands and forests, to the Nakusp Chamber of Commerce on 17 November 1960, in which he said, 'the report of the International Columbia River Engineering Board is the only one available to the public at the present time. We do not have any spare copies of this report, but it can be obtained from the Canadian Section of the International Joint Commission in Ottawa.'

At this point the Columbia scheme entered a second phase from the Arrow Lakes point of view – the public hearings phase. But the two phases were connected in the minds of the residents by one significant event. On 5 October 1960 Mr Williston had written to the Nakusp Chamber of Commerce: 'Public hearings will be held in the areas affected. If the [water] licences are granted the way will be open for the two federal governments to proceed to treaty discussions.'[1]

This was a time of particular confusion in the two-rivers (Peace and Columbia) controversy in British Columbia and there is no reason to suggest that Mr Williston did not write this in all honesty. Nevertheless his concept of proper procedure was overrun by the pace of the international arrangements and the Treaty was signed only three months later without local consultation. Thus it seemed to the people of the Arrow Lakes that to hold local hearings *after* substantial agreement had been reached by the two countries was to add insult to injury. It is true that the hearings could result in conditions being attached to the granting of the water licence, as indeed was the case. But that was not what concerned the residents of the Lakes. They opposed the High Arrow proposals as such, and they entertained no hope that the water comptroller, a provincial civil servant, could override a project already approved by his political masters. Thus the hearings which were held in the Arrow Lakes region in September and October 1961 were conducted against the backdrop of what was regarded as a broken promise and in an atmosphere of some cynicism. As one man wrote in 1970, 'They were a farce.'

Hearings were held at three points in the region: Revelstoke, Nakusp, and Castlegar. These are recounted in some detail in *Continental Waterboy* [27, chapters 5–7], and are, of course, also the subject of official transcripts. What is of concern here is how the Nakusp hearings of 29 and 30 September 1961 *seemed* to the local residents. The following impression of that appearance was gained from several sources – the *Arrow Lakes News* and several citizens who attended.

The hearing was orderly and the *News* on 5 October expressed general

1 Any use of natural waters in BC requires the issue of a water licence under the BC Water Act and this applied as a matter of course to BC Hydro in this case. Mr Williston was the minister responsible for the administration of the act, and the civil servant specifically responsible was the water comptroller.

appreciation of the way in which it was run: 'Mr A.F. Paget, Comptroller of Water Rights of Victoria, chaired the meeting and made an excellent job of it. He made it clear he would stand for no interruptions, no nonsense and the business was carried on with the decorum of court proceedings.' Further, 'it was learned that Mr Paget need not have brought the hearing to Nakusp and ... the residents of the area were even more appreciative of his decision to hold them here.' The human context therefore was by no means bad. The transcript shows that exchanges were generally conducted in a spirit of give-and-take and the chairman showed considerable understanding of the position of many people to whom public expression and formal procedure were something of a trial. Nor was spontaneous humour lacking, as provided for example by a witness who was asked how much land she owned and replied, 'a hundred acres, sir, and if I wasn't on oath it would be two hundred.'[2]

Even so, the general impression left by the hearing was not a favourable one for Hydro.[3] In the first place the Comptroller made it clear that the subject the audience most wanted to talk about and had spent much time in preparing to argue – the Arrow project and its justification – was not admissible, and even though he allowed people a great deal of latitude in their remarks about the Treaty and its inadequacies in their eyes, it was understood that inadmissible material would not go into the record of the meeting. This itself seemed to the people to imply a degree of futility about the hearing. What was the point if they couldn't discuss the question nearest their interests?

Second, the appearance and behaviour of the Authority's delegation created a bad impression. The *News* says that Hydro was represented by about a dozen people at the Revelstoke hearing, and the impression the local people seem to have formed was that they were being overborne by a battery of experts. Then there was a certain amount of legalistic, and in their eyes officious, behaviour an the part of the Authority's counsel. He seemed constantly to be jumping up and challenging people's qualifications and thus their right to express views on matters in which they happened to be vitally concerned, if not professionally qualified.

And lastly there was the distressing fact that so many of the audience's questions about their personal or communal interests could not be answered

2 A comment made to me by a perceptive resident, a native of another valley, is worthy of note here. He observed that on the whole the residents of the Central Arrow Lakes were pleasant and good tempered people, more so than in certain other valleys.

3 Strictly speaking this should read BC Power Commission. Hydro as such did not exist until 1962, as noted in chapter 13.

specifically or unequivocally. 'Oh, that's a simple engineering matter' was one frequent response that rings in many ears even today. The plain fact was that Hydro did not then have specific answers to give, and in many cases would not have them for a good half-dozen years. That was not necessarily the Authority's fault, but it gave cold comfort to the apprehensive victims of the project and created a less than helpful image of Hydro.

For their part the local people presented several excellent briefs, especially on agriculture and forestry. The statement that best expresses their sentiments was presented by Mrs Jean Spicer and reported as follows in the *Arrow Lakes News*. But first the reader should be apprised that this brief was no mere propaganda exercise. The Spicers' view *was* beautiful; their farm *was* a model of intensive production; their attachment to the valley *was* real and not untypical.

Like many others on the Arrow Lakes my husband and I live here for preference in comfort and contentment in the way of life we have chosen. We love our land and consider ourselves among BC's most fortunate citizens and that means among the most fortunate in this world.

The beauty and the climate of this valley rank among the highest. I have some authority for saying this because while I have spent most of my life in BC, I have made visits of some length to England and the beauty spots of Spain, Italy, France, Austria, and other countries, and each time I have returned to Nakusp I have realized why their beauty did not seem so superlative to me– it is because I have lived here with beauty surrounding me most of my life.

As we are now situated we feel that we have the best family farm in North America. Having started with very little money, we have put into the improving of our farm all the hard work of which we are capable, both to increase its production and to add to its beauty, with the result that we now have one of the most productive farms per acre in BC, and also one that is becoming increasingly ornamental.

The High Arrow Dam would take all this from us, and we would lose the concentrated efforts of our hearts and hands for the last twelve years.

We have built up our farm for ourselves and our children believing we would be allowed to go on living here, and I object most strongly to having it all taken away from us. Most particularly I object to losing it for a scheme which has not yet been proved to be permanently beneficial to BC. Even if it could be shown to be profitable at the present time, it is a sad thing that love of money should be put before love of country. No amount of money would ever repay us for what we would lose – our home, our livelihood, and our whole way of life.

I realize that this objection is a very small thing when viewed against the vastness of the Columbia development, but when you add to it the feeling of the many farm women up and down the lakes who feel the same way, it should carry a little weight. Those I have talked to feel almost unanimously as I do. They love their homes and their own pieces of land, they have put the best of themselves into improving both, and they feel sick at heart at the thought of leaving them, and perhaps even more sick at heart at the disruption of their family and social lives.

Dr Keenleyside says there will be quite a problem resettling some of the older people – that is putting it mildly. Through the years our little communities have become family groups with people living near their parents and so on. It would be very difficult to move these groups intact, and it would cause great hardship in many cases if they are split apart as they would be.

The general appearance of indecision and the inability to give satisfactory answers to questions in these hearings have succeeded in shaking the confidence of myself and others in the ability of the Power Commission to handle a project of this magnitude and I now have even more grave misgivings that the High Arrow and related project will end up by being a serious burden on the taxpayer and I am still more convinced that this vast High Arrow storage is not going to be of any permanent benefit locally. If High Arrow is so tremendously profitable why cannot the Power Commission offer us a bold imaginative program of reconstruction, with broad, blacktop highways, model villages and secondary industries run on the cheapest power in the world, instead of a jumble of make-shift plans qualified by 'ifs' at every turn. Are not we, the main sufferers from High Arrow, entitled to a major slice of the pie or have not my first suspicions been confirmed, and there is really no pie at all?

I sincerely hope that you will not grant this water licence which would ask such enormous sacrifices from its inhabitants.

But the long wait was by no means over in September 1961. There were still almost three years of sporadic activity to go, years full of illusions and disillusions, always at a distance, always behind an information fog. Nor did the people of the Central Arrow Lakes have solidarity in their own area or at either end of the Lakes, for there seem to have been many who regarded the Columbia proposal as a blessing.

The mainstay of political hope in the earlier part of this period was anchored in the Liberal party, then in opposition in Ottawa, and particularly in the leader of the opposition, L.B. Pearson, who on 13 April 1962 had written to the Nakusp Chamber of Commerce '... I agree with you that it is imperative to renegotiate the Columbia River Treaty.' To a lesser extent it was anchored in Jack Davis, a former official of the BC Electric Company and obviously on the way up in federal politics, who wrote to the Chamber in May 1963 appearing to approve 'changes in the present draft Treaty which are necessary to safeguard our national interests ... I prefer the approach which involves the construction of the non-controversial Treaty dams first.'

This impression of support was by no means discounted when on 6 June 1963 Mr Pearson, then prime minister, wrote to Richard Deane in Rossland, BC, 'my government intends to renegotiate certain aspects of the Columbia River Treaty.' In this, as in the previous letters quoted, there is a degree of generality which, intentional or not, provided scope for very wide interpretation of the 'certain aspects.' But in Nakusp there seemed to be reason for some confidence that might as well as right was on their side.

Not only that, but there was also the belief that British Columbia's provincial interests coincided with those of the Arrow Lakes. The government of the province had in 1962 already made a start on the huge Peace River development, which was to produce over 2 million kilowatts. It was commonly believed that British Columbia did not need the Columbia project as well. This view, however, did not reckon with Premier Bennett's mercantilistic instincts or his tremendous drive for the development of his province. At his insistence and in accordance with a permissive clause embodied in the Treaty the United States arranged to dispose of Canada's share of the downstream benefits and to recompense British Columbia for them in cash.[4] By thus exercising the prerogatives of his province in respect of its natural resources Premier Bennett outflanked the federal government and unhorsed Pearson and Davis as prospective champions of opposition to the High Arrow Dam. Thus when a Canada-BC agreement was signed in Ottawa in July 1963 and given international approval by Canadian and American representatives in January 1964, the fate of the Arrow Lakes was virtually sealed.

However the matter was not yet completely resolved, unless one is prepared to regard scrutiny by a parliamentary committee and consideration by the Canadian Parliament as a matter of form. (That one member of the standing committee on external affairs thought so – at least as regards the committee's function – was clear when Dr L.E. Kindt put to Paul Martin, the secretary of state for external affairs, a presumably rhetorical question:

4 It had already been agreed that Canada and the United States would share equally the additional power made possible at existing plants on the Columbia river in the USA. It was now agreed that Canada's half would be marketed in the United States by a US consortium of utility companies and Canada paid in cash, in advance, this lump sum being used to construct the dams. The instrument by which the existing Treaty, as yet unratified, was qualified to do this was the 'Protocol.'

'Does this not put the committee into the position of being a rubber stamp?'[5] And while Mr Martin did not accept this suggestion it was clear that the committee had under the circumstances virtually no power to amend the Treaty, although it could take the much more drastic step of recommending its rejection.) In the House itself, it could be reasoned, the Conservatives would support the Treaty, which had been negotiated and signed by the Diefenbaker government and remained unchanged in substance, while the Liberals would support the Protocol, which had been negotiated by the Pearson government and had the support of Premier Bennett. Nevertheless the hearings in Ottawa went on through April and May in 1964, during which General McNaughton fought his last uncompromising battle against the Treaty, and Mr H.W. Herridge, the perennial member for the West Kootenays, acquired or intensified a virulent personal hatred for Hydro's chairman, Dr Keenleyside. (This is not recorded as a petty triviality. Mr Herridge, an articulate man of persuasive charm, was an institution in his days as the valley's federal member, and his unrelenting and venomous attacks on everything relating to Hydro cannot have helped the people of the Arrow Lakes to accept the Columbia works.)

One more thing remains to be recorded – not a matter of substance but one which must have seemed to the people of the Lakes to be the final

5 The essence of this fascinating exchange is as follows:
Mr Kindt: ... As I understand it our function here is to improve this treaty.
Mr Martin (Essex East): No, not at all.
Mr Kindt: Well, to improve the situation with respect to Canada.
Mr Martin (Essex East): No, your function is to indicate whether you approve of what the government has done ... Any variation of it would of course involve a repudiation of the position taken by this government or by its predecessors in regard to the treaty.
Mr Kindt: Does this not put the committee into the position of being pretty much a rubber stamp?
Mr Martin (Essex East): Not at all. By careful study I think you can bring out the merits of various arguments, but we have agreed, as I stated in parliament, that after we had negotiated with the United States ... then we would enter into an exchange of notes with the United States, which we have done. But before we would ratify, we would come back to parliament and parliament could accept the course taken by the government or reject it.
Mr Byrne: I was simply going to ask the minister if when the former administration suggested that the treaty be put before a parliamentary committee, it was prepared to have it at that altered in any way?
Mr Martin (Essex East): Of course not. The treaty was signed in Washington, by the President of the United States, by the Secretary of State for the United States, by the Prime Minister of Canada, and by the Minister of Justice ... under our practice, the government of the day takes its responsibility, and having taken its position and responsibility, then it asks parliament to approve or to reject [8, p. 67].

indignity. On Friday, 5 June 1964, when the House of Commons considered the Columbia River Treaty and Protocol, only 108 members were present out of a total of 264. The Treaty passed by a vote of 92 to 16, the New Democratic party alone dissenting. It then went to the Senate on 10 June 1964 where it was not deemed worthy of a formal vote but was passed, none dissenting.

Thus ended for the people of the Arrow Lakes twenty years of waiting, of never knowing, of trusting and being let down, of being overborne, and ultimately of being ignored. For them this was only the end of the beginning of the now-you-see-it-now-you-don't dance of politicians and their advisers. But it was not an auspicious start for the last act. For now the harsh deeds implicit in the Treaty had to be done as best they might, in the presence of those who had lived through the long years and had little reason to be complaisant or co-operative with those responsible for the execution of the Columbia project.

4
Enter Gulliver

Upon ratification of the Columbia River Treaty and the Protocol amending it, the curtain came down on the prologue. As we have seen, that prologue had been a protracted, sporadic, acrimonious dialogue which had produced up to this point more kilowords than kilowatts. It had been played against many backdrops – Washington, DC, Victoria, BC, the Arrow Lakes, and finally and decisively, Ottawa. It had been largely a script of 'heavy' roles – the governments of Canada, the United States, and British Columbia – and so far the people of the Arrow Lakes had spoken only the briefest of parts. But now the prologue was over and a baleful shadow was cast across the stage at the beginning of the main act.

For this act the setting was again the lake country, and the script at last called for action in a scene which at first glance might have been taken from *Gulliver's Travels.* Gulliver was the British Columbia Hydro and Power Authority – 'the Canadian entity,' in the language of the Treaty – which had been given a central but highly circumscribed role. It was to build three large dams and any other works essential to that task; and it was to make good any damage it might do to the land of Lilliput and compensate the inhabitants for any irreparable harm caused them; *and that was all.*

The point in the analogy is that BC Hydro was indeed an actor playing from a script, a very specific and terse script, and its overall performance must be judged against the limitations of that script. It is necessary to say this not only to judge charges that Hydro should have done more than it did, but also to explain the circuitous course it had to take in attempting to transcend the limitations of the Treaty.

It had long been recognized that the new reservoirs would play havoc with the valley settlements and their communications, and these effects had been allowed for in terms of compensation (that is, money for irreparable damage) or effective replacement (for inundated roads). However, little effective preparation seems to have been made in the early planning process for broader ameliorative action. When such possibilities did emerge in due course it was realized that Hydro had neither legal mandate nor assigned funds to implement them directly, no matter how desirable they might be. Nor could Hydro, a semi-independent agency outside the departmental structure of the British Columbia government, overlook the fact that most of the extra-curricular actions it might wish to see undertaken (the building of access highways or the development of lakeside parks, for example) would fall within the jurisdiction of one or other of the established provincial departments. In short, the Authority was by no means a free agent in relation to the broader challenges of the Columbia River project.

What were these challenges? In the first place, over 500 million dollars were to be spent on the project.[1] It is true that this total was to be spent at three widely separated points and over periods ranging from three to nine years. Nevertheless, the total was very considerable and Hydro's economists estimated in 1964 that an average of five million dollars a year would be spent in the Columbia region. (In the event this sum must have been closer to ten million.)

Another measure, and one probably more meaningful for the Columbia region, was the work force to be employed. Peak employment and the approximate duration of the three dam projects were estimated in 1964 (Table 1). So much work could not be done and so many men housed, fed, and serviced, without a considerable amount rubbing off onto the region. And the first of the challenges was to maximize the rubbing off. Much of the rubbing off was obvious and to be expected, such as the incidental expenditures made by the workers on personal needs, recreation, gasoline, and so on. But much of it also consisted of deliberate decisions by Hydro to achieve its ends in ways which would best serve the surrounding communities. For example, development of new communities, assistance in the financing of a hospital extension at Castlegar, contribution to a community recreation hall at Duncan, and the preservation of a prized community ball park at Revelstoke were all decisions which left something permanent and useful in the region when Hydro's problem could have been solved in less constructive ways. Usually it was merely a matter of taking the humane and constructive alternative, and in general this *was* done.

1 This is not put forward as the 'cost' of the Columbia project, but merely as an order-of-magnitude figure to indicate the scale of the project and its impacts.

TABLE 1

Dam	Construction period	Peak force (all tasks)	Camp forces
Duncan	4 years	700	400
Arrow	5 years	1400	300–500
Mica	9 years (dam only)	2000	2000

The second challenge, however, was different in that it demanded deliberate action by Hydro in areas beyond its Treaty responsibilities. Had it viewed its task through the single lens of the Columbia River Treaty it would, for example, have merely replaced inundated sections of road leaving the region with a patchwork of old and new roads. Such an approach would have been unimaginative and short-sighted for two reasons. First, the Arrow Lakes region was one of the most neglected in the province and badly needed better roads and communications. Second, it was anticipated that the new dams and lakes could become tourist magnets, as similar works had always proved to be in the United States, and would add a new element to the economy of the region and the province. But this situation could not materialize unless access roads were built and provisions, such as parks and campsites, were made for the accommodation of visitors.[2]

Since such extra-curricular works were neither legally nor financially within the competence of the Authority, it was necessary for Hydro, once its proposals had been sketched in outline, to seek co-operation from the provincial government. This part of the story is described in chapter 7. The point here is that these actions did constitute a reaching out beyond the given and the mundane by Hydro.

But beyond these two challenges there was, at least for those who could conceive it, a third – the human challenge. The condition of the Arrow Lakes settlements and the temper of their inhabitants in 1964 have already been described. It seemed clear to many that the valley was to be ruined, that nothing good could come out of the whole nefarious affair. It is true that the element of opportunity in the scheme had been pointed out by Dr H.L. Keenleyside, Hydro's chairman, in his public utterances in the region. But many people were in no mood for optimism.

For those of humanistic temper there seemed to be an overriding task to be done: the task of re-energizing people, of helping to restore their faith in the future of the valley. Was this part of Hydro's philosophy, one of its avowed objectives? It was not. It is true that it could have been implied from

2 Nearly 60,000 visitors were recorded at the Arrow dam in 1966.

Dr Keenleyside's speeches, although these were couched in hortatory rather than sympathetic terms. But nowhere in the official record will there be found such an aim, and for good reason. For one thing the people themselves would probably have received it with derision. For another, Hydro would probably have decided, as it did later in like circumstances, that such an explicit objective would be distorted, flung in its face and used against it. And in any event such an idea, spoken, would have been totally foreign to the English-Canadian temper. The whole situation militated against a *stated* objective of this kind.

But the real problem lay much deeper. It is one thing to have visions and ideals for yourself; quite another to have them for others. In particular, how does a corporation set about helping people who are being dispossessed by its own actions, especially when there is quite a gap in attitudes and standards between the urban 'helpers' and the rural people to be helped? The situation is pregnant with possibilities of misunderstanding, of raw nerves and ham-handed idealism. Tom Joad pungently describes the recipient's view of that situation in *The Grapes of Wrath*: 'Doin' good to a fella that's down an' can't smack ya in the puss for it. That's preachin' [22, p. 28].[3]

Was there then no possibility of such a concern being exercised? There was, of course, but it had to be expressed largely in doing the essential tasks with efficiency, patience, and understanding. Thus it fell largely to the Hydro field staff whose tasks brought them into personal contact with the people of the valley on their own ground. At this level, man could at least identify with man and only the most callous could be unaware of the stress which the displaced people were experiencing, even when that expressed itself in hostility or cynicism. If Hydro is judged to have emerged with credit from its exercise in the Arrow Lakes, it will be largely to the credit of its field men – its appraisers, engineers, planners, and information officers – who did their difficult jobs, for the most part, with understanding and humanity.

3 Another comment on the menace of the altruistic zealot is made by Jon Gower Davies [11, p. 219]: 'men motivated by concern and love for fellow human beings are notoriously incapable of even listening to, let alone accepting, criticism. As H.G. Wells said of Beatrice Webb: "P.B.P., she boasted, was engraved inside their wedding rings, Pro Bono Publico, and she meant it to be no idle threat".'

5
Feeling the wind

I joined the staff of the BC Hydro and Power Authority in May 1964, assuming responsibility for the planning of the resettlement program. As soon as possible thereafter I set out for the Arrow Lakes to conduct a 'horseback survey.' The purpose of this was to assess for myself the overall situation as a basis for the resettlement program. I had by this time reviewed the available written material which Hydro had collected a few years earlier, and this provided a useful starting point.

I called on all the people who held positions of trust and responsibility in their communities, on public officials and also on some of the known opponents of the Arrow project. I visited homes, read the local newspapers, walked the streets, drove on the back roads, and in effect tried to *feel* the situation and all its nuances for myself. It was, of course, a highly subjective, relatively unsystematic, exploratory process, which involved a considerable degree of personal excitement and stress as I tried to understand and to assess the meaning for Hydro of the mass of 'facts' and viewpoints which inundated me during the two-week period.[1] It was inevitably a risky process in that one could very easily come to false or naive conclusions. Admitting this, and

1 I was often reminded of the wry comment, attributed to an English physicist, that human knowledge is of two kinds: theories, which nobody believes except the men who formulated them, and facts, which everybody believes except the men who last investigated them. The truth of many situations in the Arrow Lakes, whether pre-Treaty or post-Treaty, is hard to establish. Without disrespect to any of my informants and collaborators it is necessary to say that not only do most of us see for ourselves only a very limited amount of 'the action' but we tend to see in it only what we *want* to see.

remembering also that the conclusions drawn from such an exploration should always be tentative and subject to review, the utility of such a reconnaissance cannot be over-emphasized.

In any event I did get some feeling for the region and especially its people: who really counted and who did not; who was merely puffed up and noisy; who was at all representative; what the local concerns and differences were. In turn, some of them got to know me and took note of the fact that for the first time someone of some responsibility was asking them about *their* views and needs (before the Treaty was signed Hydro's surveyors and engineers could not be forthcoming with the local residents about their doings). The immediate result of this survey was a memorandum dated 14 July 1964 to the chairman of the Authority. Meaty and condensed as it is, it introduces in some fashion all the topics pursued in this book and is therefore reproduced in its entirety.

THE BACKGROUND SITUATION IN THE ARROW LAKES

1 *Local attitudes*

The local attitude varies from place to place depending on the anticipated impact of Hydro's works on the area. However, it can be said without any doubt that there is no *basic* hostility to the project or to Hydro although there is a great deal of apprehension as to the effect of the works on individual properties and lives. Furthermore, since this has been the case for at least four years, some people, especially older people, are obviously feeling acute strain, and all are nervous, suspicious, and an easy prey to rumour and emotional appeal. Hydro is not being blamed for this situation, which the people realize is nobody's fault, but the important thing is that they are reacting to the unknown. I am convinced that Hydro can easily dispel these attitudes if, in carrying out its programs, it adopts an outgoing, co-operative approach to the people, and in particular, keeps them fully informed of its programs and intentions.

2 *Population types*

From Hydro's point of view the people of the Arrow Lakes can probably be divided into three broad categories. (*a*) Those who are self-supporting, mainly through employment with Celgar – often amplified by small-holding and tree-farm operations. These consider themselves tied to the region and will probably resettle themselves spontaneously, given suitable compensation. (*b*) Those who are not self-supporting, mainly older people and pensioners, who are often both indigent and ailing. Many of these are likely – as evidenced by a recent survey taken in the Edgewood area – to expect low-rent housing to be provided by Hydro. (*c*) A small residual group containing other types, mainly true farmers and 'aesthetes' who have sought out the Arrow Lakes area for its special environmental qualities. Both of these groups seem to doubt that the future Arrow Lakes can supply their needs.

In the first group especially there is widespread acceptance of the project as potentially beneficial and in any case inevitable, and there are signs of readiness to adjust to it, given the necessary leadership by Hydro. These people are almost all firmly rooted in the region because of their jobs, because of social or sentimental attachments, or because of the region's climate, which is widely appreciated. They know that the works will affect them considerably, and are naturally anxious about these effects, but many of them see clearly that it will be a richer, more stable, and less isolated place than before. This leads me to believe that except for a few requiring medical attention or unable to stand the strain of waiting and wondering any longer, almost all of the people displaced by flooding will wish to remain in the Arrow Lakes area.

3 *Spontaneous resettlement*

I got the strong impression that those who are able will resettle themselves spontaneously, given certain conditions: (*a*) adequate compensation, *to be settled as quickly as is humanly possible*; (*b*) provision of substitute land, house-moving service, removal costs; (*c*) knowledge of new highway locations to guide their relocation decisions; (*d*) knowledge of Hydro's land 'take'; and (*e*) enough time so that they may establish new homes in stages, and in particular avail themselves of the 500-dollar winter building rebate.

In view of the utter desirability of such initiative, everything possible should be done to create conditions encouraging spontaneous resettlement.

4 *Compensation*

At the moment confusion and distrust centre around the subject of compensation. Some hold that Dr Keenleyside's recent statements on this subject are at odds with earlier statements by Mr Williston. Also I believe that our last statement has *seemed* contradictory and theoretical to the people, no matter how logical and sound it may have seemed to us. We talk about fairness, suggesting market values; they know very well that there has been no market for properties in the Arrow Lakes for years. We talk about a few special cases and exceptions to this general approach; they know that there are lots of them and are worried about them. Furthermore they have long memories of the Power Commission's opportunistic approach to the negotiation of line easements in the area, in which owners of similar properties received vastly different payments, depending on their alertness and toughness.

The crucial question hanging over the region is 'What will I get for my property?' and it is crucial not only for the individual but also for Hydro because (*a*) it will determine what people do for themselves in the way of resettlement and therefore, in reverse, what they will expect Hydro to do for them and (*b*) it will determine the whole atmosphere in which Hydro carries out its works – whether against a background of satisfied people resettling themselves and co-operating actively, or against a background of hostility, obstructionism, jujitsu, and legal actions.[2]

I am convinced that this situation could be improved immediately, without prejudice to the appraisal program, if the Authority would publicize a general statement on compensation along the following lines: (*a*) that it is trying to determine, professionally, a fair value, not to obtain the best deal it can for itself; (*b*) that appraisers will not be empowered to bargain, although adjustments may be made if agreed by the Authority; (*c*) that removal and other justified resettlement expenses will normally be allowed; (*d*) that there are several ways of assessing value and that the most appropriate way, or ways, will be used in every case; (*e*) that Hydro is well aware of the effects of the last few years on property values in the Arrow Lakes area and will make allowance for them; (*f*) that in cases where market value of an old home is not enough to purchase another home Hydro will take steps to see that shelter is provided; and (*g*) that special care and accommodation will be provided for older people and those unable to look after themselves.

It is an interesting sidelight on the question of compensation that the few prospective 'scalpers' in the area are well known and regarded with some amusement by their fellows. I take this as evidence that most of the people are both fair-minded and realistic.

5 *Restitution*

I am convinced that by continuing to use the word 'compensation' we are blinding ourselves to our real problem. To express this as a proposition which everyone in the region would accept: no one should be worse off after flooding than before it. This definition suggests that we should be thinking in terms of *restitution* – making good, restoring – rather than compensation, which is generally taken to mean money. This is especially important in the Arrow Lakes, firstly because many people are concerned about *shelter*, which they now have although compensation dollars may not enable them to replace it anew; secondly because in many cases dollar values will be difficult to determine and potentially contentious. I therefore suggest that we make a practice of distinguishing between the two

2 See for example, the *Nelson Daily News*, 25 June, regarding proposals by the Canadian Legion to provide legal aid for veterans so that they 'will not be at a disadvantage negotiating with trained (and presumably predatory) officials of BC Hydro.'

terms and preferably use *restitution*, which reminds us of our fundamental responsibility and of the several ways of discharging it – of which dollar compensation is only one.

What does restitution imply in practical terms?

1 Since many people would have preferred to be left undisturbed, and a few probably profess the same while hoping for considerable improvement in their habitation, the basic approach should be one of *substitution* as far as possible: by making available equivalent parcels of land and by moving *or being ready to move* existing dwellings.
2 There will probably be some able-bodied people whose houses cannot be moved and who claim the right to an equivalent roof. Without attempting to be exhaustive I suggest three possible approaches to this problem: provision of houses acquired in cases of dollar compensation, provision of new houses on a rental basis, or provision of assistance in acquiring loans for private construction of new houses.
3 The older people who do not wish to be re-established as above should be offered specially-designed, low-rental accommodation, attached to the nearest community. (Incidentally these people need special reassurances as to the Authority's intentions, since they feel particularly vulnerable and apprehensive.)

These proposals imply the following actions by Hydro:

1 Acquisition of land for 'residential' purposes within the region. Some of this will be acquired involuntarily in the process of buying severed parcels; some will have to be purchased in addition, especially in existing communities. Whether this action will extend to the building of so-called 'model communities' it is too early to say.
2 Provision of substitute farms, with the help of the BC department of Agriculture. This should not be a great task as the number involved will be small and those wishing to continue farming will be active and self-reliant.
3 Thorough investigation of house-moving techniques and movability appraisal.
4 An inventory of houses in the flood areas, which are capable of being moved, should be prepared.
5 The process of resettling old people will not be simple. First, their total needs must be broadly and sympathetically assessed (for example, their financial situation and medical needs). To tackle this we should use the social welfare and public health services in the region. The welfare case-workers know many of the people involved, and both the regional welfare administrators involved (Okanagan and Nelson) have expressed their willingness to co-operate with the Authority. Secondly, even when the need is clear, many older people may require demonstration and persuasion to settle in group housing. This implies a program of films and visits (for example, to the Kam-

loops housing project), which could be undertaken by the information services group in conjunction with the Central Mortgage and Housing Corporation and the University of British Columbia's extension department.

6 *Critical land operations*

The steps suggested above apply primarily to the Central Arrow Lakes area, where the bulk of the flooding will take place. However, there are two critical areas in which Hydro should concern itself with land acquisition and development, namely Revelstoke and Castlegar.

In relation to the size of the community, and local topography, the amount of flooding in the Revelstoke area will be considerable. The people involved will probably wish to resettle locally and will cause a considerable demand for land in an area which is already burgeoning with motel construction under the impact of the Rogers Pass highway and which may be due for a bout of land speculation, if that is not already happening.

Hydro has a serious interest in this situation. First, it cannot expose itself to any charge that it purchased property at pre-Columbia values and then left the people to purchase land at post-Columbia prices inflated by its own actions; secondly it should not, for its own sake, pay inflated prices and thus promote inflation. The obvious solution is for Hydro to acquire land for its own restitution purposes. If these lands are strategically located and proper arrangements made with the city for services, this could mitigate inflation, exonerate Hydro, and also promote efficient, good quality growth in Revelstoke.

In Castlegar the situation is even more critical, although Hydro is not directly involved in the municipal areas. Our plans envisage the employment at the dam site, only four miles from the town, of a peak work force of 1400 men, of whom 900 to 1100 are not expected to be accommodated in construction camps. This presumably does not take any account of supply, service, and other secondary workers who will come in to support the construction forces. But allowing only for the families of the primary workers, we can envisage an influx of 3000 people into an area whose total population is now only about 2500; and a demand for 1000 living units in a community whose total excess capacity at the moment has been estimated as 75 units.

Clearly Hydro cannot stand aloof from this problem and its contribution can probably be made best by direct participation in the land market.

7 *Community plans*

One factor of some significance for Hydro is the condition of local government in the Arrow Lakes. This consists only of the city of Revelstoke and the villages of Castlegar and Kinnaird, the rest being unorganized – although Nakusp may soon decide to become a village. All of these are small and served by non-professional, general-factotum staffs; and they are bedevilled by the existence of fragmented boundaries, all having unorganized fringes around them, Castlegar being further complicated by the presence of two bickering village councils. Where there is no organized government, as in Nakusp, communal problems are met by *ad hoc* societies or boards.

In all of the three major communities – Revelstoke, Nakusp, and Castlegar – Hydro will inevitably be involved either in works within the community or in negotiations over the effect of its operations on local services and facilities. In either event it is imperative, whether to look after its own interests competently or to deal fairly with community claims, that Hydro should know precisely how its works affect the community and what it should do about these effects. Also, it is desirable that the local councils – and other statutory bodies, such as school and hospital boards – should act as responsibly as possible in matters which affect Hydro. (To cite one example, the village of Kinnaird completely bans trailers within its area.)

I believe that the interests of Hydro and the communities can best be served if Hydro encourages the preparation of comprehensive plans for the affected communities. Yet it should not infringe or *appear* to infringe on those communities' autonomy by advising them itself; and equally it should be in a position to uphold its own rights in any argument with the community.

These considerations suggest that Hydro should offer to assist these communities by contributing substantially to the employment of independent planning consultants. These consultants would be instructed to prepare plans for the development of the whole community, to be presented to both Hydro and the councils concerned. In order to achieve full impact – for absorption of ideas and experience by councils is slow, and implementation of plans takes years – the consultant should be retained, probably throughout the construction period, to assist with implementation of the plan once it is prepared.

All this raises a general question of some importance to Hydro since it will clearly be bombarded with requests and proposals for help and involvement: 'What is Hydro going to do for the communities it affects?' I suggest that in the first place Hydro answer this with a principle: 'Hydro will not do for any community what it ought to be doing for itself, but it will make good any damage it causes; it will contribute generously where its operations will clearly affect community facilities or the community's ability to support these facilities; and it will, where necessary, help the community to help itself by insuring that it gets competent and impartial advice.' This principle, which was adopted very successfully by TVA, will make the communities stand on their own feet, improve their ability to govern themselves, and at the same time provide a reasonable community environment for Hydro to work in.

8 *Area prospects*

The Treaty works will trigger immense changes which will necessitate readjustments on the part of individual citizens, organizations which carry out community undertakings – municipalities, school boards, hospital boards, cemetery boards, recreation commissions, etc. – and major employers such as Celgar and the CPR. At the moment only Hydro, as the initiator, is in a position to estimate what the prime changes will be, such as: increases in population through the influx of construction and supporting forces; redistribution of population as a result of flooding; local economic opportunities presented by Hydro's operations; long-term economic changes and opportunities, including tourism and recreation, caused by the improvement in highway communications.

For many reasons – for its own information, for the guidance of other bodies serving the region, and as a matter of constructive public relations – I suggest that Hydro arrange for studies of the economic and population outlook for the region, and that it seek the co-operation of major employers such as Celgar and the CPR in doing so. These studies should then be widely distributed throughout the region as part of Hydro's public information program.

9 *Public information program*

In my view the greatest need at the moment is to broaden the public information program now under way. This is necessary both to gain the confidence and co-operation of the people and thus give us a favourable environment for our works, and to enable them to relocate themselves and thus minimize our need to do things for them. Also, if carried at the grass roots, it holds a further potential benefit to Hydro, namely feedback of local intelligence, enabling us to deal more sensitively with local feelings and often to anticipate them.

As I see it this program should: (*a*) operate at the grass-roots level in *formal* co-operation with the engineering, planning, and appraisal functions; (*b*) involve regular and direct dissemination of information to local residents; (*c*) provide a local intelligence service to Hydro's staff; (*d*) undertake public presentations and discussions of Hydro plans; (*e*) undertake specific educational and demonstration programs, such as those connected with resettlement of old people.

It is my feeling that for obvious reasons beyond its control prior to the signing of the Treaty, Hydro has often been or has appeared to be on the defensive. It has therefore invited suspicion and attack. The only way to change this image is to be as outgoing and co-operative as possible. The need is to establish the people's confidence in Hydro as a constructive force in their lives, and as a real, visible force at their own level. I have not the slightest doubt that this can be done and that it could – to put it in money terms – save Hydro millions of dollars.

10 *Clearing*

In view of current suggestions that, while clearing all merchantable timber below the flood line in the Arrow Lakes, we leave the balance for a five-year period after flooding to see what Nature will do for us, free, I feel impelled to make the following observations:

1 The Arrow Lakes are 'working' lakes and will be even more so after flooding. They are heavily used, especially by Celgar, and it is expected that they will be increasingly used for pleasure boating and fishing in future.
2 The Arrow Lakes area has a relatively mild climate and has frozen over (in the Nakusp area, at least) only twice in the last sixteen years. Since natural clearing depends on ice action, the outlook for effective natural clearing seems slight.
3 For the first few years after completion of the dam the Arrow Lakes will undoubtedly be a magnet for tourists. It would be fatal to the region's image if during these years it presented a dead-forest appearance or were plugged with debris.
4 As a result of the Authority's statements to date every one I met expects the Arrow Lakes to be 'cleared,' that is, completely. Any modifying proposal would be regarded as a gross breach of faith.
5 I feel that, of all the lakes concerned in the Treaty, the Arrow Lakes are not the place to 'take a chance,' especially when the odds are not favourable.

I am aware of the thought that the proposal might save the Authority 'millions of dollars'; on the other hand I believe there are weighty reasons for doubting both the practicality and the wisdom of the proposal. I therefore suggest that very serious study be given to clearing in the Arrow Lakes before a final decision is made.

11 *Recreation*

Since there are few established recreational facilities on the Arrow Lakes now, presumably Hydro has little responsibility for restitution.

The Arrow Lakes may experience considerable growth in recreational use. The Kootenay Lakes are said to be dangerous and 'not popular'; the Okanagan is 'too popular'; while the Arrow Lakes will become more accessible and better known. It seems also that due to local topography, there are several areas of outstanding micro-climate and shelter characteristics on the Arrow Lakes – Deer Park, Renata, and Nakusp for example.

It seems that the Castlegar-Renata area is considerably used and highly regarded by the people of the Castlegar-Trail-Nelson complex, thus accounting for at least part of (local MLA) Brothers' insistence (which appears to be accepted as gospel in that area) on the maintenance of a road to Deer Park. Having visited them, I feel that the post-flooding sites at both Renata and Deer Park, though limited in size, will be exceptionally good for recreational use, and the question of maintaining an access road – difficult and costly as it will undoubtedly be – should not be decided on grounds of economy only.

The careful reader will have noted a considerable difference between the historical situation sketched in chapter 3 and the assessment of local attitudes presented in this report. He will therefore not be surprised to know that when I wrote the latter I did not know the history of the local hearings. Had I known it I might have been rather less sanguine about the human relations aspect of the program.

For all its shortcomings and its rather ingenuous optimism this report gave rise to many useful actions. Several of these could be classified as exercises in communication: the *Property Owner's Guide* (chapter 6), economic impact studies, and *The Columbia Newsletter,* which was mailed to every householder in the area and ran through thirty issues between August 1964 and June 1969. Another action with a large element of communication in it was the decision to hire independent planning consultants for Revelstoke, Nakusp, and Castlegar. This seems to have been quite useful. Perhaps one result, although it is impossible to document, was that Hydro had relatively little trouble from these communities. I like to think, however, that the cause of competent self-government was advanced a little by the efforts of these conscientious consultants. Certainly one thing cannot be denied, namely their independence. In this respect the Revelstoke case proved embarrassing both to Hydro and to me. The consultant there, a friend of my own and one of the world's most stubborn people, concluded that Hydro ought to construct a low dam across the Columbia near Arrowhead in order to maintain a lake rather than a widely fluctuating river in front of Revelstoke. Hydro's engineers blew their fuses. This would have necessitated a dam a mile long; would have further raised the flood level at Revelstoke where Hydro was already having a worrying time with dikes and a railway bridge; and according to our engineers would have altered water levels to the point of necessitating re-approval by the U.S. government. Needless to say the dam was never built.

The report also precipitated local land acquisition and development programs (chapter 7); plans for provincial recreation areas (chapter 7); and the tree-clearing controversy, which had a history of its own (chapter 11). The comments on compensation were received by the appropriate officers with something less than bubbling enthusiasm. Nevertheless they presaged very clearly some of the conflicts and problems which arose later (chapters 6 and 15).

For all the dangers inherent in superficiality, this broadbrush treatment of the Arrow Lakes seems in retrospect to have been useful and productive. Most of all it pointed out, and suggested specific means of dealing with, the inevitable relationships between the Columbia project and the people and institutions of the Arrow Lakes country. Equally important and no less complex it pointed out working relationships both within Hydro and between it and the provincial government which deserved attention.

For me the immediate result of this survey was a sense of direction which was reflected in the planning program from that point on. Secondly, it resulted in the establishment of a small planning office in Nakusp. This was a one-man show for the first winter, but was amplified by the employment of three short-term people for the following summer.[3] Their instructions were to get to know intimately the people and the land and to prepare plans and programs for the resettlement of those wishing to stay in the region. In the event they provided planning, public relations, and intelligence functions which served Hydro well.

Many months were to pass before most of the suggestions made in the report would materialize. However, one over-riding question demanded early attention by the Authority. That was the question of compensation principles, to which we now turn.

3 Without intruding on the course of the story I should acknowledge the sterling work done by the 'one-man show,' Gerry Fitzpatrick. A young man of quite unusual common sense and integrity, Gerry braved the psychological frigidity of the first winter, while his wife collected bruises on her hips as she learned to live with two lively sons in a tiny trailer. Perhaps they and the three young men who supported them the next summer all benefitted in that they, like me, were not 'regular' Hydro employees. Thus, they came with open eyes and no worries about status, promotion, or hierarchy to distort their views of the situations they were called on to assess. In their quiet way, they performed a very valuable function and did it well.

6
The root of all evil?

Undoubtedly the issue of greatest consequence to the individuals affected, and therefore the touchiest job facing Hydro, was the acquisition of properties located below the reservoir flood line. This was not only a task of considerable size (about 1300 properties were involved[1], but one which governed the timing of several stages of the Columbia project. Properties on the dam site had to be acquired immediately and land on the reservoir floor had to be purchased before clearing operations could be carried out. In addition, homes affected had to be bought so that their owners would know how much capital they had to invest in new homes, for this would govern their ability to co-operate with Hydro in resettlement planning. Furthermore, people could be expected to be fractious until they knew. For both sides, therefore, timely acquisition of property was crucial.

From Hydro's point of view much more was at stake than just the expediting of other parts of the project. In one sense Hydro's reputation and the image of the provincial government hung on this program. The actual conduct of the operation, a far bigger task than Hydro or its progenitors had undertaken before, was therefore a very serious administrative responsibility.

The first question, since Hydro had only a small land staff, was whether it should be an 'inside' or an 'outside' job. Contract appraisals were not unknown and some of the large real estate and appraisal firms would have

1 1280 ownerships (3200 parcels of land) and 71 flowage easements. This involved about 2000 people, including 615 households, of which 260 were on farmsteads or small ranches. The land area was 33,500 acres, of which 9000 acres was Crown land.

been delighted to be commissioned. However Hydro thought it would lose control of a very sensitive operation if it depended on others for this work. It was probably true that the job could be blitzed; but at what cost to all concerned? The first decision therefore was that Hydro should do the job itself.

This was only the beginning. Staff had to be found from all over the country, for suitable people were scarce; they then had to be scrutinized, checked, and briefed on their responsibilities. Workable arrangements had to be hammered out for liaison between the field staff, – who knew the realities of each case, and the back-up staff at head office in Vancouver, who held the ultimate responsibility for approving offers. Before long it became necessary to shift some responsibilities and discretionary powers to the field office in order to expedite the operation.

Inevitably there were problems. The whole process took time. The program seemed to crawl along in the early days and took many months to get into high gear. There were a few mistakes in staffing. One veteran employee proved rather abrasive and had to be retired. Another took his own life after becoming improperly involved in contract administration. Since he was a man of great drive and energy, this was a grave setback to the property acquisition program, for which he was responsible in the field. But judging by some of the comments made in the 1970 survey his case had an even more serious effect on Hydro's image.

To right the balance however, it is only fair to point out that in the opinion of the Vancouver press representatives who visited the region in 1966 Hydro's field men were generally respected. Furthermore those who had direct knowledge of their work, especially in the early days when the situation was rather tense and the few available men were under great pressure, testify to the devotion and endurance of the first staff members.

They worked from early morning until long after dark, writing reports in lonely hotel rooms and doing what most people would regard as a thankless task with remarkable fortitude. Nor was this always done without personal cost. Friends of the employee who took his own life have told how he was often physically sick at the end of the day as a result of emotional strain. So much for the vampire image.

As far as the job itself was concerned the general character of the Arrow Lakes country and its houses has already been described. But one thing more needs to be said: there had been no effective market for property in the Arrow Lakes for many years. Thus the mainstay of the appraiser's normal approach, demonstrable market value, was non-existent in the Central Arrow Lakes and had to be sought in nearby areas.

Communal property was another problem. There was a minimum of formal organization in the Arrow Lakes. None of the communities were then incorporated, nor were their cemetery boards, or community hall boards. Thus in a legal sense Hydro had frequently no 'party' to deal with, and it should be said it took no advantage of that. In addition communal works, for example community halls or water systems, had often been the product of volunteer labour without benefit of niceties such as drawn plans, which meant of course that there were no records. Not that these situations lacked humour. Hydro's staff still recall fondly the appraisal of one venerable community hall. One of the appraiser's standard items was 'sanitary facilities.' In this case the answer was 'indoor outhouse,' a very proper description for a very proper six-holer.

One basic step taken at the beginning was a background study of conditions and land values in the adjacent Kootenay, Okanagan, and Slocan valleys. It was not pretended that conditions in any of these valleys were precisely similar to those in the Arrow Lakes, but they did present a reasonable range of situations into which some of the displaced people might be moving and of property values they might face. When this was announced (*Columbia Newsletter,* No 1, August 1964) it was acknowledged that the Arrow Lakes had been under threat of flooding for many years and it was stated that allowance would be made for this.

A second step was the publication in September 1964 of *The Property Owners' Guide* (reproduced in Appendix 1) and its distribution to all householders. This booklet was an attempt by Hydro to outline the property acquisition process, and to reassure people by giving them some idea of how they would be treated. This idea had not been received with enthusiasm by all members of Hydro's staff. There were those who felt it unwise to commit themselves to print, believing, not without reason, that anything they might say would be used against them. And laudable as it was as an exercise in open communication the *Guide* foreshadowed at least a couple of problems.

The first lay in Hydro's insistence that it would change an offer only 'if discussions ... show that some element of value was overlooked or that we erred in some other way,' at the same time refusing to present the breakdown of its offers. This could be interpreted only to mean that Hydro, not being willing to give a detailed statement but being willing to 'discuss' the situation, would only enter into a party-type guessing game with the property owner in which he would ask questions and the Hydro representative would answer only yes or no. In fact, Hydro officials admitted that if an owner was smart he could find out substantially what allowances had been made, a very disturbing admission in light of the fact that people concerned were by and large simple people, not skilled in matters of real estate or the art of cross examination.

The second problem lay in the semantic fog produced by the concurrent use of three key words. Hydro would 'discuss' and it would 'negotiate' but it would not 'bargain.' Quite apart from the tendency of these words to overlap in meaning, in common usage there was the simple fact that, whatever words were used to describe it, a process of accommodation took place whereby Hydro and a property owner reached agreement. Was the process 'discussion,' 'negotiation,' 'bargaining' (which is after all not necessarily a sinister process), or a miraculous kind of silent osmosis? Or was it 'bargaining' if the owner proposed the idea, but 'discussion' if the Hydro representative did? The people affected clearly couldn't care less what the word was. Call it, if you will, the 'non-bargaining process', it amounted to the same thing in the end.

These preparations, however, merely set the stage for the long, piece-by-piece process of inspecting, appraising, negotiating, and acquiring property. The process was a play in itself, lacking neither incident nor drama. The first player on the scene was Dr Hugh Keenleyside, who very shortly after the ratification of the Treaty felt that he, as Hydro chairman, should appear in person in the Arrow Lakes. His message was one of reassurance combined with sternness. He used the words he had employed when defending the Treaty in Ottawa, the only kind of language anyone could possibly use at that stage, 'fair and generous.' Having said this he went on to make it clear that Hydro had no intention of acceding to unreasonable demands, apparently a shot across the bows of certain American speculators.

The difficulty was that terms like 'fair,' 'generous,' and 'unreasonable' could be interpreted in Humpty Dumpty's words: 'When I use a word, it means just what I choose it to mean.' The inhabitants talked of *replacement* regardless of circumstances ('a roof for a roof') while Hydro talked of *value* as a market concept and therefore strictly related to time and place. The first viewpoint was well illustrated at the first meeting addressed by Dr Keenleyside at Needles when he was pressed for a specific assurance that lakefront land would be valued at the same front-foot price as in the Okanagan Valley. From the questioner's viewpoint the paramount consideration was replacement; from Hydro's the question had to be judged in light of the fact that the Okanagan was more populous, more accessible, more productive, drier, blessed with warmer water, and several hours' driving time closer to Vancouver.

But it was not merely that two very different views could be brought to bear on the question of value that made property appraisal a difficult task. The circumstances of the task made it doubly touchy. It was often impossible for inspections to be made privately.[2] Neighbours usually got to know. In-

2 It may also be pointed out that the telephone system, a euphemism at that time, featured party lines and (very) human operators.

evitably comparisons were made, valid or not. And even if the property owner kept his own counsel, that did not prevent the rumour mill from grinding out its own versions of the 'deal.' Occasionally a case would even pop up outside the region, like one which occasioned the following item by Hydro in *Columbia Newsletter*, No 11, 7 June 1966.

NEWSPAPER STATEMENT INCORRECT
We'd like to set the record straight concerning the purchase of a 100-acre dairy farm from James McKinnon, Revelstoke. A story originating in the *Vancouver Sun* stated that BC Hydro originally offered Mr McKinnon $100,000 for his dairy business and later raised the offer to $227,000.

No offer of $100,000 or any amount close to that figure was ever made to Mr McKinnon. Discussions leading to purchase of his property were completed within a 24-hour period and the original offer by Hydro was very close to the amount actually paid for the property.

We are concerned about the erroneous publicity because of the disturbing impact it could have on property owners whose properties have not yet been purchased.

At this time, in fact, rumours and editorial criticism were so widespread that Hydro wrote an editorial in the same *Newsletter*.

We are concerned about the publicity appearing in a number of newspapers criticizing the job that Hydro is doing. Some of the criticism has been justified and we welcome it, but a large part of it has been based on misinformation, misunderstanding and exaggeration. The result is an extremely distorted picture of the situation.

This matter is of grave concern to us because it imposes even greater anxiety on the property owners still waiting to reach an agreement with us. Their position has been difficult enough without this added burden.

Of the 1300 property holdings affected by three projects, more than 800 have already been purchased. We know from direct contact with them that the great majority of these property owners have been satisfied with the settlements we have reached with them.

We urge those property owners still waiting to reach a settlement with us to keep an open mind, to view the repeated criticisms by a few people with reservation, and to judge the situation for themselves when they have had personal experience with our field representatives.

One contributor to the boiling of the compensation pot was H.W. Herridge, the member of parliament for the Arrow Lakes, who was still fighting the project tooth and nail. It was to be expected that the region's political representatives would try to ensure the best possible treatment for their constituents, but in Hydro's view Herridge's tactics were irresponsible and likely to raise false hopes and unnecessary animosities. On July 3 1964, for example, he entered an item in the *Arrow Lakes News,* inviting comparison between property values in the Arrow Lakes and the environs of Ottawa, as if the two regions were remotely comparable in terms of population, growth rate, or property market activity.

By contrast the local politician who emerged with reputation enhanced was Randolph Harding (NDP), then incumbent in the Kaslo-Slocan provincial riding and later member of parliament for the federal riding. Harding fought for his consitituents regardless of their political allegiance; he questioned, needled, and harassed the government in the legislature; and he interceded directly with Hydro on behalf of his constituents, quietly and effectively, with dignity and responsibility. Despite his status as a highly critical member of the opposition. Harding gained Hydro's respect and admiration.

But value appraisal was in many cases only the beginning of the job for Hydro. For example, some of the displaced people receiving welfare payments lived in their own homes, and although many of these were small, old, and decrepit, their appraised value might amount to thousands of dollars. Provincial welfare regulations were such that the receipt of any substantial capital sum would automatically disqualify the recipient for welfare payments until he was again reduced to a state of need. Even more serious for many, such disqualification would automatically cut the recipient off from medical benefits.

In such a case routine payment of compensation would have wrought considerable distress upon individuals, and damaged Hydro's image. On becoming aware of this danger Hydro took the matter up with the welfare authorities and it was arranged that a period of grace would be allowed, long enough for the recipient to find a new house.

A somewhat similar situation could have arisen from the fact that the whole process of inspection, appraisal, checking, discussion, and acceptance often took quite some time to complete. During this time people frequently required cash to buy or put a down-payment on a new property. In such cases once the general level of the compensation was clear Hydro arranged to make a substantial proportion of it available in advance of final settlement. Not a big thing to be sure, but an indication that Hydro was not a soul-less monster.

Despite the story told in chapter 12 Hydro did take special care of old and needy people. Among other things it employed a fatherly retired civil servant, William MacGillivray, to look after them. One of his main tasks was to help find them new homes and to do this he drove them on many long journeys into neighbouring towns and valleys.[3] Hydro believes that no older person displaced by the Columbia River project lacked a comfortable home.

One of the most imaginative steps taken by Hydro was the appointment of an 'ombudsman' or, more formally, a special commissioner, for the Columbia project. This was the brainchild of Dr Keenleyside, who at the same time realized that his proposal would need very careful implementation if its objectives were to be fully realized. The facts of the matter and reasons for it were set out in the *Columbia Newsletter*, No 5, 19 February 1965.

We are grateful to Chief Justice J.O. Wilson of the Supreme Court of British Columbia for selecting Judge M.M. Colquhoun for the important role of Special Commissioner for the Columbia projects.

Over 2000 people will have to move as a result of the construction of the three Columbia Treaty dams. We have promised these people that they will be treated fairly and generously. So far the program has been working remarkably well, but we realize it is always possible that a mistake may be made or that some people may feel that they have been unjustly treated. That's why we asked Chief Justice Wilson to select a distinguished citizen to act as a kind of referee to hear complaints and to advise us as to actions we should take.

The terms of reference for the Special Commissioner (which have been approved by the Chief Justice) are:

1 On request the Special Commissioner will advise persons whose rights or interests are to be affected as to the proper representations to be made and the proper course of action to pursue before or during the process of negotiations for purchase by the Authority.
2 When asked to do so by the Authority, or by a person affected, the Special Commissioner will present to the Authority such considerations as may appear to him to affect any rights or interests of the person concerned.
3 The recommendations of the Special Commissioner are to be made only for the help of the individual affected and the guidance of the Hydro and, if a process of compulsory acquisition follows, will not be acceptable as evidence.
4 The Special Commissioner will normally examine complaints in relation to the Hydro's financial offers only in those instances in which the complainant has reason to believe that some significant aspect of his case has been overlooked by the Hydro officers who have made the proposal.

3 MacGillivray's work was appreciatively mentioned by several people in the 1970 survey (chapter 14).

5 The services of the Special Commissioner will be rendered free to the persons who request them.

Behind the manner of this appointment lay the realization that at the time – winter 1964–5 when relatively few property settlements had been completed and tension was rising – such an offer might be regarded as a spurious PR gimmick. To be taken seriously it had to bear the stamp of impeccable impartiality. This led the chairman to approach the chief justice of British Columbia, who suggested Judge Colquhoun for the post as well as concurring in his terms of reference.

It would scarcely be surprising if, nevertheless, the people of the Arrow Lakes were suspicious of this move at the time. I well remember the reply given me when I asked one of the Hydro field staff how he thought the special commissioner was viewed by the people. 'Oh,' he said, 'they think he's just a Hydro pussycat,' his meaning being as clear as his metaphor was odd. Nevertheless the Judge heard fifty-five cases in all and in every case Hydro accepted his recommendation, which was invariably on the side of generosity.

The evidence cited so far suggests that Hydro of its own volition did many humane acts to ease the plight of those it uprooted. However, as corroboration it may be worthwhile to add here accounts of the Arrow Lakes scene by Tom Hazlitt, a critical young reporter for the *Vancouver Province*.[4] The first, written on 2 July 1964, gives a good view of the problem and the atmosphere which confronted Hydro at the start of its work.

ARROW FOLK IN QUANDARY

How much is home worth?

In the valley of the Arrow Lakes the cold, precise laws of economics have always been an enemy. And now those same laws are about to dictate a dramatic end to a way of life.

Two thousand people are caught in a classic conflict. On one side: the dam and shattering attendant developments which the majority of law-makers have found desirable, necessary and profitable.

On the other side is a manner of living which may be slow and inefficient. But it is a life in which most residents have a vested interest and which many honestly prefer.

4 Frank Rutter writing for the *Vancouver Sun* about the same time in 1966 reported in much the same terms as Hazlitt, but in order to avoid tedious repetition his articles are not reproduced here.

It is only in the past few weeks that the truth has begun to sink in that the old days are truly gone. And only now are people realizing that while some of them will profit, a great number will be hurt.

BC pledge

Throughout the long negotiation of the Columbia River Treaty, officials of the BC Government and BC Hydro have repeated one theme concerning the people who will be displaced. Dr Hugh Keenleyside, co-chairman of BC Hydro, has said repeatedly the people will be treated fairly, sympathetically and generously.

He has also said that special help will be made available to old people to assist them in re-establishment. There will be no formula, but each case will be settled on its merits, with due attention paid to intangibles like sentimental attachments, years of toil, employment, and income.

Spelled out

There seems no doubt but that these principles will be honestly and humanely applied.

But the tragedy lies in the fact that these promises have come to mean one thing to the politicians and administrators responsible and quite another to the farmers, loggers and old-timers who will be flooded out.

Rightly or wrongly, many people of the Arrow Lakes have come to believe they will receive what they term full replacement compensation. Under this line of reasoning, a man who owns outright a six room house, a couple of barns, 30 acres of land and a bit of waterfront should be moved to a similar holding or given enough money to establish himself in the same fashion.

This is definitely not the case.

In the past week or so, the property owners affected have received letters setting forth the true state of affairs.

The letter, signed by Dr Keenleyside, says representatives of BC Hydro's land division will determine the fair market value of each parcel of land involved, then will make offers of purchase to the owners.

One case

It has not escaped the Arrow residents that fair market value and so-called replacement value are two very different things.

In fact, land and buildings which are about to be flooded have no market value, fair or otherwise. However, a fair estimate of value can be made by taking the tax assessment, comparing land sales in adjacent areas, and adding something for the intangible called 'special value to owner.'

In the view of BC Hydro officials, this treatment is fair and equitable, and certainly in line with expropriation procedures in Canada. But in the view of many property owners it is a disaster.

Take the case of Nick Makarewicz, father of six, a ferry operator by day and a farmer the rest of the time. For his regular eight-hour shift he gets an average salary. He works hard, all members of his family work hard, but the rewards are high. He walks to work and puts his car money into tractors and equipment. He never buys milk, eggs, beef or vegetables, which most people figure results in a saving of $500 per year, for eight people, or $4,000. He sells beef cattle and timber.

Others' problems

In city or town Nick Makarewicz would be fortunate to make $100 a week, assuming he could find a job. But in his own private empire he lives like a king on prime waterfront property, has no security problem, and figured on putting all six children through university.

Because of his zeal in putting the farm in shape, Makarewicz will probably get higher compensation than most, but his chances of building a comparable life with the proceeds are slim.

It could be argued that the Makarewicz dilemma is a special case. BC Hydro officials are fond of saying that the majority of farms are marginal operations and many, in fact, are not farms at all but residences, the owners of which have long since given up farming for more lucrative work in the woods and mills.

Real values

This is quite true. Many of the farms are run down and neglected, and many of the residents do earn a good living, often on the payroll of the Celgar logging division.

But it does not necessarily follow that they are just itching to trade the old family spread for a crowded duplex in town.

There are advantages to living on a marginal farm. For one thing it is paid for, and until recently the practice of going into debt has been considered one of the more serious forms of sin in the Arrow Lakes. The barns may be falling down and the whole thing needs a coat of paint, but many of these people consider themselves proprietors of country estates. Kids have horses of their own and enough wood to cut to keep them out of trouble.

The proceeds of the farm operation may be small in terms of cash, but this is an isolated valley and a lively barter economy keeps living standards high. Mrs Jones makes good butter which she trades with Mrs Smith, who has an orchard, and both deal with Mrs Black, whose eggs taste wonderful. This sort of thing has little market value, but it stretches the pay cheque.

The so-called marginal farmers of the valley are quick to claim that their farms are uneconomic rather than unproductive.

Residents also claim that their district has been deliberately depressed with a view to just the kind of deal now shaping up.

On balance, it appears the residents of Arrow Lakes will get fair compensation and fair treatment.

But the way of life – independence, privacy, the ripple of water on the lake and the colt in the far pasture – these things are dead, and there will be many who mourn their passing.

On 16 May 1966 Hazlitt was writing again.

TWO-FISTED FOLKS ARE HARD TO UPROOT

Clouds of smoke hang heavy over the beautiful valley of the Arrow Lakes, where more changes have occurred in the last six months than in the past hundred years.

Most of the smoke comes from slash clearings along the lakeshore, where all night long, men with bulldozers feed bonfires as part of a giant clean-up job.

But some of it comes from the remains of houses and barns, where in some cases the hopes and hard work of generations are put to the torch in fiery sacrifice to the god called progress.

Today the battle lines are drawn. The people are on the move, and the blue staff cars and trucks of BC Hydro move through the old townsites like warrior ants in search of prey.

Although rumours fly thick and fast in the Arrow Lakes country, it is difficult to find bona fide cases of hardship or bureaucratic mismanagement.

Hydro officials admit that in the mammoth job of uprooting a whole countryside – a countryside inhabited largely by two-fisted individualists – some mistakes have been made. But, they insist, the rule books have been stretched on occasion to rectify these, and the bulk of displaced persons are satisfied.

In the offices of BC Hydro here in Nakusp, one hears a story of orderly negotiations and sound business practice not untouched by the qualities of mercy and imagination.

But in the beer parlors, the quiet side roads and back kitchens of the country people, things are quite different. Charge and counter-charge echo back and forth with the same persistence and frequency as the steamboat whistles of a generation ago.

From this welter of conversation – some of it pretty wild – there emerges a pattern of legitimate complaint.

On 17 May:

THERE WILL BE BLOODSHED: HYDRO ‘GANGSTERS’

‘It's this scorched earth policy that frightens people. It's getting worse every day – homes burning, and old widow ladies standing out in the snow watching their belongings go up. Somebody's going to get hurt one day, and then there will be bloodshed in this valley on top of everything else.’

The speaker was a bespectacled farmer-logger, apparently in his right mind and apparently well-informed.

'I tell you,' he went on, 'I tell you those Hydro land agents aren't anything of the sort. Gangsters, they are, specially imported gangsters and black-mailers to boot.'

The conversation is extreme, but typical of the endless talk one encounters in the more remote sections of the Arrow Lakes.

It goes on and on, one shocking 'fact' piled on top of another with obvious sincerity.

A non-critical tourist from Calgary or California would come away convinced that the darkest deeds of the Middle Ages are being perpetrated wholesale on the long-suffering citizenry.

A reporter checking rumours of bureaucratic mismanagement quickly fills a notebook with such 'facts,' but must then check back laboriously to find out what really happened.

There is usually a grain of truth, explainable in itself, but built to magnificent proportions as the story passes from one pocket of habitation to another in an area where communication is still in an undeveloped state.

The really wild rumours move like the wind of the Arrow Lakes, which is fast and unpredictable.

But under the wild talk there are serious complaints, put forward quietly by responsible people.

Basically, these are the causes of trouble as Hydro officials go about their land-assembly task:

– There is a deliberate lack of any announced yardstick in figuring property values.

– Property owners can cite what appear to be scores of inconsistencies in settlements already reached.

– Property owners claim Hydro uses time a a bargaining agent, on the theory that the big Crown corporation can afford to wait it out much easier than a small farmer or logger who has to find a new place in which to earn a living.

– The so-called scorched earth policy is a fact in some places where Hydro officials consider it dangerous or unwise to leave an empty house on its newly-acquired property.

– Hydro officials refuse to disclose the basis on which they make offers.

This last item is the cause of more trouble than all the rest put together.

For example, the land agent will say that an offer of $10,000 is based on the price of land, house, buildings, waterfront and the disturbance factor. But he won't tie down the cost of any separate item.

Residents say this is unfair and leaves them completely in the dark as to what their values are.

It also removes an ingredient of comparison on the cost applied to barns and the like, although the Arrow Lakes people compare virtually everything that happens.

The property owners claim Lands Minister Williston promised them that this practice would cease, but nothing has happened yet.

However, the much-maligned Hydro officials have their own side of the story, and this will be presented in the next article.

And finally on 19 May:

In the brand new offices of BC Hydro – well above floodline – there is a special room lined with maps and well filled with card indexes and filing cabinets.

This is the land department, where the financial fate of thousands of Arrow Lakes residents is weighted and measured.

To hear some residents talk, you would think this a star chamber set-up inhabited by parsimonious officials determined to pay the least possible compensation for valuable land and buildings.

What actually goes on here? How do the Hydro land agents go about setting a price on homesteads which vary from wheezy old mansions to log huts, and farmland that runs the gamut from highly productive orchard to poverty stricken acres suitable only for the production of boulders?

The first step is the appraisal, which takes the form of a bulky questionnaire complete with pictures of the home in question, barns, out-buildings and all the rest.

Once the description is complete, the land agent evaluates the features of the property concerned, in line with values in neighboring valleys.

Because the Arrow Lakes people have lived for years in the shadow of the impending dam, there are very few local property sales which can set a pattern.

To this point the investigation follows the lines of a normal real estate deal.

But these people have to move, so the guidelines must differ. The land agents add something for cost of moving, for disruption and for land use.

The eventual total and all pertinent data then go to Vancouver, where a special staff compares it with settlements already reached in the area and with values elsewhere.

All this checking and crosschecking takes time, which sometimes leads to the charge that Hydro utilizes the time element as part of the bargaining procedure.

Finally the offer goes to the property owner concerned. Very often it is considered too low, or rejected flatly.

At this point the process of 'non-bargaining' begins.

According to the terms of reference set down by the authority, land agents may not haggle. Theoretically the offered price is final and can be upset only by the findings of an arbitrator in expropriation proceedings.

But in actual fact, changes can be and are made if the property owner can show that some feature of his property has been neglected. The property owner is also encouraged to go into Hydro offices, where he is shown extensive files of property which he could reasonably purchase with the amount of money available.

For a vigorous young logger with a tumbledown home, the Arrow Lakes displacement can be a chance to get out from under and start anew.

But for older people who expected to live out their days on the old homestead, displacement is indeed a problem.

Hydro officials admit that in these cases the amount paid for 'disruption' is sometimes inflated, because the market value of the property simply isn't enough to procure equivalent living accommodation.

It is this intangible assessment of circumstances which leads to charges that there is no rhyme nor reason to Hydro offers.

It's the old dilemma of balancing the need to guard the public purse against the possibility of causing undue hardships, and every case is different.

Little things sometimes play a big role in the 'non-bargaining' process.

One elderly woman placed great value on her bathtub – the finest bathtub in all the Arrow Lakes. Hydro enabled her to take it with her.

The process of hoarding things against a rainy day is second nature in the Arrow Lakes, so there are cases on record of citizens labouriously packing old lumber from their purchased homes over mountain ranges to a new site.

And there is the delicate matter of saving face. The farmer who has stormed the countryside declaring that he won't settle for less than $30,000 may in fact settle for a good deal less, providing he gets something. This is handled by the last minute 'discovery' of some intangible which permits a minor upward revision of the purchase offer.

Hydro officials claim they are fair and generous without being extravagant – and they have the files which tend to bear them out.

But they agree with critics in one important respect.

The old communities are disappearing, the old associations are gone and a leisurely way of life is dead.

For this there can be no compensation in kind or in money, and to this extent the people of the Arrow Lakes are the victims of the common good.

It is the accepted thing in some circles to decry the work of the daily press. Nevertheless in this case it is significant that two reporters from competing newspapers, Hazlitt and Rutter, should both report in nicely balanced terms. Both found dilemmas; both found blacks and whites; and both refrained from resounding judgments.

It is worth mentioning, by the way, that there was some organized opposition to Hydro, principally by a group known as the Arrow Lakes Property

Owners Protective Association. This group organized a demonstration at the Arrow dam site in October 1965 and thereby earned quite a bit of publicity. They are also credited by Hydro with having propagandized widely against the Authority's program and having stirred up a degree of recalcitrance in many people. Certainly in places considerably removed from the region the Arrow Lakes program attracted fire, notably from Ma Murray, the pyrotechnic publisher of the *Bridge River News.* It should be admitted however that almost *any* program of the Bennett government was liable to send Mrs Murray into orbit, and perhaps the Columbia program should not have felt especially honoured by her fulminations. There was also some coherent opposition from a group of Ukrainians south of Revelstoke where no fewer than ten cases had to be dealt with by expropriation.

These observations make it clear that it is wrong to stigmatize opposition as perverse or wicked, as bureaucrats tend to do. Where does neighbourly solidarity end and organized resistance begin? When does firm conviction become irrational obstinacy? And anyway, why should anyone expect *rational* behaviour under such circumstances? It is clear from the records that some people displaced by the Arrow Lakes project were unable to accept the inevitable with equanimity. To that extent they are more to be pitied than pilloried for they lost not only home and community but personal serenity as well.

The views of some of the displaced people in 1970, two years after the effective completion of the project, are recorded in chapter 14. They tend to reflect the situation sketched by Hazlitt. But what is important at this stage in the narrative is to establish the climate which prevailed in the Arrow Lakes for some four years. This climate stemmed very largely from the question of compensation: whether it was adequate, whether it was consistent, and how the business of negotiation was actually carried out. It enveloped everything else Hydro did in these four years, and is worth remembering throughout the chapters that follow.

But first it is worth pointing out that even in human terms the processes of taking properties and resettling people were not all funereal, nor did they always find the dispossessed on the side of the angels. A rather humorous memorandum illustrates the point. It was written by Bert Watson, a discerning Hydro staff member of humane disposition. Names, places, and prices have been changed in this version but the essence of the situation remains untouched.

RE: THE JOHANNSONS OF BURWOOD

I travelled with the Johannsons to Canoe Monday to seek potential relocation sites.

We were met at Canoe by Mr Pepper, a real estate man who arranged to visit a house in the town. The house, about twelve to fifteen years old, was not in the best condition, but was pleasant, roomy, and conveniently located. It was rather obvious that Mr Johannson rejected the property before examining it inside; indeed, I feel he was prepared to reject it even before he arrived in Canoe.

While in Canoe I viewed, from outside, a replacement property the Johannsons had selected on a trip through the area recently. This property is for sale at $20,000 according to Johannson. It is, I expect, no more than two years old, and is apparently a good and substantial house. Even so, my layman's guess is that $20,000 is a rather high price for this place.

I formed the opinion that Mr Johannson has set his cap for this house and will exert all pressures to get it. He realizes that BC Hydro considers $12,000 a generous offering for his existing property but, of course, is in total disagreement.

Mr Johannson has a frustrating defense which is difficult to puncture. This is his wife's apparent condition, which is used to rule out settlement in most areas. The only place they've found where Mrs Johannson is comfortable is in the Canoe area. And the only thing acceptable to them there is a house which is worth nearly twice the value of their present place when very generously estimated.

I cannot fathom this medical conundrum; but I can't dispute it either. The same climatic circumstances and conditions cannot be duplicated, says Mr Johannson, in Vernon, Kelowna, or Penticton, where there is too much pollen; in Kamloops where it's too hot and too cold; in Salmon Arm, Enderby, etc., where there's too much farm dust; in Revelstoke where there's too much snow; in the Fraser Valley where it's too low; in the East Kootenays where it's too high; in Vancouver where it's too wet; or on Vancouver Island (well, who'd want to live there?) Indeed!

To cap this a very revealing story was told of the Peace River about this time. It concerned a worried trapper who asked a Hydro engineer how much he thought he might get for his trapline. 'Oh, I guess they'll give you what it's worth,' said the engineer ingenuously. 'Hell,' said the trapper, 'I'll want a damn sight more than that.'

With this we shall leave our very human beings of both camps and step chronologically back into our tale to June 1965.

7
The broad brush

Having felt the wind, we started to prepare public documents which would tell the people of the Arrow Lakes as precisely as was then possible how the Arrow reservoir would affect them and their homes. (Stakes showing the future high water mark had previously been driven into the ground at many points around the lakes so that most people had some idea how the scheme would affect them. But of course many of the stakes had been removed and there were many areas of uncertainty at this time.) The first document published was a broad-brush report entitled *The New Outlook for the Arrow Lakes* which was mailed to every home in the affected area in June 1965. This is reproduced almost in its entirety on the following pages.

THE TREATY DAMS AND THEIR EFFECTS ON THE REGION

The Treaty dams

The major works which will change the face of the Columbia basin are the three dams to be constructed under the Columbia River Treaty, namely the Mica, Arrow and Duncan Dams. Of these the Arrow Dam will flood the most inhabited land and will therefore necessitate most reconstruction.

Reservoir levels

The Arrow Lakes will be used for the storage of water. Thus every year the reservoir will be filled by the spring flood and will then be drawn down as required by the Treaty. The level of the reservoir in any month will fluctuate from year to year, but it will be highest during the summer months, which are important for recreation and tourism. Normally the reservoir will be full during these months, unless there has been an exceptionally dry winter.

Elimination of floods

The Arrow Dam will control the floods which used to plague the Arrow Lakes Region from time to time. Previously the flood level and flood damage in any year could never be predicted; from 1969 onward the maximum water level will be known and there will be no dwellings below that level to suffer damage.

The new levels and their land effects

Today the Arrow Lakes experience an extreme range in water level of about 40 feet. When the Arrow Dam is in operation they will have an extreme range of about 76 feet, the full reservoir level being some 36 feet higher than the previous maximum flood level. At no time will the water level fall below the minimum level under natural conditions.

The new high water level and the effects of wind and wave will render some land uninhabitable; and in certain areas we must acquire additional land to allow for unstable banks or for difficulties in maintaining road access. As a result land will be purchased to the following minimum elevations: from Arrowhead to Revelstoke, 1455 feet; in the Narrows area, 1460 feet; elsewhere in the reservoir, 1453 feet. However, each piece of land is unique as regards soil, slope and exposure to waves, and additional land will be purchased wherever it is necessary to ensure that the area remaining will be safe.

We propose to buy all the properties in the areas shown in Diagram 6. The inclusion of the Arrow Park area requires explanation. The fine silty soils of this area will be saturated as the Arrow reservoir rises and will become unstable when the water level is drawn down. This is expected to result in landslides extending considerable distances back from the shorelines. Also, these circumstances will make it impractical to provide access to the area by ferry.

TOMORROW'S REGION

In the face of these changes, a great deal of thought has been given to the future of the Arrow Lakes Region. The most important factors for reconstruction will be as follows:

Highway network

The new highway network, to be built through the combined efforts of Hydro and the Department of Highways, will be of the greatest importance to the Region. The major elements in this will be as shown on Diagram 7.

As a result of this new network the speed, continuity and safety of travel

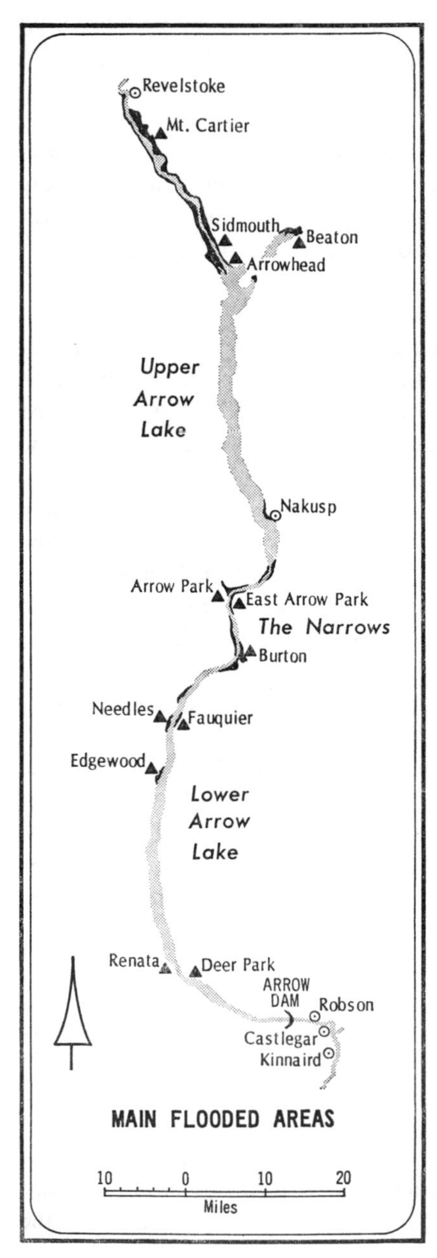
Revelstoke
Mt. Cartier
Sidmouth
Beaton
Arrowhead
Upper
Arrow
Lake
Nakusp
Arrow Park
East Arrow Park
The Narrows
Burton
Needles
Fauquier
Edgewood
Lower
Arrow
Lake
Renata
Deer Park
ARROW
DAM
Robson
Castlegar
Kinnaird
MAIN FLOODED AREAS
10
0
10
20
Miles

DIAGRAM 6

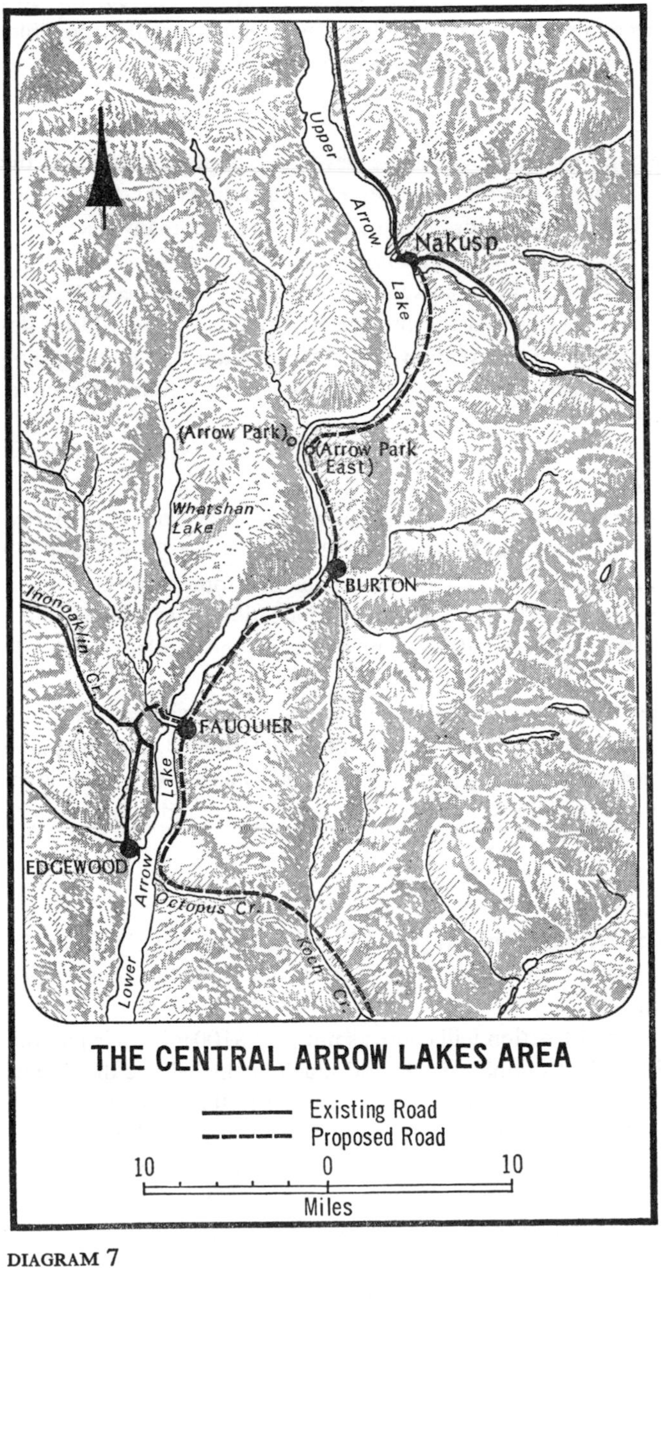

Upper
Arrow
Lake
Nakusp
(Arrow Park)
(Arrow Park East)
Whatshan Lake
BURTON
Inonoaklin Cr.
FAUQUIER
Lake
EDGEWOOD
Arrow
Octopus Cr.
Koch Cr.
Lower
THE CENTRAL ARROW LAKES AREA
Existing Road
Proposed Road
10
0
10
Miles

DIAGRAM 7

into and out of the Edgewood-Nakusp area will be greatly improved; the cost of travel will be reduced; a wider choice of outside supply centres will be possible; and Nelson, Castlegar and Trail will become more accessible.

Parks and beaches

Good parks, beaches and campsites could be developed at several spots at the new high water level. These features, together with attractions like the various hot springs, will result in the Region being able to provide many recreation attractions both for its own inhabitants and for tourists.

In order to make full use of the opportunities, sites at Syringa Creek, Renata, Deer Park and Demars will be set aside for beach parks and these will be developed by the Department of Recreation and Conservation. Other promising sites will be investigated by the Department this summer and, if found attractive, will also be developed.

Land for resettlement

In the spring of 1969 a new ring of waterfront sites will emerge around the Arrow Lakes. Most of these will be owned by Hydro or directly by the Crown and will be made available for resettlement at soon as possible. In some cases this might be almost immediately; in some, as soon as new road locations have been decided; and in others, only after a number of years have passed and the land is clearly safe for settlement.

In order to make the most of these land resources, sites will be dealt with systematically. First the best use of each area will be determined; then a system of priorities will be set up to allow for the claims of displaced residents, community and service organizations, commercial enterprises and other private citizens.

Economic opportunities

The economy of the Arrow Lakes Region will benefit enormously from the construction of the Treaty works and, both during and after the construction period, from tourism.

In the next 20 years construction will cause as much as $100 million in payrolls alone to be spent within the Columbia Basin and much of this will be distributed widely throughout the Arrow Lakes Region. In addition to the dams themselves, surveys, clearing, road projects, the construction of new communities and other tasks will give employment to many men, who will require accommodation, food, supplies and services of various kinds. Local enterprise within the Region should be able to supply many of these needs, thus adding to the prosperity of the Arrow Lakes communities.

The new highway network will open the way for tourists and holiday-makers.

A large volume of tourist traffic will be assured by the attraction of the dams, at which we will provide reception facilities for visitors. The new network will also bridge the gap between two trans-continental highways carrying hundreds of thousands of tourists every summer.

Tourists spend money mainly on lodging, food and automobile needs, and – if they can be persuaded to stop over – on shopping, entertainment and recreation also. Thus new opportunities will arise in the Region for stores, cafes, service stations and motels, both existing and new. There should also be new business for holiday resorts and ranches and for the sale of curios, handcrafts and local produce.

A NEW SETTLEMENT PATTERN

Where should people, especially those whose homes are affected, fit into these plans? Some guidance on this question can be obtained by looking back to the past.

Over the years the automobile and the road have replaced the steam boat and the river; the axe has given way to the power-saw and the team to the logging truck; the working radius has been stretched from a few miles to 45 minutes' driving time; and the working unit has grown from the small timber lot to the very large tree farm.

But these changes have been superimposed on a settlement pattern which has changed little in the past two generations, for the old days left enduring marks on the Region. Many of the original communities have shrunk – or even disappeared entirely – although the original building lots remain; most orchards, with a few exceptions such as Renata, are abandoned and cleared land supports only a few horses or cattle; most river landings are deserted; the houses are often heavy with years and many are derelict. In other words, for reasons of necessity or sentiment many of the residents have retained the old settlement pattern. But the original reasons for that pattern vanished long ago.

Today's opportunities

The raising of the water level will wipe out much of the past; much more important, however, it now offers those who must move a unique opportunity to build vital new communities based on the circumstances of today, not of yesterday.

The resettlement plans of some people are now becoming apparent. For example, our studies suggest that some people will resettle as close as possible to their former homes; some, especially older persons, will leave the Region entirely; and others will move to the larger centres of Revelstoke, Castlegar and Nakusp.

These trends are to be expected. However, between Edgewood and Arrowhead a challenging alternative is available. Much of the communities of Edgewood, Needles, Burton, Arrow Park, East Arrow Park, Beaton and Arrowhead will disappear entirely. The choice facing their residents is: whether to remain as near as possible to their accustomed localities or to take full advantage of the situation by settling in completely new communities.

Their choices will depend partly on whether they wish to live close to their jobs and on whether they prefer rural or community life. Nevertheless, two facts should be considered carefully before vital resettlement decisions are made:

(*a*) Many people today expect an increasing range of services and conveniences from their communities – a doctor, a hospital, a high school, churches, a range of stores, radio and TV repair services, telephones and a curling club, for example – but these can be provided only where there are enough people to support them.

(*b*) The automobile and good roads enable people to live in larger communities and travel considerable distances to work, thus reducing the need for small settlements tied to job locations. (It is equally possible, of course, for people to live close to their work or in rural areas and travel to the communities for their services.)

These facts suggest that in the Edgewood-Nakusp area those who wish to enjoy the best available range of community services should first consider settling in Nakusp, which has a range of services unrivalled within 70 miles.

On the other hand, for those who do not wish to settle in Nakusp, the fewer new communities there are, the better equipped they could be. Perhaps 150 families may settle in new communities. If they were to settle in three communities containing 30, 50 and 70 families respectively, not one of these could support much more than a general store, a garage and a two-room school, and none would have much to offer the surrounding countryside. But if all the families were to settle in one community it could support more services more efficiently, serve the surrounding area better and have more to offer the traveller and the tourist.

Alternative sites for new communities

In the Edgewood-Nakusp area there appear to be only three places suitable for the development of new communities (Diagram 7).

Edgewood: A pleasant site is available on the tongue of land between Eagle Creek and Inonoaklin Creek. This site, which is already accessible to Vernon, will also have good access to Castlegar and Nelson when the new Koch Creek road is built. It would serve the Inonoaklin Valley farming area. However, since it is several miles off the main highway a settlement there would probably remain relatively minor.

Burton: Several suitable sites are available for a new community, all with nearby land for rural settlement. However, in view of the existence of Nakusp on one side and the greater growth prospects of Fauquier on the other, Burton also would probably remain a minor community.
Fauquier: There is a good site for a new community north of the ferry route, with nearby waterfront and ridge sites for rural homes. According to official records, it enjoys the best local climate in the area – almost three inches less rainfall than Edgewood and eight inches less than Nakusp. A settlement here could act as the supply centre for the Inonoaklin Valley. Most of all, being located at the key highway junction it would be accessible from all directions and would receive *all* the tourist traffic passing through the Region.

Even under the most favourable circumstances a community at any of these sites would be small at the start, offering only limited services to its residents. Considering the future as well as the present, we believe Fauquier is the best available site.

However, it is not for us to decide how or where people should live. Consequently we look forward to hearing the views of those concerned on the location of new communities.

What should a new community be like?

An example of a new community designed for 150 families[1] is shown in Diagram 8. It should have the following characteristics:

1 It should be located and laid out to take advantage of views, lake frontage and other natural features.

2 It should have a well-designed centre containing the central facilities of the community – stores, bank, post office, church, community hall, hotel – together with parking space and a public park. This centre should be the most accessible point in the community and closely connected to the main road.

3 The school should be convenient to residential areas but located away from the main highway.

4 It should have utilities suited to its size and ground conditions: probably a piped water supply; septic tanks, provided the ground is porous; telephone and electric power; and, preferably, paved streets.

5 It should be developed compactly, with a minimum of empty lots, to minimize the cost of services and their maintenance.

1 A note in retrospect: this may have been an unfortunate choice of size in that it may have given some people a vision of a highly improbable community. It was over-optimistic to expect that there could be such unanimity among the prospective settlers. Ah, hindsight!

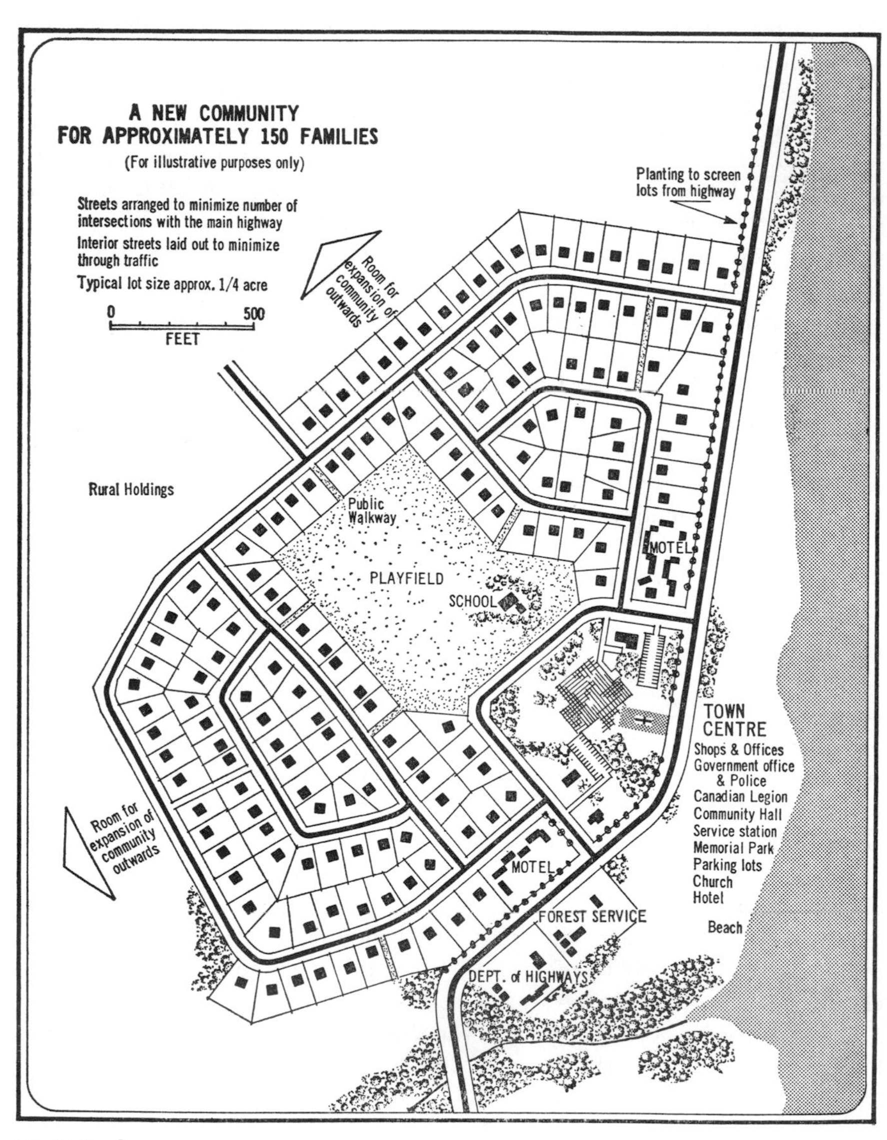
A NEW COMMUNITY
FOR APPROXIMATELY 150 FAMILIES
(For illustrative purposes only)
Streets arranged to minimize number of intersections with the main highway
Interior streets laid out to minimize through traffic
Typical lot size approx. 1/4 acre
0
500
FEET
Room for expansion of community outwards
Planting to screen lots from highway
Rural Holdings
Public Walkway
PLAYFIELD
SCHOOL
MOTEL
Room for expansion of community outwards
TOWN CENTRE
Shops & Offices
Government office & Police
Canadian Legion
Community Hall
Service station
Memorial Park
Parking lots
Church
Hotel
MOTEL
FOREST SERVICE
DEPT. of HIGHWAYS
Beach

DIAGRAM 8

6 The lots themselves could vary in size depending on the desires of prospective owners, but many people would presumably want purely residential lots no bigger than they could easily maintain.

However, new communities may not fill all resettlement needs, for there will be some who prefer to settle on relatively large lots in rural areas. We will give them first choice of the stock of land which we will own when our land purchases are complete.

Residents' role

We have attempted to provide information that will help displaced residents to decide where they wish to resettle. In addition there will be opportunities for questions and public discussion. After that, those concerned must make their decisions.

This we must stress. Building new communities cannot be a one-sided business. Our resources will be necessary to help create them; but those who will live in them must first say what they want and be prepared to work with us to achieve it.

THE NEXT STEP

Public meetings are being arranged at points throughout the Arrow Lakes Region to give residents an opportunity to ask questions and to discuss local situations with our representatives.

Following these meetings, some time will probably be required for those concerned to discuss the situation among themselves and possibly to form local groups and appoint spokesmen. As soon as possible after that we will proceed to find out what the individuals and groups facing resettlement wish to do. To accomplish this we may hold further meetings or conduct personal interviews.

When all this has been done we will immediately prepare final plans for new communities, land disposal, housemoving and all the other action programmes involved.

In the meantime this Plan offers food for thought and for decision. The next step lies with the people of the Region.

Simple as this report may seem, its birth was not an easy one.[2] The essence of the problem was that raising the top water level by thirty-six feet would do two things: it would displace over 2000 people, and would greatly reduce

2 What follows is an analysis of the working process as I experienced it. However, an inkling of difficulties at the board of directors level is given by a retrospective note to me by Dr Keenleyside: 'You are not, I think, aware of the trouble experienced in getting the Hydro Board to approve anything as "extravagant" as *The New Outlook*, or the development program in general.'

the amount of land available for resettlement in the valley. That supply was already very limited; just how limited no one then suspected.

The first survey of basic data had revealed the upsetting fact that in keeping with the main (engineering) thrust of the project up to this point the contour maps which had been made of the Arrow Lakes area covered only limited areas above the high water level. In particular, some of the most probable resettlement sites were not adequately mapped. Much more serious, however, and much less quickly remedied, was the fact that no specific soils examination had been made of the new shoreline.

The first difficulty was soon overcome and caused no delay. The second, however, involved detailed investigations by outside experts and was still not completely resolved as late as November 1965. The reason for concern was that many of the slopes at the foot of the mountains consisted of silty soils whose stability would change radically when saturated by the rising waters. Dry, the slopes were completely stable, apart from some erosion at the river's edge; saturated, they would be both heavy and weak,which was expected to result in the collapse of large masses of soil. That this was no figment of an expert's imagination had been made very clear on the Columbia south of the border. There some massive 'alcove' slides had taken place which affected land as much as half-a-mile back from the water's edge.

The reports of the soils experts, when they dribbled in over the months following, were disturbing. They put out of bounds almost all of the strip land, especially in the Narrows, which we had hoped to use for scattered resettlement. They cast grave doubts for a considerable period on two of the principal sites for new settlements, Fauquier and Edgewood, and contributed to the long delay in the completion of resettlement plans. This in turn greatly upset the people concerned, especially the impatient band at Edgewood who not unnaturally concluded that Hydro was stalling and had no intention of encouraging resettlement there. In fact we were assuring people in public as late as May 1965 that there would be lots of land available for resettlement, a situation which did nothing to enhance our credibility when the engineering facts ultimately became available. Most of all, the reports unexpectedly turned thumbs down on West Arrow Park, necessitating total abandonment of that community, contrary to the expectations of both the inhabitants and ourselves.

One of the greatest difficulties which Hydro faced in the planning stages was that of effective collaboration with the provincial government. Yet this was vital to a complete development program rather than just a patch-up job. The main elements in such a program were completion of the highway system both within and beyond the Central Arrow Lakes, and development of lakeside parks and camping grounds.

One of the most important of these difficulties concerned the site of the bridge which was to cross the Arrow Lakes at Fauquier. This location had already involved a choice by the highways department, in that an alternative site just below Burton had been considered and rejected. However, slow as the site investigations were, Hydro had always been led to believe that the final outcome was not in doubt, and the *Columbia Newsletter*, No 10, in February 1966 announced that work on the bridge would start that same summer. Apart from its significance to the provincial highway network and to the Arrow Lakes region this bridge was crucial to the presumed advantages of the Fauquier resettlement site, advantages which Hydro continued to stress throughout the time of resettlement decisions. However, the promised bridge has not been built to this day.[3]

Apart from this difficulty, the main elements of the overall highway system were reasonably well understood at the field engineer's level – 'reasonably' because although rough cost-benefit studies showed where the highways ought to go from a functional point of view, there were two important qualifications affecting the southeast connection. The first was that no detailed survey had been made of the Koch Creek route. Thus the engineering implications and cost of the route were not known, and in that extremely rugged mountain country with an estimated peak elevation for the highway of about 6000 feet, construction costs could be very high indeed.

The second was trouble of an entirely different kind – political opposition at the Castlegar end of the lakes to the Koch Creek route. One of the 'casualty areas' of the Columbia project was the thin ten-mile ribbon of development north of Castlegar. This contained a mixture of development, mainly summer cottages for Castlegar and Trail residents, some permanent housing, a couple of little beaches, a tiny cluster of homes, and a combination general store/restaurant/boats-for-hire operation at Deer Park. Hydro proposed to replace the original road only as far as Syringa Creek, where very steep and rocky slopes would have made housing impossible and highway construction extremely expensive. Many local people opposed the Koch Creek proposal in favour of a lakeside road running all the way from the Arrow dam to the central area of the lakes. This opposition would not have been unusual (every district has its own interests and its own pet project) but for the fact that the local MLA, a member of the provincial cabinet, continued to support this proposal even after an apparently firm decision had been made by the department of highways and presumably the cabinet.

3 One reason seems to have been unusually poor foundation conditions; another the onset of 'tight money' and the fact that to make complete sense *both* the bridge *and* the costly mountain route to the southeast would have had to be built together.

However, the seesaw of political uncertainty became somewhat wearing for those concerned with timely production of plans.

The second element in the provincial segment of the proposed regional development program consisted of four lakeside park sites (designated by Hydro staff) which Hydro acquired in the course of its land acquisition program. The Authority proposed to donate these sites to the provincial government on the understanding that they would be developed as parks by the department of recreation and conservation. There was no disagreement with parks branch officials, but they were in no position to commit themselves on the nature and timing of side development. To that extent Hydro's position was again somewhat tenuous.

Apart from such difficulties at the working level, Hydro's real need was to obtain a firm commitment from the provincial government to the regional development program, since without its co-operation no firm plans or public statements could be made. Dr Keenleyside therefore took the matter up with Premier Bennett. As a result the Columbia Ministers Committee was formed consisting of the ministers of highways, lands and forests, municipal affairs, agriculture, and recreation and conservation, chaired by Dr Keenleyside. This committee considered the program formulated by Hydro and presumably agreed to it, for the program was tentatively allocated a special five-year capital budget of some twenty million dollars. The highway and park decisions already described were therefore 'made' and included in *The New Outlook*, which was then given wide publicity throughout the lakes.[4]

Just about this time, however, the provincial government apparently began to be concerned about the extent of its capital spending, for early in 1966 the committee seems to have 'died' and its program with it. In the meantime, Hydro had in good faith announced the agreed plans for parks, highways, and the bridge, none of which materialized within the construction period of the Arrow project. Again, and through no fault of its own, the Authority lost credibility in the Arrow Lakes.

The New Outlook for the Arrow Lakes showed what was to be done in that region. It did not show a number of other matters which were investigated and for some reason or other did not ultimately feature in that plan. Some of these are worthy of mention.

4 Perhaps it was merely because I was so keenly awaiting decisions from it that this committee, like the proverbial watched kettle, seemed to move so slowly. I suspect that meetings were difficult to arrange. In any case, there appeared to be no interdepartmental staff work attached to it, and it seemed that nothing was happening. In the meantime the clock was ticking on and the Arrow Lakes inhabitants got less patient and more suspicious.

FISH AND GAME

At the request of the BC fish and game branch a study was carried out by the branch, at Hydro's expense, of the implications of the reservoir for wildlife and fish. This showed that the immediate Arrow Lakes area was of minor significance for wildlife, which was scarcely surprising in view of the very small amount of land affected and the vastness of its hinterland. Consequently no action on wildlife was necessary.

The fish situation was slightly different. The Arrow Lakes were never known as fisherman's country as were the Kootenay Lakes, but they did sustain some trout fishing at certain spots. These spots depended on the mountain streams tributary to the lakes, where the sand and gravel fans built up over the centuries supported spawning. These fans, however, would now be under thirty to forty feet of water in the spawning season and would be useless for that purpose. New fans would undoubtedly form over a long period but in the meantime little could be done to conserve the small existing fish stocks.[5]

It may be noted in passing that circumstances were quite different on the Kootenay Lake, which was affected by the Duncan Dam. Here the fish (Kokanee salmon, a land-locked species) were both plentiful and renowned for their sporting qualities, and the dam would sit right on top of the principal spawning grounds. A fish census program, started in 1965 by the fish and game branch, led in 1966 to the installation of an artificial spawning channel just west of the dam. This new channel, a multi-looped bypass about two miles long, was lined with the same type of smooth gravel as the original spawning ground, very carefully graded to a mix and texture which the fish could adjust to make small pockets for their eggs. The channel was a great success from the first; the survival rate in the spring following the first spawning season in the fall of 1967 was three times the survival rate under natural conditions.

ARCHAEOLOGICAL STUDIES

It was known that there had been some activity in the Arrow Lakes by Indian tribes. For example the lakes were said to have taken their name from arrows shot into trees at one point on the shore, and at another point there

5 At least this is the way it appeared in 1965 when it became clear that the fish and game branch had neither basic data nor funds to acquire the data. Certainly, nothing had been done by 1970.

TABLE 2

	Lots created	Houses moved in	Houses built
Robson (Castlegar)	52	18	26
Nakusp	25	9	6
Revelstoke	7	3	0
Christina Lake	11	—	—
TOTAL	95	30	32

were rock paintings. Studies were undertaken by archaeologists from the University of British Columbia which found and examined some Indian camp remains at the south end of the lakes. It was concluded that the lakes had never been settled but had only been traversed by Indian tribes in transit between the Okanagan and Kootenay Lakes. No further action by Hydro was deemed necessary.

MOSQUITOES

One question which had concerned Hydro at one point was the possibility that the falling of the lake level might leave pockets of marsh land which would act as a breeding ground for mosquitoes. Checking with the department of agriculture revealed that breeding took place around June when the reservoirs would almost invariably be full. So this did not appear to be a real danger, and in fact in 1970 several people reported that mosquitoes were not nearly as bad as before.

LAND AND HOUSING DEVELOPMENTS

It is worth recording that, in addition to the new communities which it developed in the Central Arrow Lakes, Hydro undertook a considerable program of land and housing development at several points. The extent of this program is shown in Table 2.

8
People and plans

The New Outlook for the Arrow Lakes did four significant things: it pinpointed the areas which would be wiped out by the new reservoir; it gave an overall view of the Arrow Lakes region as it would be on completion of the work, including possible sites for new communities; it gave the displaced people a general idea of what Hydro was willing to do to establish these new communities; and it committed us to meet the people face-to-face in order to work out resettlement plans with them. It was intended to be a thoroughly positive and helpful document, and to that end it had certainly committed the Authority to specific actions. And this involved Hydro in signing a blank cheque, for at that stage no one knew how many people would choose to resettle and therefore how much this policy would cost.[1]

But there were matters of some delicacy involved: advising without appearing to dictate; and refusing to be bulldozed by some of the inhabitants who, without benefit of facts, had already made up their minds what to do. Hydro's staff knew the facts and something of their significance and to that extent had a clear obligation to give advice. Specifically that advice, put in the form of a question, was, 'Why not build one community of some size instead of several hamlets of minimal strength?' A reading of *The New Outlook* will show how many ways were found of offering that advice:

1 That did not mean, of course, that there were no views on the subject within Hydro's staff or within the provincial civil service. The water comptroller, no stranger to the Arrow Lakes, once told me that there would be no need for new communities as the people of the lakes would be only too glad, given a chance, to 'get the hell out of it'.

historical exposition, a listing of the values of the larger community, and passing reference to some of the drawbacks of very small places. But having said these things Hydro declined to play God: 'it is not for us to decide how or where people should live. We look forward to hearing the views of those concerned.'

This is the kind of step that one can take only out of conviction, without having any real idea how it will go down. There were those who held that, given inaction on Hydro's part, both the people and the problem would go away; and it is possible that only a little more uncertainty, confusion, and worry might well have discouraged many to the point of giving up. And there were those who could not see the point of it all: 'Just tell them what you're going to do and they'll fall in line if they want to and go away if they don't.'

As it was, I had scarcely set foot in the Arrow Lakes area when I was set upon by residents of Edgewood and invited to meet them in the Legion Hall. At that meeting it was stated very strongly that however the rest of the Arrow Lakes might feel on the subject of resettlement the people of Edgewood were unanimous that they were going to resettle right there. But especially for the neophyte in the region this had several bothersome aspects. The first of these was that their wishes were being expressed in total absence of knowledge about the future of the region, about new roads, bridges, land supply, or Hydro's resettlement policies. The second was that it appeared the Edgewood proceedings were being dominated by one man, Bill Haggart, the local forest ranger and a man of strong views and vigorous expression. There was nothing wrong about either the views or the expression; the question was: did they represent the feelings of Haggart's neighbours as well as himself? We were not sure, especially since at one point in our meeting with them the Edgewood people had laughed out loud at one of his more high-flying claims (to the effect, as I remember it, that the rest of the world, or at least the world of Needles and Fauquier, would soon be beating a path to the door of New Edgewood). We remembered too some neighbourly nudges (the penalty of a small community?) and reactionary glances as Bill expounded his faith. Were the troops behind their leader or not? There were other voices which advanced the view we ourselves came to hold: that it was time for the people to abandon their outpost mentality and pool their resources in one new community. And lastly we were told that half a century before there had been a settlement on the spot designated for New Edgewood and that it had been abandoned because of the intolerable downdraught which funnelled through the narrow neck of the Inonoaklin Valley at that point. (We were unable to confirm this but it troubled us at the time.)

With all these considerations in our minds, as well as our natural reluctance to father a white elephant at Hydro's expense, we decided that we would postpone any commitment until the picture should become a little clearer; that is, until we had garnered the views of the Edgewood inhabitants individually once they had all the facts before them. As it turned out this was not a comfortable stance to maintain, for our first meeting had been held in August 1964 and *The New Outlook* was not released until June 1965, although our plans had been ready since January 1965. There were two compelling reasons for this delay. One was the time required to engage the Columbia Ministers Committee and get it committed to the program ultimately outlined in *The New Outlook.* The other was considerable doubt for some time about the stability of the banks at the New Edgewood site. The soils experts' first report was that the banks would have to be so flat and would leave so little width in the tongue of land that settlement would not be possible. It was only a second examination that led them to conclude that their first findings were too cautious and that a community could indeed be developed there.

But no matter how compelling the reasons, the hiatus from August to June was a long one, overlapping from one construction season well into another, and the conclusions of the people concerned can be imagined: Hydro was stalling; the image of the 1961 hearings was the true one after all. Nor was this feeling dispelled by the hopeful announcements made in all good faith by the *Columbia Newsletter* from time to time that the promised plans were just around the corner.[2]

But this byplay was merely an embarrassing prelude to the sequence of events we had planned, starting with the publication of *The New Outlook.* This sequence was: (1) to prepare and publicize a general plan; (2) to present the plan and discuss it in public meetings; (3) to interview every family affected and attempt to determine its plans for resettlement; (4) to prepare specific resettlement proposals based on these surveys and have them approved in principle by Hydro; (5) to present these proposals to the groups concerned for information and discussion; (6) to seek specific commitments for land from prospective settlers; and (7) to design the new communities based on these commitments.

This sequence was carried out as planned with no serious delay. By midsummer 1966, almost three years ahead of the scheduled filling of the

2 The *Newsletter,* No 2, 18 September 1964, forecast public meetings on the plan 'around February and March'; No 5, 19 February 1965, said that we would be announcing all plans 'in another month or so'; No 6, 28 April 1965, announced that a general plan had been completed and 'will be presented in the near future.' The best laid plans ...

reservoir, development of the new community sites was underway and about half of the available lots had been committed. In fact, construction of some houses had actually started by about that time, so that the main objective, not to lose a construction season, was achieved. However, it would be wrong to suggest that the process flowed on without incident. The whole operation became easier as time went on because, no doubt, we and the people got to know one another and because Hydro's proposals became more specific with the passage of time. From the start meetings were well attended; in fact I suspect there was an element of community entertainment about them, if not Roman holiday, an analogy I carefully eschewed lest there be any loose thinking about Christians and lions. One interesting thing was that it was never necessary to call a public meeting in any formal way. (The only newspaper in the central Arrow Lakes was a weekly and thus no help for publicizing short-notice meetings.) We simply checked and arranged casually with the apparent spokesman and the bush telegraph did the rest. The Arrow Lakes society was certainly not based on paper.

The only really tense meeting was held at West Arrow Park, and it was tense for good reason. At the beginning of the project and in the absence of advice to the contrary we had assumed that West Arrow Park would constitute one of the more useful resettlement areas in the region. It was an assembly point for some of Celgar's most productive forest areas and afforded access to some of the most attractive upland meadows in that part of British Columbia. But as the preliminary river bank surveys progressed it appeared that a large cloud hung over not only the riverside area but also much of its hinterland. As more detailed examination went on the cloud darkened. The silty nature of the river banks was clearly apparent, but the planning staff was not ready for the final verdict that massive 'alcove' slides extending as much as half a mile back from the existing river bank were feared. Nor was this the only cause for concern. The slide might also cause a wave up to forty feet high in the Narrows. In view of this and the continuing uncertainty attached to the new river banks, the department of highways refused to operate a ferry service in the area. But of all this the people of West Arrow Park knew nothing.

I looked forward to the West Arrow Park visit with trepidation. At the same time it appeared essential that a face-to-face meeting be held in which Hydro's sense of responsibility and good faith could be demonstrated and the inhabitants' questions answered. And questions there were.

Of all the bare and age-worn community halls in the Arrow Lakes this one seemed that night to be the barest. And the people who packed the long lines of benches and chairs and leaned against the walls were the least familiar to me and the most strained. The general tenor of the meeting was set when one man asked if they might tape my remarks: they were going to anyway, taking no chances of misunderstandings or of promises made and 'forgotten.'

I reminded them of our promise to give them the facts they would need, and apologized for being the bearer of bad news. I told them simply that West Arrow Park as they knew it would cease to exist. A silent shock-wave ran through the meeting, but they said nothing. I told them why. Then the questions started. There were good, searching questions coming from intelligent and vigorously independent people who were in the habit of doing for themselves anything that had to be done. The only specific question I remember now was typical: why couldn't the department of highways operate a ferry in the Narrows in a fifty-foot range of water level? It was being done in the Yukon – why not here?

I gave them my well-prepared reasons, wrung from our engineers and from *their* consultants, and in the end they were accepted. The only semblance of a scene was staged by the local school teacher, an 'outsider,' who delivered an impassioned speech of indignation and made his exit, dragging his small son with him, all of which was totally ignored by the meeting. Even so, there were undercurrents in the hall of which I was happily unaware: a small group of men strategically gathered at the door had been quietly debating whether I should be tarred and feathered or merely thrown in the river. Saner views prevailed however and the evening passed without incident.

I must pay tribute to these people. Few of them were young. Several had lived there for upwards of fifty years. Now the very land they had broken, as well as their homes, was to be violated. They took these blows with remarkable fortitude and later issues of the *Columbia Newsletter* reported some of the oldest of them re-established and looking forward undaunted to a new life on the 'wrong' side of the lake. For example, the *Newsletter,* No 20, November 1967, quotes Alex Mauchline: 'I came here from just outside Glasgow, Scotland, in 1909. A strong wind brought us across the ocean – most of it was from people telling us about the fortune we could make growing fruit on the Arrow Lake. But when the men saw the timber and bush that had to be cleared before a fruit tree could be planted, most of the men got to work in the woods, or moved to the towns and went back to the trades they had in the old country. We had a good life in West Arrow Park, and were sorry to leave.' Mrs Mauchline agreed: 'But now we're here in Nakusp and comfortable, and we like it. Some of our neighbours came here too, and that makes it nice. But I wish I were a few years younger because I see a real future for this area, with all the new and improved roads and the dams for tourist attractions ... This country is a real sportsman's

TABLE 3

Households	1965 estimate	1970 approximate
Fauquier	50	40
Burton	25	18
Edgewood	12	27

paradise, and it won't take the tourists long to discover it once the roads are fixed.' That was the true spirit of the Arrow Lakes.

Some of the problems inherent in the first surveys of resettlement intentions are worth mentioning. These surveys were essential as a basis for plans for new communities, but at the beginning they suffered from certain drawbacks which, quite apart from the pressure of time, made a mockery of any thoughts of refined survey methods.

The first difficulty was that at the time of the early surveys a great many people had not yet been compensated for their property and therefore did not know what their working capital would be. Compounding their difficulty, it was not then possible for Hydro to be specific about the cost of lots in the proposed new communities. At that stage also uncertainty about the intentions of neighbours and friends may have inhibited responses. This is not to imply that people did not know their own minds or were bound by the decisions of others, but simply that they were conscious of their communities as factors in their lives. But most of all we were conscious that we were asking people to state their intentions regarding things that were quite unreal at that stage. It is true that we used air photos and scale models to identify the new community sites. Nevertheless, people were being asked not only to imagine that their own familiar communities did not exist but to visualize hypothetical communities which would be set in a radically altered landscape.

The cumulative effect of these difficulties for those whose responses were now required can well be imagined. For us the need to know was nevertheless compelling. There was therefore no alternative for the survey staff but to listen carefully to people's problems and their analyses, to answer questions as honestly as possible, and to try to sense the probably decisive considerations in each case.

It is interesting to compare the estimates of households made after the first round of individual visits in the summer of 1965 with the occupancy figures of summer 1970 (Table 3).[3]

3 At least part of the difference between these two sets of figures is due to the fact that we gave no thought at the beginning to renters, that is, those who did not own property.

The process of determining the probable resettlement pattern went on for a full year. *The New Outlook* was published in June 1965, after which door-to-door surveys were conducted. This was followed in January 1966 by a preliminary statement of Hydro's plans entitled *New Communities for the Arrow Lakes* and in June 1966 by a supplementary report which showed detailed lots and prices in all three new communities.

A year after the preliminary survey the situation was considerably improved for people's decision-making. The compensation program was more than half complete; the new sites were visible; the cost of lots was known; and some people had made their decisions and invested in buildings or foundations. In short, the people of the valley, as well as Hydro, were getting on with the job.

9
The new communities

When all the broad-brush work had been done the development of the new communities loomed up as the next job.

Sketch plans were prepared by Hydro's planning group on the basis of the results of the intention surveys and somewhat rough ground information. These plans were then handed over to the reservoirs engineer for engineering design, followed by development by contract.

These communities were equipped by Hydro with services and facilities appropriate to their size and to modern standards. All have modern water systems, but Fauquier alone required storm drains and a piped sewer system (leading to a sewage lagoon) because of the impervious nature of its subsoil. All have power and telephone services, those at Fauquier being underground. Each community has an elementary school, a community hall, at least one church, and a park. There are stores in all three and post offices in Fauquier and Edgewood; the latter also retaining its Red Cross outpost hospital.

Fauquier built a nine-hole golf course, the first in the central Arrow Lakes, intended to serve all three communities. When Hydro learned that 2000 dollars had already been raised towards such a project by the residents it offered to contribute 15,000 dollars, plus water supply, engineering assistance, and the land at a yearly lease of ten dollars. Later, it contributed an old school building for a clubhouse.

Most of the houses were built at least in part by their owners, but Hydro re-established thirty-seven sound houses it had acquired, many of which were sold back to their original owners and to others. (As the 1970 survey showed, this seems to have been a very satisfactory part of the program.)

So once the plans were made, based on consultation with the people concerned, everyone settled down and lived happily ever after? Well, not exactly ...

After the series of meetings in the summer of 1965 it was reported to the chairman that the meetings had gone over 'quite well' but the attitude of the residents was 'show me.' This was in fact only the beginning of a three-year process of community-building which varied greatly from place to place. Burton developed relatively painlessly; Fauquier developed slowly amid considerable frustration to its residents; and Edgewood was enveloped in protest and controversy from beginning to end.

It may be that the major factor in all the troubles was simply the time required to get the essential things done. The longer it took to complete the compensation process, build roads, and establish the visible infrastructure of the new communities, the longer the period of indecision, turmoil, and trouble for the people concerned. This was by no means unforeseen. But clearly time was not the only factor.

It will be recalled that in the spring of 1965 the minister of highways announced the 'decision' to build a bridge across the Lakes at Fauquier. This was discussed in matter-of-fact fashion as a fait accompli in the *Columbia Newsletter,* No 10, February 1965. But the bridge was never constructed. Neither was the Koch Creek highway shown in *The New Outlook* as connecting Fauquier to the Nelson-Castlegar area. These were crucial links in the regional framework and governed the prospects, both relative and absolute, of Fauquier. With both bridge and highway constructed Fauquier would have been the fulcrum of the region, enjoying the benefits of three-way accessibility and tourist flow. Under these circumstances it seemed reasonable to assume that the people of the Inonoaklin Valley might have oriented themselves a little more to Fauquier and a little less to Edgewood. Edgewood itself might have appealed to somewhat fewer people and Fauquier to more. With no bridge the whole pattern reverted to the status quo in which Edgewood had long been the service and social centre for the Inonoaklin Valley.

On the basis of the ostensibly firm highway decision Hydro had committed itself to support of Fauquier and soon gave physical expression to that commitment by starting site development as planned. But continued delay and the apparent abandonment of the bridge gave rise to new forces and consequences, which are well described from Hydro's viewpoint in a letter sent to the minister of lands and forests on 12 May 1967 by the manager of Hydro's land division.

Before Dr Keenleyside left on vacation, he called Mr Gaglardi [minister of highways] and urged that a public announcement be made without delay regarding the intention of the Government to build the Needles Bridge. Our concern in the matter is twofold:

(*a*) The philosophy behind our community resettlement program is that the numerous scattered communities that presently exist should be replaced by one major community (Fauquier) and two minor ones (Edgewood and Burton). Many people on the west side of the lake who formerly favoured Fauquier are now looking to Edgewood as a place to reside, to the point that we are under considerable pressure to expand Edgewood. We still believe our original concept was correct but the announcement a year or so ago that the bridge would not be built knocked the props out from under it. A firm announcement now that the bridge will be built would be of great assistance.

(*b*) This is the year when most of the displaced people have to make the decision where they will live. At the moment we think many people on the west side of the lake are being strongly influenced by the propaganda of a vociferous group who are urging them to reside in Edgewood. An immediate announcement on the bridge might influence them to make a decision that will be in their best interests in the long run.

This letter serves to re-introduce two matters which bear on the history of Edgewood's development. Both have already been mentioned in connection with the development of the Arrow Lakes plan: first, the long delay in producing a plan for Edgewood; second, the role of William Haggart. The first had probably implanted in the minds of the Edgewood people an attitude which was to be strengthened by many subsequent events as they interpreted them. The feelings of the people will be quite clear from the correspondence which is cited later; the significance of Haggart's participation might as well be established now.

William Haggart was forest ranger in charge of the BC forest station at Edgewood for almost twenty years before his retirement in 1965. His general vigour and refreshing directness apart, he was a power to be reckoned with on the Edgewood scene because of the responsibilities that attended his office. As forest ranger he administered grazing permits on Crown land; he controlled the use of forest service equipment (boats, trucks, bulldozers, etc.) which can be crucially important in times of crisis in rural areas; and he had the power to press men into service for fighting forest fires. In a rural setting these are no mean powers, and when they belong to a man of strong but pleasant personality they confer on him considerable stature and authority. Despite this it seems from the records that a succession of Hydro representatives had reservations about Haggart's credibility.

It will be recalled that in 1965 Hydro's planning staff came to suspect that Haggart was given to overstatement and did not command complete support from the Edgewood community. In June 1967, when the planners had long gone from the scene, one of Hydro's new representatives observed in a report to head office: 'Mr Haggart is a strong spokesman for the New Edgewood Community Development Committee – but I do not believe his views are completely supported by all members of his Committee.'

The purpose of this recital is not to denigrate Haggart but to establish the image he had created in the minds of Hydro officials, bearing in mind that he was the most active, visible, and articulate champion Edgewood had. The clear import of this is that Haggart was hoist with his own petard – not disbelieved but always discounted to some extent. In the context of Edgewood's two years of development this was probably not unimportant, for the situation contained all the elements of a vicious circle: Edgewood had, in its view, good reason to distrust Hydro; Hydro had, in its, good reason to distrust Edgewood. This was the backdrop to the period during which New Edgewood took shape.

Round one was fought over the BC Forest Service Station relocated at Fauquier but originally located at Edgewood and presided over by Haggart until his retirement in 1965. The correspondence which follows tells the story as it shuttled from the Lakes to Victoria and back, and up and down the administrative ladder in the process.

From Hydro's field office to the manager of the land division, 23 September 1966:

I today learned, with disappointment, that the BC Forest Service intends to retain its Edgewood Ranger Station at Edgewood rather than move to Fauquier. This also means that Fauquier would lose the three homes which the Forest Service intends to build for its employees.

I feel we should do all we can to locate the Ranger Station in Fauquier as originally planned.

From the manager of the land division to the chairman, 27 September 1966:

We have certainly been counting on having the Forest Service Ranger Station located in Fauquier along with the three homes which would be associated with it. Would it be possible for you to speak to Mr Williston in an effort to direct these facilities back to Fauquier where we feel they properly belong?

And, finally and conclusively, from the manager of the land division to the Nakusp office, 5 October 1966:

Dr Keenleyside informed me this morning that Mr Williston informs him that neither he nor anyone in his Department in Victoria has heard of any plan to locate the Forest Service facilities in Edgewood. Insofar as they are concerned, these buildings are to be located in Fauquier as originally planned.

Round two was fought on a much broader base. It was started by a broadside from one of Edgewood's most respected citizens to the minister of lands and forests, Mr Williston, on 15 March 1967.

Dear Sir:
A number of my neighbors in Edgewood and vicinity have asked me to inform you of a very obvious rising tide of bitterness and frustration among those who will presently be compelled to remove and find new homes before the flooding of the Lower Arrow Lakes becomes fact.

We know the BC Hydro and Power Authority is responsible to implement the damming and flooding of the lake. We wonder if you are fully aware that in the minds of many people BC Hydro and Power Authority is synonymous with Social Credit Party? The business ethics used by BC Hydro here are bound to reflect credit or otherwise on our government whether justifiable or not.

You will readily appreciate how exasperating it is for a person to write BC Hydro, only to receive such a long-delayed reply that they come to believe BC Hydro is completely indifferent to their problems or dilemmas, to say nothing of common business courtesy. Or when someone, having completed preliminary business with a BC Hydro official, believing they have reached an emphatic understanding, is approached by another Hydro employee, who, they discover, is not bound by what was previously understood, but dissolves and dismisses the situation in his favor by declaring that Mr So and So is no longer with the BC Hydro.

Incidents of business methods and dealings, not to the credit of BC Hydro, are topics of everyday conversation. You will readily understand that the unfortunate incident relating to the late T.G. Mead, has had a tendency to confirm the details of such incidents as factual.

As far as can be ascertained, the BC Hydro and Power Authority has not initiated any plan to relocate either the BC Forest Service or the Red Cross Outpost Hospital in the new townsite of Edgewood. According to rumor the BC Forest Service is to be relocated in Fauquier. Such a move would locate this branch of the Forest Service in territory which is under Celgar management, and put the Lower Arrow Lakes between it and ninety per cent of the forest area which it controls. Hastening to a fire would necessitate crossing the lake by ferry which is delayed for as long as one and one half hours by log booms being towed down the lake.

We feel that unnecessary hardship is being imposed upon people here. Two brothers aged eighty-four and ninety-two are a case in point, yet our senior

1 The Narrows, 1964

2 The end of an era: the passing of the *Minto*

3 The Hugh Keenleyside Dam (formerly the Arrow dam)

4 The new waterfront at Nakusp

5 New Burton, looking south

6 New Edgewood

7 New Fauquier

8 The end of a chapter

citizens had been led to expect special consideration in their problems of moving and relocating.

Mr Williston, we believe you are an honest man; that you will stand behind your statements made here in Edgewood. We therefore take pleasure in extending to you an invitation to visit us here as soon as it can be arranged, that by frank discussion, we may be assured of the integrity and honest intentions of our Government and the BC Hydro and Power Authority.

We realize that you must have a busy schedule, but trust you will make every effort to accept this invitation to visit us in the very near future.
Yours Sincerely,
Ernest J. Donselaar

These charges were examined in detail by the manager of the land division, who replied on 11 May 1967:

Your letter of 15th March to the Honourable Ray Williston refers to delays on the part of the Hydro Authority and to the use of business methods which reflect discredit on our organization. I do not believe that the examples you have given in your letter justify the charges you have made. I think there is some justification for the complaint over delays particularly over the past few months when we have been striving to overcome the loss of our senior man in the area. Mr Watson is taking over the work and I can assure you that there should be an early speed-up in our program. It should be remembered, however, that real estate work requires great care and attention to detail and undue haste can only result in problems.

I reject altogether the suggestion that we are using improper business methods. You say many people are loath to complain because of fear of reprisal. If you or any member of your group has any legitimate complaint regarding our business methods or the tactics employed by our land representatives, I would be glad if you will ask them to get in touch with me. I will then arrange to meet with them on one of my trips to the area and hear their complaint first hand. These people need have no fear of reprisal.

Round three introduced a new but durable element – the charge that Hydro was stifling the development of Edgewood by limiting the supply of serviced land for building. A report to head office dated 20 June 1967 by one of Hydro's information division staff described this problem.

On two occasions I was told that Edgewood people had been assured early in negotiations that if the residents wanted Old Edgewood completely replaced it would be done ... and the Honourable Mr Williston was reported as having agreed several years ago that it seemed reasonable to expect BC Hydro to replace Old Edgewood on a one-for-one basis.

Don Williams claimed he had a number of letters applying to purchase lots in the new townsite ... I urged him to present them without delay to Nakusp Lands Office, explaining that BC Hydro needed such proof of demand for lots.

Several persons in the area told me that they had no quarrel with families who wished to move to New Fauquier, but they resented any attempt to direct them to that new townsite ... They added that some five persons in Needles had some time ago incurred their displeasure by attempting to pressure them into changing their plans to move into New Edgewood ... 'You can't push people around or into where they don't want to go,' three members of New Edgewood Committee declared. I explained BC Hydro's responsibility to make fully known all the advantages and expectations for New Fauquier, so all families could make their selections with full knowledge.

One resident of New Edgewood asked why BC Hydro had made ample provision for expansion at New Fauquier and at New Burton – but was unwilling to do the same for New Edgewood ... All that I could say was quickly discounted ... Another resident said: 'BC Hydro can spend an extra $15,000 on a golf course for New Fauquier, but seems unwilling to spend another $1,500 to meet the requests for extra lots in the New Edgewood townsite.'

In reply to my query as to why people of Edgewood seemed inclined to write direct to BC Hydro, Vancouver, or Victoria Parliament Buildings, three residents claimed that until recent months their letters and questions to Nakusp office went unanswered, and the men they telephoned at our office never called back ... However, they admitted the situation had improved recently.'

Ultimately the manager of the land division met the Edgewood committee in Edgewood, and on 15 August 1967 recorded in his diary:

Insufficient lots: The Edgewood Committee stated that with the number of unfilled applications for lots on hand the present supply of lots will be exhausted and there is no room for expansion.

Our records at the present time indicate nine outstanding applications for lots at Edgewood for which we now have four uncommitted lots, but that of the nine applications only one is from a displaced person, three are from tenants and five are from people outside the area altogether ... However we said if we were furnished with reasonable evidence of a demand for more building sites (particularly if the demand comes from displaced people, and even if some of the displaced people may be renters, provided they are renters of reasonably long standing) we are prepared to recommend that steps be taken to enlarge the present community.

A decision followed when on 11 September 1967 the chairman approved this recommendation by the manager of the land division:

Until recently we have been in the position of having more available lots left in the new community than we had applications to purchase. The situation has now changed. We have eighteen lots in the new community and all but four have been purchased. We now have eighteen unfilled applications to purchase lots. Of these six are former displaced property owners and four are displaced tenants of sufficiently long standing to deserve consideration. The other eight applicants are considered ineligible for lots. The time has now come when we should proceed with the above expansion.

In round four in the summer of 1968 the subject is the same as in round 3 – requests and rebuttals on the provision of more *lebensraum* for Edgewood. Norman Robinson, a Hydro field engineer with a blunt no-nonsense style, replied on 7 June 1968 to Mr Donselaar, who had again been drawn into the fray.

There are at least nine unsold residential lots in Edgewood at this time. The subdivision of additional residential lots, as you request, is not warranted.

Of the few remaining families to be settled none have requested to be established in Edgewood. Further, there are some privately owned homes in Edgewood being offered for sale. In these circumstances it appears there is no need to place houses for sale in Edgewood on a speculative basis.

Houses located below the full reservoir level are being sold for salvage or relocation. We have encouraged the sale of these houses to persons wanting to settle. Recent examples in the Edgewood area have been Mr Settle and Mr Milne, whom we assisted in finding accommodation. These men purchased houses at a nominal sum and setting up of the buildings is now in progress.

Prospective house purchasers might find an advantage in following the example of Mr Milne and Mr Settle.

By this time the temperature seems to have risen in Edgewood to the point where the ladies felt compelled to get into the act, as shown in a letter to Mr Robinson from the Women's Institute dated 12 July 1968.

On behalf of the Women's Institute, I have been instructed to write you concerning houses for rent in the Edgewood townsite.

From time to time, it has been noted that BC Hydro has moved a number of houses to Fauquier and that many of them are being rented.

The housing situation in Edgewood is most critical. Numerous men who have obtained work here are being forced to leave because no living accommodation is available for their families.

As an organization that works for the betterment of the community we would like to know why some of these houses are not being placed in Edgewood? Why are we being discriminated against? The Development Committee here has been asking for this accommodation and are not able to get any results. Why?

We urge that you make some effort to see this situation is remedied. We had houses here before that people could rent and we only ask that we have them now.

If no action is forthcoming, we will be forced to publicize this in every newspaper in the province. We feel that we can not sit back any longer.

On 22 July the manager of the land division met Donselaar and Haggart and recorded in his diary:

I was asked if Hydro could move houses to Edgewood to take care of demand of rental housing. I asked if demand was coming from displaced owners and was told it was not. I said Hydro does not recognize any responsibility towards others than displaced property owners and certain long-term tenants.

I was asked if Hydro could make more lots available for prospective purchasers and pointed out ten still available. These said to be rocky and discouraging. I suggested reducing price instead. They said this might be an answer.

But as an anticlimax, on 28 October 1968 one of Hydro's field staff reported:

Heavy demand for rental accommodation at Fauquier and no demand at all in Edgewood. Requests for rental housing to be made available in Edgewood appear to have little justification. No applications for prospective tenants. Of three salvage houses moved to Edgewood by Messrs. Milne and Settle only one was occupied.

This gives some idea of the stormy history of the development of New Edgewood. By comparison Fauquier's experience was relatively tranquil, though not without its ups and downs. On 16 June 1967 Hydro's information officer in Nakusp was reporting:

Here is needed a speeded-up development program. Prospective residents are beginning to lose faith in BC Hydro's promises for the model townsite and in Hydro's ability to produce. Time after time our work has seemed to stop because of lack of workmen, materials, decision, or ruling of Department of Highways.

It was pointed out to me that the Commercial Area planning, carried out recently, could – and should – have been done in the winter. Repairs and renovations to 'moved in' houses should have been carried out months ago. Newly-built houses and grounds are not as attractive for buyers as they could be. Windows are broken; most windows are so dirty you cannot see in, and when you can, the scene is one of discarded boxes and strewn materials.

As long as no stores are in the new townsite, residents will hesitate to move in.

Development Committee feels so many changes are made at Vancouver in programs that local Land people cannot speak with full authority. Under the impression that decisions cannot be made by Nakusp Land force.

Relaxation in building standards is needed to encourage growth at New Fauquier ... and we will have to ease our standards on the type of buildings to be moved into the townsite in order to encourage young people, who do not have the money to either buy our houses or build their own.

Delay in registering the legal plan for the townsite was cited as 'still another instance of BC Hydro's ineptitude.'

Members of the Centennial Committee are anxious to get ahead with clearing for the golf club at New Fauquier and the moving of the golf club house ... This work is being held up because Hydro has not completed purchase negotiations with property owners.

Delay in building a community hall at Fauquier is also a sensitive point with prospective residents.

Just ten days later, however, the same observer reported: 'Pleasure with the way in which development programs for New Fauquier are beginning to move was expressed by the New Fauquier Development Committee ... The competition to select a new name for the community is to close early in July, then a petition for change of name will be circulated.'[1]

A year later however, Don Underwood, writing for the Fauquier Development Association, was complaining that the other communities were being developed first and expressing dismay over the delays which Fauquier was suffering. In the same vein one of Hydro's field staff noted in September 1968 that charges of 'inefficiency and inconsistency were being levelled at Hydro. Also, echoing the Edgewood theme it was complained that lack of housing for rent was inhibiting the growth of Fauquier.'

In comparison with its sister communities New Burton seems to have achieved its rebirth with a minimum of travail. It is almost anti-climatic to

1 The name Fauquier, derived from one of the pioneers of the area and pronounced locally in English rather than French fashion, seems to have produced four-letter associations in many minds. Hence the move towards a more comfortable name. To the best of my knowledge nothing ever came of this move.

record the comments of one Hydro representative on 16 June 1967:

This is the happiest of the three new townsites, and there is a growing undertone of pride. The crash program to put the new ball park, sports ground and concession stand in shape for the May 24 holiday festivities helped BC Hydro's cause, I feel.

It will be apparent that the new communities were not born without birth pangs and that from Hydro's point of view there were many slips between cup and lip. Thus there are reasons and lessons to be sought. The main discrepancy between plans and fulfillment lies in Fauquier's under-performance and Edgewood's over-performance. Why so?

Fauquier's difficulties seem to have been three. First, the failure to build the bridge and the southward highway deprived the Fauquier townsite of much of its *raison d'être*. This was a crushing blow, but by the time it fell Hydro was irrevocably committed to the development of Fauquier as its main thrust. But as the pendulum swung away from Fauquier it automatically swung towards Edgewood, for between them lay the Inonoaklin Valley, which could be served by either. Ties of tradition, and some of kinship, inclined the valley people towards Edgewood, but the die was cast when a ferry instead of a bridge was interposed between them and Fauquier.

But this was probably not the only factor. Comments made in the 1970 survey suggest that some prospective Fauquier residents changed their minds as the townsite emerged slowly and in desultory fashion. And, possibly even more important, the coherence and sense of identity that marked the Edgewood community throughout seems to have been lacking in Fauquier. There was a greater mixture of local origins among its residents and a greater range of personality types and ambitions. Most of all, there does not seem to have been a commonly accepted leader.

No such drawbacks applied to Edgewood. The site was well known and had been chosen by the people themselves prior to the advent of Hydro; no mean advantage. The resettling group were all Edgewoodites, who seem to have maintained their sense of community not only among themselves but with the Inonoaklin Valley. The site was much smaller and sat on a promontory based on sand and gravel, so that no drainage or sewerage works were required; thus it could be developed and settled with a minimum of delay. But favourable as these conditions were, they may not have been the crux of the matter. This was probably the presence of William (Bellwether Bill) Haggart, combined with a sense of grievance which united the community and caused it to fight for its future. This has nothing to do with the rights and wrongs of the prolonged arguments between Hydro and the Edgewood people. It has to do only with their reaction to the wrongs and adversities they saw and conquered. (Arnold Toynbee would have been delighted.) Haggart's role has been attested by some of his fellow residents, and nobody who knows his bluff and breezy personality will doubt that his part in the struggle was a crucial one.

One thing deserves to be noted. The correspondence at several points makes it clear that there was some bitterness between the communities of Fauquier and Edgewood, arising out of competition for growth and out of a mutual sense of grievance against Hydro. The point is that community-building is a stressful experience, as is the task of resettlement for each person. The records suggest that Hydro personnel became a little impatient with the residents, especially in the case of Fauquier, for their slowness in accepting community responsibilities. This may well have been an insensitive judgment arising from failure to reailze how great the burden is on those who have to struggle both with home and garden building and with the task, psychological as well as physical, of rebuilding a community.

Something of the essence of the three new communities emerges from the story of their symbols. We conceived the idea that it might help to establish the new communities if each were offered a symbol of its own choosing to mark the beginning of a new life. Burton chose an earthy ensemble of stone and timber, presumably symbolizing mining and forestry, which now bears an appropriate plaque. When I saw it in the summer of 1970 it was almost obscured by long grass. Fauquier adopted a pair of slender concrete pylons, symbolizing the historic 'Needles' – a pair of long sandpits which used to project out into the narrow channel of the lakes nearby and gave the area its name; these were suggested, however, not by the residents but by a history-conscious Hydro engineer. Edgewood moved its original cenotaph, accepted one thousand dollars in lieu of a symbol, and used that sum to purchase the materials for a tennis court for its young people, which the community built itself. Need more be said?

It will have been observed that the process of building new communities was a difficult one, not unmarked by human fallibility. Nor did Hydro emerge unscathed in the summer of 1970 from the comments of hindsighted individuals in all three communities. But it will not be overlooked by any fair-minded observer that Hydro *did* fulfil its undertakings (although the provincial government did not); that the new communities are by no means unsuccessful as such; and that in building and equipping them the Authority showed both generosity and understanding. In the arena of human affairs, where crystal balls are customarily cloudy and saints and heroes conspicuous by their absence, that is not a record to be ashamed of.

10
The dead and the living

One of the saddest aspects of developments such as the Columbia is that not only the living but even the dead are affected by them. In the case of the Arrow reservoir no fewer than eleven cemeteries were affected. In addition to these, there were three which had already been abandoned.

The task of dealing with cemeteries is a delicate one, not merely for reasons of religious belief or personal sentiment but also because the laws governing them are usually strict. Also time and circumstance often conspire to make the task difficult. Records may be poor or non-existent; graves may be unknown and unmarked or may not correspond with records; next-of-kin may not be found; legal formalities of incorporation and ownership may never have been seen to.

Even if none of these possibilities exist there may be very real differences in conviction about what constitutes respect for the dead. If there is no physical or public health reason should graves be moved? If a cemetery is liable to be exposed at certain times of the year should it be made 'properly' visible or, as far as possible, part of Mother Earth? To ask the question is to provoke the controversy.

Clearly the task facing Hydro on the Arrow Lakes required patience, tact, and compassion. But it also required administrative care and attention to practical detail. One village took strong exception to a proposal to cover its cemetery with graded stone which would soon be indistinguishable from the ground around it. Another declined to make its cemetery available for the reception of relocated graves as it had relatively little space remaining. (So Hydro developed a new one.) Nor was the subject absent from the we/they struggle in the early days, when it was possible for a young woman to stir a crowd by crying, 'We are not just to be thrown out of our homes. Now it appears we can't even *die* in peace!' (However, even this subject had its lighter moments. After embarking on the development of one new cemetery we received an angry letter from the owner of the neighbouring property, who complained that his prospective bride would not tolerate the idea of living beside a cemetery and that his romance was 'off.' Several months later, however, the grapevine told us that the lady had given hostages to fortune and was happily ensconced in that very house, cemetery and all.)

Hydro's cemeteries program turned out to be larger than had been anticipated. This was mainly because of unforeseen bank conditions, which necessitated the complete removal of three additional cemeteries.

The first task of Hydro's staff after assembling available data was to visit each cemetery board, where one existed.[1] Records, such as they were, were scrutinized and questions of policy discussed. Frequently it was decided to hold wider meetings, advertising them, and writing to known next-of-kin. People were given the choice of having their relatives' graves moved or leaving them undisturbed if that was possible. Requests to move graves to special cemeteries were honoured. Undertakings were given that all moved graves would be fully protected from erosion, and plaques would be arranged to commemorate flooded cemeteries. Arrangements were then made for Hydro to acquire the cemetery in order that it might be legally closed.

As a matter of interest, the actual steps involved in each case were:

1 to assume ownership of the cemetery, paying compensation as required
2 to apply to the public utilities commission for permission to close it
3 to circulate the proposal with a final notice to all next-of-kin who could be reached
4 to publish notices in the local papers, calling for information on graves for which no next-of-kin had yet replied, and announcing the intention to close and cover the cemetery
5 to prepare, and in due course place, a memorial plaque
6 to establish survey markers for the boundaries of the cemetery and to identify every possible grave on the ground by the use of low-level aerial photography
7 to make final preparation for removals, including arrangements for re-interment in accordance with the wishes of the next-of-kin
8 to carry out the final operation of clearing, levelling and covering the cemetery

The program in the Arrow Lakes was carried out according to plan, without a hitch and without incident.

1 This program was assigned to the planning group and was ably and successfully administered by Walter Parker.

11
On clearing

One of the most important decisions Hydro had to make was whether to clear the reservoir area of its tree cover immediately or to postpone it for a few years. This was a question of some financial importance to the Authority; figures suggest that the clearing of the Arrow reservoir cost about fifteen million dollars. It was also a question of both practical and emotional significance to the people of the Lakes and one they really knew something about, for they made their living from logging. And lastly, from the outsider's point of view, it was invested from the beginning with a certain amount of administrative confusion. In other words it contained all the ingredients of trouble.

Action was officially initiated on 17 August 1964 when the comptroller of water rights wrote to Hydro:

The storage of water in the Arrow Lakes is authorized by Conditional Water Licence No 27066, of which clauses (1) and (*m*) state as follows: (1) The licensee shall clear the reservoir in the manner and to the extent as directed by the Comptroller ... (*m*) The licensee shall provide public access to the reservoir area as may be directed by the Comptroller. Pursuant to clause (1), the Comptroller of Water Rights hereby directs that the reservoir shall be cleared as follows:

GENERAL CLEARING REQUIREMENTS

1 All economically merchantable timber shall be salvaged prior to commencement of storage in the reservoir
2 All trees, brush, stumps and snags exceeding two inches in diameter and

exceeding five feet in height below elevation 1446 feet shall be knocked down or cut at a height not to exceed two feet or the diameter of the stumps, whichever is the greater

3 This knocking down or cutting shall be completed not later than five years after the initial filling of the reservoir, except that in areas to be designated clearing shall be carried out prior to commencement of storage

4 Debris resulting from clearing shall be disposed of either by burning or by floatation after flooding ...

5 Dead trees on land surrounding the reservoir below an elevation of 1450 feet and located within 100 feet of the highwater line shall be felled within ten years of initial filling of the reservoir

SPECIAL CLEARING REQUIREMENTS

1 Plans showing areas requiring special clearing treatment, shall be filed with the Comptroller of Water Rights not later than December 31st, 1965. These plans shall specify the clearing treatment to be carried out to achieve the following objectives: (*a*) to preserve the appearance of portions of the reservoir near settled areas; (*b*) to preserve the appearance of portions of the reservoir near settled areas or main highways or other areas of public use by the removal of stumps; (*c*) to provide public access to the reservoir for recreational purposes; (*d*) to provide safe waterways for commercial and recreational use

2 Special clearing treatment shall be carried out as specified in the plans and specifications as approved by the Comptroller of Water Rights

This directive deserves attention both for what it did and what it did not say. It established the water comptroller as the ultimate authority for approval of clearing plans. It stated in technical terms what was meant by minimum-standard clearing. It acknowledged that 'special clearing' might be necessary in certain areas (unspecified). It did not say, nor should it have said, *what* standards were to be applied *where* or *when*; these were properly decisions for Hydro.

There need be little wonder that this produced confusion. The person who wrote to Hydro would be told that (*a*) the standards had been laid down by the comptroller (*b*) the clearing plans were subject to the comptroller's approval – both true. The person who wrote to the comptroller would be told that the responsibility for clearing plans was Hydro's and that he only set standards to be achieved – both true. This resulted in correspondence such as the following letter from the Inonoaklin recreation commission to the comptroller in November 1964.

Dear Sir:
This Recreation Commission strongly protests your proposed method for clearing the Arrow Lakes reservoir.

We in this area have a very good example before us of what condition a lake is left in after it has been cleared by your proposed method. We, of course, refer to clearing of the Whatshan Lake. It is now nearly sixteen years since it was cleared and they are still piling and burning. The beaches are covered with stumps and debris. Up until the last years the lake was unsafe for boating. The fishing was reduced and what fish were caught were of an undesirable weight and appearance.

We feel that the Arrow Lakes with its vast area will be left in a worse condition. Boating and fishing, tourism and living facilities will be practically eliminated for at least ten years.

We strongly recommend that you reconsider your proposed method of clearing and that you fall, burn and clear all materials prior to flooding. This would leave a recreational area BC could be proud of.
Sylvia Underwood

To Mrs D.E. Underwood:

Dear Madam:
I judge from your letter that you have some misunderstanding about the authority and responsibility of the Comptroller of Water Rights with regard to the clearing of reservoirs. The Comptroller is not charged with the responsibility of carrying out clearing or of specifying the method by which it is to be carried out. This is the responsibility of the BC Hydro and Power Authority. I can only impose a standard to be achieved, and in the case of the Arrow Lakes reservoir, this standard has been set at complete clearing within five years of the creation of the reservoir. Although the deadline for the completion has been set at five years after initial filling of the reservoir, we have always been aware that practical considerations would result in much of the clearing being carried out prior to flooding. The additional period of five years was allowed in order to provide for some flexibility in the program of clearing in order to avoid any unnecessary expenditure of funds ... You will note, however, that control has been retained by the Comptroller of Water Rights over the areas in which delayed clearing will be permitted ...
Gordon J.A. Kidd

Mrs Underwood's letter gave a special reason for the residents' alarm. Whatshan Lake had been a favourite picnicking and fishing spot for the people of the valley, and it had one great advantage over the Arrow Lakes in that it was relatively warm. As both parties point out it had not be cleared when developed sixteen years earlier for power purposes, and its attractiveness had been greatly diminished. Fish had been affected, shore access had been made dangerous and difficult, and the appearance of the lake had been impaired. Thus the people knew very well whereof they spoke. In addition there had been a public outcry in the province a few years earlier about other power reservoirs which had, in one sense, been *too* successful: it had resulted in one lake (Buttle Lake on Vancouver Island) being cleared to standards which many considered too fussy and too expensive. Thus there had been both a public backlash against previous practice and a quieter backlash against the most recent practices.

Into this situation I wandered by chance in June 1964 when I saw two communications which caused me some concern. One was a draft copy of the comptroller's proposed clearing conditions, the other an internal memorandum from Hydro's lone forestry expert. The latter spoke happily of the savings which would accrue to the Authority as a result of postponing some of the clearing for five years. Not having been involved in the issue, I reacted to this by a brief caveat on 25 June which said in part: 'I would stress the importance of aesthetics during the years immediately following flooding. These will be 'rush' years for tourists and will establish the image of the new region in the public mind. While savings to the Authority are important, so also are the image and long term outlook of the region.'

On 17 August however, the forestry expert and I received a curt memorandum which requested his recommendations 'on a program for carrying out the Authority's obligations' and mine 'concerning areas within which special clearing should be carried out.' This presumably meant 'Cobbler, stick to your last.' But in the meantime I had discovered that postponement of clearing was being taken very seriously, and was now linked to the plausible idea that in the Canadian climate nature in the form of ice would do the clearing for us, given time. Furthermore it seemed that all the opinions which would be expressed had already been expressed in favour of postponement and it was put to me quite brusquely that if I did not agree I would have to 'show them.'

As a result I undertook some research on my own, writing to power and recreation authorities across the country, and in particular trying to get evidence from knowledgeable people in the Arrow Lakes. The latter were, of course, completely biased because there was only one view in the Lake country and that was for complete and immediate clearing. The Vancouver experts on the subject, a large firm of forestry consultants, made no bones in private about their views (they were strongly for clearing) but did not want to be quoted because they were trying hard to be hired by Hydro yet did not wish to appear to be setting up jobs for themselves to do at a percentage fee.

Among my respondents the 'nature will look after it' concept did not find many supporters. Probably the strongest view was expressed by a BC forester of considerable experience:

I would not think that anyone with eyes to see would still be advancing the line that reservoir clearing will take place through natural action. We have, in British Columbia alone, an abundance of flood-killed areas where, after upwards of sixty years, the natural clean-up has not taken place. One can cite numerous examples where messy dead material is still firmly fixed in place: reservoirs of the Lower Mainland, the small irrigation reservoirs of the Okanagan Valley, big reservoirs such as the Alcan development, smaller reservoirs such as Lower Campbell, Downton Lake – anywhere you care to look. As the Okanagan Section of the Canadian Institute of Forestry said in writing to the Water Comptroller in 1961: 'We submit that visual inspection of past dam projects reveals that nature has been most unco-operative in her clearing attempt, and that eventually man will have to go back and clear up his original mess.' A Royal Commission Report on Forestry in Ontario decries the habit of flood-killing and shows pictures of extensive flood-killed areas in Ontario which are *not* cleaning themselves up.

I believe there is no argument for natural clearing other than a reduction in cost of the power project. In the long run the loss to the country of other benefits from reservoir projects far exceeds this gain for the power interest.

This, however, was only one aspect of the whole issue. That issue I attempted to deal with in a memorandum to the manager of the land division dated 10 December 1964:

I have a number of strong representations to make on the proposal that clearing might be delayed in certain areas for a period of five or more years.

I appreciate that any delay in expenditures is normally financially advantageous to us and that we earn money thereby. However, it seems possible that we could actually *lose* money by postponing clearing. In any case several factors must be considered which might far out-weigh immediate dollar considerations.

Short, unpredictable working season

Once the reservoir is in operation, it will not be possible to predict in advance what the level of the reservoir will be, what areas will be accessible for clearing or for how many months. However, it is a fair assumption that normally only about two months will be available for work in areas above the 1400-foot elevation.

Poor ground conditions
Much of the ground in the Arrow Lakes ... will be saturated and will remain wet as the water table behind it continues to discharge following the fall of the lake. Much of this is silty, sandy ground which is known to be soft and sometimes unstable. Since the lakes are relatively low in elevation and do not have very severe winters, the ground does not become frozen to depths capable of supporting heavy, moving machinery.

Bad working conditions
First, the trees, standing or fallen, will become completely saturated and also impregnated with silt. This affects saw teeth and makes cutting costly and slow. Second, and especially in these long narrow lakes, existing drift (of which there is a great deal) and slash from logging and clearing operations will create a tremendous tangle in areas of both standing and fallen trees, which is very dangerous, difficult and costly to work in.

In other words, any work not done prior to flooding will have to be done later under the worst possible conditions, leading inevitably to higher costs.

Short burning season
Once the reservoir is flooded and trees are saturated, burning will be difficult, if not impossible, in the short winter season available especially since much of it consists of absorbent cottonwood and other deciduous trees.

The debris problem
Recent experience in Saskatchewan is illuminating. At the Squaw Rapids Reservoir some 40,000 acres of forest were cleared. The forest cover is very light and is probably what we would call 'brush.' The situation today can only be described as a shambles. This originated from several years delay (1959–62) in getting started, which resulted in only one year being available for clearing and burning. This turned out to be a wet year and burning was largely unsuccessful. The results appear to be as follows, according to Saskatchewan government officials:

1 'The shoreline is ringed by logs, debris, and submerged trees for upwards of 150 feet out from the water's edge. Rafts of debris travel the reservoir. Snags appear over most of the water surface.'
2 The one private beach development has been hemmed in and the Department of Natural Resources has not been able to undertake any recreational development.
3 The Saskatchewan Power Corporation's great fear is of debris plugging the emergency spillway to the Torch River.
4 Two tugs are presently working trying to remove debris in front of the major structures, and it is understood that two more will have to be ordered.
5 'We have approximately 2000 acres of close-packed free floatage which to

remove completely and burn will cost $800 per acre. We have also 4000 acres of trash which is "hung-up" but which may have to be removed in later years.'

If the Arrow lakes drift and slash are not burned on the spot, their amount will be 'enormous' – the word used by Consolidated Services in their 1961 report to us. If, as I understand, it took two years with a dragline to clear the slash from the 2500 acre Cheakamus reservoir, what can we expect on the Arrow Lakes, with 20,000 acres to clear? If 40,000 acres of brush in Saskatchewan produced 6000 acres of water-borne trash what would 20,000 acres of Arrow Lakes cover produce? *Five square miles* of floating trash.

This question of scale must be related to the shape and circumstances of the lower end of the Arrow Lakes. At Syringa Creek, where the lake is around a half mile wide we propose to boom debris and burn it on a relatively small headland. At the same time we must maintain a navigable channel for Celgar's log-booms. Beyond this is the damsite area – a natural bottleneck only a few hundred yards wide – which must accommodate the handling of both boats and log-bundles; which will be a tourist attraction; and which therefore must not become littered or plugged with debris.

These considerations suggest that we must do our clearing and burning in the four pre-flooding years to minimize the debris problem.

Effects on the lakes and their image

If the lakes are not cleared ahead of flooding two things will happen which we should not tolerate:

1 Navigation in the lakes, especially in the very narrow area at the dam, will become very difficult. This will affect all who use the lakes – Celgar, Forest Service fire crews, air pilots, tourists, boaters and local residents – making many essential jobs dangerous, if not impossible.
2 The lakes, which will undoubtedly experience a flood of visitors in the years following completion of the dam, will be full of debris for the first five years of their new life. The tourist image of the area would be damaged from the beginning. This would be both unfair to the region and contrary to what we keep saying about the beneficial effects of the project on the area.

Furthermore, in view of our repeated and unqualified assurances about clearing, postponement would certainly be regarded – in fact is now being prematurely attacked – as a breach of faith on our part.

Effects on future clearing jobs

The Arrow Lakes is only one reservoir area. After it will come Mica, Libby and others which may be much more significant in terms of money-saving than the Arrow reservoir. On the other hand the Arrow reservoir is a most sensitive one owing to (*a*) the presence of many people along and adjacent to it, (*b*) the fact that it will be accessible to general traffic when new highways have been completed. If we were to save a ha'p'orth of tar at Arrow and cause further outcry on an already emotional subject, we might very well spoil the ship for later projects on which clearing could with good reason be postponed.

Conclusion

I draw your attention to two final quotes from Saskatchewan:

1 'every scrap of timber is being taken out of the South Saskatchewan Reservoir.'

2 'We are still of the firm opinion that, solely for the production of power there was no need to clear the reservoir ...' However, 'in another location where the reservoir could be serving other purposes such as recreation, transportation, domestic or industrial uses of water, we would expect that complete clearing down to mineral soil could have been required.'

My view is that before we entertain any proposal to postpone clearing on the Arrow Lakes we should be sure that it would result in a saving in money; that we could handle the debris problem; that the broader policy aspects of the proposal are fully known to the Authority.

This brief seems to have had some effect in what have been described as 'hesitations in Victoria and battles in the Hydro building,' for shortly after this the Authority announced that it would entirely clear the Arrow Lakes prior to flooding.

Before leaving this subject it is only fair to mention two aspects of the clearing job which reflect credit on Hydro. The task was one of considerable size and variety: 40 square miles of land were cleared, spread over 300 miles of reservoir perimeter, and this employed a total of 2000 men and 300 machines through 83 contracts. BC Forest Service officials have reported that despite the immense amount of burning which had to be done the job had an outstanding fire-control record, only two fires 'getting away' at all. They also report that Hydro performed very thoughtfully in another matter which had traditionally plagued regions such as the Arrow Lakes: control of payment to contractors in order to ensure that they do not bilk their subcontractors and loggers. By judicious hold-backs the Authority ensured that there was a minimum of 'robbery' of the smaller people in this way.

Finally, a wry note from Dr Keenleyside '... we were widely criticized for doing *too good* a job – the fact that teen-age girls went around collecting sticks and branches seemed to enrage some of our colleagues and others.' But from the Lakes themselves in the 1970 survey three people went out of their way to commend Hydro for the competence of its clearing program.

12
A plethora of problems

While the resettlement of displaced people was probably Hydro's most dramatic problem, it had many others to contend with. For many of these it could have been argued that Hydro had no legal responsibility, a matter of some potential significance, for the Authority as a Crown corporation could act only within its given powers, and could be challenged in the courts if it appeared to act beyond those powers. For other problems it could well have been argued that Hydro had no moral responsibility either, for although there were strains that were undoubtedly caused by the project in towns such as Castlegar, these towns clearly benefitted in some ways (or perhaps, *some* people in them benefitted) by money spent by the work forces. However, these arguments had to be weighed against the very cogent factor of public opinion. What did Hydro *seem* to be doing, and was it possible to make a plausible case for the Authority? These were salient questions, particularly at the start of the project, local feeling being what it was, and if Hydro decided in any situation that discretion was the better part of legalism or of thrift, it was not for lack of either understanding or principle. The Columbia project was not undertaken in a social vacuum, and it was often a question of which was the best rather than the right thing to do.

SCHOOLS

School problems arose in all of the three main areas on the Arrow Lakes, all for different reasons. In the Central Arrow Lakes the problem was replacement of schools in flooded areas, and this was solved by compensation or by moving the school buildings.

In Castlegar the problem was that the number of children attending school had bounded upwards to the great dismay of the local school board, and a check of the school records showed that temporary residents had contributed to much of this increase. Legally Hydro could have washed its hands of the problem because the temporary construction works lay within the school district and would be taxed for school purposes like any other property. In addition, when the dam and its ancillary works were completed they also would be taxable and would add immensely to the district's assessed value.[1] However, strenuous efforts by the school administration through double shifts and the re-opening of an abandoned school tided the district over the first crucial year and gave its prearranged building program time to take effect in the next year.

At Revelstoke a different problem threatened. This arose out of the work on the Mica Dam eighty-six miles north of the city where a largely self-contained construction village had been built. Hydro had accepted full responsibility for elementary school children by building a two-room school in the village, but had no plans for any high school facilities. The trouble started when the project manager forecast the presence of two dozen children of high school age in the fall of 1965, and endless trouble from the wives in the camp if a suitable arrangement could not be made for their education. Daily commuting was out of the question over such a road in such a climate (almost forty feet of snow was recorded at Mica Village in one winter). The Revelstoke school board set about finding suitable lodgings in the city for the anticipated youngsters and was satisfied that it could cope with the problem. In the event only three or four children turned up in the first year. No problem.

HOSPITALS

Hospital problems arose in both Castlegar and Revelstoke. Hospital boards in both cases feared that their limited facilities would be swamped either by injuries arising from the construction operations or from normal illness of the workmen and their families. The two situations were, however, quite dissimilar and gave rise to quite different solutions.

The common element was agreement that in serious construction injuries the important thing was prompt first aid, a minimum of intermediate han-

1 In any event this particular district was by no means badly off as a result of the presence of Celgar's new saw mill and pulp mill nearby. However, a subsequent amendment of the municipal act specifically exempted the dams from school taxation, causing deep resentment on the part of the co-operating school boards and indirectly giving Hydro yet another black eye.

dling, and speedy transport to the nearest hospital capable of dealing with them. At Mica Village there was also the consideration that in such an intimate, closed-circuit sort of community, major accidents would have serious effects on the morale of the resident families and preferably should not be treated in the village itself. There was also the awful possibility, always present in the case of tunnelling works, that a whole shift of men might be involved in one accident. In both cases therefore, stress was laid on adequate first aid provisions, availability of a doctor, and means of evacuation. At the Arrow dam this was no problem, for there were two substantial hospitals accessible by road within about thirty miles.

The Mica site presented a much more formidable problem partly because of the serpentine nature of the eighty-six-mile mountain road to Revelstoke, and partly because of the limited capacity and facilities of the antiquated hospital there. Two possibilities remained: the use by ordinary aircraft of the Mica airstrip two miles away from the dam site, or point-to-point flights by lands and forests helicopter, if one could be summoned quickly enough. In addition it was essential again for reasons of morale as well as treatment, to provide for the immediate needs of the families at Mica. Thus a resident doctor was installed by Hydro at the village in a two-bed 'hospital.'

At Castlegar however a crisis showed signs of developing. The small local hospital (thirty-three beds) was already being used at an occupancy rate of more than ninety per cent and thus could truly be said to be full. (There were beds in the corridors, which made the point dramatically.) A planned extension of the hospital was still 'in the works' between the health authorities in Victoria and Ottawa, which seemed to be light-years apart, and no timely assistance could be anticipated from that source. Fear had already been expressed by some local residents that they might not be able to obtain treatment in their own hospital because of its preemption by Arrow-based workmen and their families. This took place in the early days of the Arrow project (summer 1965) when suspicion and resentment were widespread, and there was reason to believe that real trouble might break out if prompt remedial action were not taken. No one who has lived in a small community in times of stress will underestimate the speed with which news can travel, whether fact or rumour, and the emotional voltage which can build up.

Under these circumstances Hydro agreed to build a ten-bed extension to the hospital at its own expense, thus not only discharging any responsibility it might have, but also bridging over the long gestation period of the extension planned by the hospital board.[2]

2 Hydro did recover a federal subsidy of two thousand dollars per bed, but paid the balance itself.

A TRAILER PARK

All the communities directly affected by the Columbia project were small, and had only limited ability to absorb the impact caused by the influx of large numbers of workmen. One such impact resulted from the tendency of the modern married construction worker to bring his family along with him in a trailer or mobile home.

By the summer of 1965 accommodation in Castlegar had become very scarce, a matter brought home to the community when the school board complained of losing teachers because of the cost of housing. At the same time a survey carried out by Hydro suggested that a shortage of trailer sites might also develop. Hydro therefore planned to forestall such an emergency by developing a substantial trailer subdivision, which might later be turned over to the village of Castlegar for normal residential purposes. With this in mind the only really suitable piece of property in the area was identified. A beautiful piece of abandoned orchard land, the site had only one drawback – it was just outside the village boundary, which meant that the village council could not spend public funds to maintain and service it even if it were given to them. A public vote would be required to annex it and officials were uncertain as to the reception a plebiscite would receive if it were thought by the voters to be for Hydro's benefit. These difficulties were discussed privately with the village council; a detailed site plan to accommodate 160 trailers was prepared which would preserve most of the trees and provide for ultimate reversion to single-family development; and arrangements were worked out by which the village would be given the land fully serviced and in return would maintain it (that is, collect garbage, police it, and plough the roads in winter), and collect the trailer rents. In return the village would acquire title to the land, a valuable addition to the village which would swell its coffers considerably, and would be helped by Hydro to acquire several key lots which would allow it to develop a highly desirable park in the middle of the village.

At the crucial moment when Hydro moved to option the land, which had been valued at eighty thousand dollars, two countervailing events happened simultaneously. First, it became apparent that another interest had just been acquired in the land. This was made known by the new owners, a triumphant young man and wife who demanded one hundred and sixty thousand dollars for the land and sat back waiting for the grapes of entrepreneurial virtue to drop into their mouths. Secondly, Hydro received a well-documented letter from the local trailer court operators association pointing out that new courts were being developed in sufficient number to meet the anticipated demand, and protesting the proposed invasion of their market. In this situation Hydro was glad to be relieved of the burden of well-doing.

DIKING

At Revelstoke a very considerable problem, and a choice, faced Hydro because of the relatively low level of much of the land; and land is scarce in that mountain-ringed location. Had it taken all the land below the high water mark Hydro would have destroyed quite a proportion of the town's supply of both land and housing. It would also have inundated the community ball park and part of an already small golf course. Studies showed that it would be more economical to protect the housing areas by diking, provided that the banks were not too porous. Drilling showed that diking was feasible, so the dikes were built, thus serving the purposes of both Hydro and the city. But that was only the beginning of a much more extensive program of land conservation, and by the time it had met all the problems Hydro had diked and improved the ball park, diked the golf course and participated in a land consolidation arrangement which doubled its size, and had saved and improved the local airport by raising the runway fifteen feet. (The latter was almost mandatory since there were no satisfactory alternative sites in that rugged country and the airport was also important as a part of the provincial airstrip network.)

A WATERFRONT SCHEME

At Nakusp a similar problem arose: how to protect the steep forty-foot-high bank which edged the town only a block away from the main street. Consideration was given to flattening the slope, which would have meant taking a long strip of built-up land half-a-block wide. It would also have meant the end of the venerable Leland Hotel, a much-added-on-to institution whose roller-coaster floors had known the tramp of generations of heavy boots ('Caulks and spiked shoes must not be worn') and whose beer parlour had provided liquid solace to the thirsty owners thereof.

With a weather eye on all these things Hydro's engineers ultimately decided on a rather unusual form of protection – a soil-cement sloping wall 2000 feet long wrapped around the point. This single decision had some highly beneficial side effects for the community, for the old foreshore had served many barely compatible purposes: as the boat dock (the centre of the community in the sternwheeler days), railway sidings, a logged-off swimming area,[3] and the village dump (not in close proximity of course).

3 Nothing illustrated the difference between the 'cultures' more than this swimming

A new swimming beach was provided along with the wall, and a new and less conspicuous site was found for the dump.[4]

There was at the beginning a great outcry against this proposal, based largely on inadequate information. In fact the village council was at one point proposing to hold a plebiscite on the question. In the event the new wall was built with a promenade along the top and an extensive sand beach beyond. It is quite extensively used, and is believed to be regarded with pleasure by most of the inhabitants.

ADMINISTRATIVE MINUET: RONDO ANDANTINO

This section outlines the case of the Revelstoke Museum, a splendid example of administrative mazemanship. As far as Hydro was concerned this arose in the fall of 1964 when it seemed that two separate but concurrent aspirations might profitably be made to supplement one another. First, Hydro was at that time considering establishing an information centre near Revelstoke for the benefit of the travelling public, with the thought that this might be expanded to contain the main exhibit of the whole Columbia project. Simultaneously, on one of my 'pastoral visits' to Revelstoke I became aware of the aspirations of a lively and tenacious group of citizens, the Revelstoke Historical Association. This tiny group was convinced that more strands in the web of British Columbia's romantic past could be found and woven into a stirring tapestry in the Revelstoke area than anywhere else in the province. Furthermore, being doers as well as dreamers they had already amassed a considerable collection of artifacts which filled the basement of a small downtown building; and they had their eyes on bigger quarry: log houses and barns to be acquired by Hydro, abandoned mining gear scattered all over the local mountains, railway engines, saw mill relics, and so on. Impressed, I advised them to write to Dr Keenleyside, himself a student of history, and make their case to him. Thus started a four-year, desultory

pool. The old foreshore was rough, dirty, pebbly, and exposed, and the water was cold – all to a point which caused some of Hydro's officials to snort derisively when replacement was requested. But it was used happily and extensively. The boys walked the circumscribing logs with glee and dived off the mooring posts with trepidation, which was no less than they could have done in an Olympic pool.

4 A dump is a must for a new rural community; the shielded city-dweller might overlook this, the small-town man never. (Correction: As I write, Toronto is still in the throes of a prolonged garbage strike.) It reminds me of a piece of sage advice given me by one battle-worn provincial planner, wise in the ways of the BC interior. 'Always allow for a Dogpatch in your resettlement planning,' he said. Fortunately this is possible in the spacious if rugged country in that part of BC, but as an admonition it could well be pondered by many city planners contemplating urban renewal schemes.

rondo which illustrates the fate of issues, even small ones, that do not fit clearly into an existing pattern of administrative responsibilities.

To understand it at all it is necessary for the reader to interpolate at various points letters or conversations not specifically mentioned in this account (which is based only on Hydro's files) and sometimes to imagine that certain actions may have taken place which are not recorded at all. Also, to follow the tale without cynicism it is necessary for the reader to remember that the prime reason for the confused sequence of events and the long gestation period involved was that Revelstoke was too small and poor to develop a museum on its own, and it was not the responsibility of any other body to do it. Hydro's general terms of reference clearly could not be stretched to embrace the kind of museum envisaged; and the BC department of recreation and conservation, which until then had been one of the weakest and lowest-spending departments of the provincial government, was not funded to do it in the face of the many projects it would have liked to undertake across a vast province.

But on with the tale. And in order to maintain a speed of at least *andantino* rather than *andante doloroso* the events are treated in telegraphic style.

23 November 1964: Keenleyside to Revelstoke Historical Association (RHA): acknowledges RHA letter re museum proposal; says he is considering exhibit of Columbia project and discussing matter with department of recreation and conservation; acknowledges possibility of joint plan for maximum benefit to Revelstoke
1 March 1965: RHA to Wilson: could we incorporate our museum into Hydro's information centre plans
4 March 1965: Wilson to RHA: trying to arrange a meeting with provincial secretary
14 April 1965: Keenleyside to Black (provincial secretary): expresses interest in mooted museum because (*a*) it would be logical place for Columbia exhibit (*b*) Hydro would contribute buildings and effects. Suggests feasibility study and offers to participate in any meeting called by Black
30 April 1965: Keenleyside to Black: acknowledges letter from Black stating intention to call meeting, and delegates Wilson to attend
18 May 1965: Wilson to Wallace (deputy provincial secretary): stresses urgency on account of vandalism and need to safeguard good houses for museum use
29 July 1965: Wilson to Keenleyside: Revelstoke group arranging temporary storage but transportation costs beyond them: suggests fund of $500 to support this. Keenleyside agrees

9 August 1965: meeting called by Black: all parties agree broadly on idea: department of recreation agree to have historic sites officer (HSO) investigate in September, his report to enable Black to ask Cabinet for funds for full planning study
24 September 1965: HSO, having investigated, recommends preservation of specific houses acquired by Hydro
30 October 1965: department of recreation sends to Hydro confidential copy of enthusiastic report by HSO on museum concept
17 December 1965: Wilson to Wallace: expresses surprise over telephone news that 'submission will be made to treasury board in January proposing that provincial government match any contribution Hydro may make to a regional museum at Revelstoke' and points out that Hydro can only contribute land and/or buildings acquired as part of normal Columbia program
12 August 1966: Wallace to Fitzpatrick (Wilson's successor) asks Hydro to donate designated thirty-two-acre site (No 1) for museum
30 August 1966: Fitzpatrick to Hydro's Columbia projects committee: asks for policy decision on Wallace request, which would cost Hydro $80,000 to $100,000. Request refused
31 August 1966: Fitzpatrick to Wallace: sorry can not donate: site too valuable; try again
26 September 1966: Wallace to Fitzpatrick: suggests another site (No 2), ninety acres
12 October 1966: Gross (manager of Hydro's land division) to Wallace: this site is of no concern to Hydro; suggest you look for Crown land, possibly Mount Revelstoke Park
26 October 1966: Kiernan at Hydro directors' meeting suggests that 'unless Hydro has made a definite commitment to contribute a site the RHA request be declined'; agreed

A year passes
8 August 1967: RHA to Keenleyside: recounts history of proposal as of November 1964, describes progress in collecting material and asks for definite decision
24 August 1967: Keenleyside to RHA: sees little chance of Hydro contributing and suggests RHA go ahead independently

Eight months pass
18 May 1968: RHA to Williston (minister of lands and forests): recounts history of proposal and asks that committee established by Black in 1967 request new site from Hydro

23 May 1968: Williston to RHA: will discuss with Kiernan
29 May 1968: Wallace to Keenleyside: asks whether new twelve acre site (No 3) owned by Hydro would be available for museum
4 June 1968: Gross to Keenleyside: reviews history of proposal; advises that value of new site is $18,000
7 June 1968: Keenleyside to Wallace, advises that new site is valuable for residential development and wonders if another site more accessible to tourist traffic could be found
26 June 1968: Gross reports to Keenleyside on a telephone conversation in which Kiernan suggests that if Hydro will donate the site his department will raise funds for a museum building (RHA now under notice to vacate its storage building by September)
3 July 1968: Gross to Kiernan: relates decision of Hydro management committee that Hydro will not donate site but will transfer to department of recreation if given a credit against which it might purchase Crown lands as required (Note: This was an established policy of Hydro's)
8 July 1968: Kiernan makes his proposal to Hydro directors (that is, that Hydro donate site); board resolves to convey land subject only to granting of credit equal to site value
12 July 1968: Gross to Kiernan: relates decision of board to Kiernan and advises that site value is $18,000
23 July 1968: Kiernan to Gross: 'when I have had an opportunity to discuss this matter further with my colleagues I shall write you again'
6 September 1968: Kiernan to Gross: 'My colleague, the Honourable Ray Williston, has agreed to establish a credit on behalf of Hydro for the sum of $18,000 in consideration of the twelve acres ...'

The layman may well shake his hand in wonder at such gyrations and ask whether the gordian knot could not have been cut in less than the four years required by this bureaucratic shell game, especially when Kiernan and Williston were both active members of Hydro's Board of Directors. (Did Mr K., minister, one wonders, write himself letters as Mr K., board member? Parkinson where art thou?) Clearly it could. But short of special sanction and budget the problem was in fact a complex one, and the student of public administration will ask many more questions and possibly pose some speculative answers. He may suggest that Hydro was concerned not only with the legality of its actions but with the question of precedent, in relation to other Columbia communities on one hand and departments of the provincial government on the other. He will ponder the strength of the different participating departments in terms of budget and freedom of spending, and note without amazement that it was lands and forests which ultimately found the eighteen thousand dollar credit demanded by Hydro, credit which cost it nothing in dollar terms. He will observe that while 'departmentality' is an annoying disease in the absence of a common purpose or a means of resolving conflicts, there are many ways of skinning a cat, as the ultimate solution showed. He will ponder the constant flux between and within the various agencies and will speculate as to who drafted who's letters and to whom he had spoken by telephone before drafting them. He will reflect on the many points in an organization at which concern and imagination can be excercised, directly or indirectly, even by humble actors. He will ask when the department of recreation, which did not start the hare, felt committed to the idea and how it happened – by constant internal nagging or because of a plea by a cabinet colleague? Did the persistence of the Revelstoke Historical Association ultimately pay off in its appeal to the minister of lands and forests?

The answers to most of these questions may never be known, but the student knows that the records are really a sort of palimpsest, for beneath the formal, top-level letters lie layers of drafts, memoranda, telephone calls, and conversations, casual or contrived, over beers or cocktails, and that these reflect the passions, perceptions, and prejudices of many men at many levels. This is so at any time. Given an orphan issue in a complex structural situation the problem merely becomes a little more difficult and the minuet a little longer.

Postlude

When this book (started in 1970) was being finished in 1972 I thought the museum issue was resolved. How little I knew. First I learned that the minister of recreation and conservation had at last stated (in December 1971, three years after the conclusion of the original rondo) 'the Government's intention to create a Provincial Park' on the Revelstoke site and that Hydro's parcel was purchased by the government in January 1972. Then in November 1972 a friend in Revelstoke, one of the stalwarts of the Revelstoke Historical Association, brought me up to date with a letter which deserves to be recorded as a fitting finale to the minuet and as a proper tribute to the redoubtable members of the association.

In August of this year, having tried to foist it off on first the Regional District and then the City of Revelstoke, the area known as Columbia Village was finally, by Order-in-Council, declared a Class A Historic Provincial Park. With which a mighty weight fell off the shoulders of the R. and Dist. Hist. Association, which through the years, dealing with Hydro and Province, had well earned the name of Hysterical Society. From now on, it is anybody's guess what happens. The land is saved. The enormous shed is stuffed in an orderly manner with all kinds of goodies, which are listed. Would you like a stuffed elk head, or a chamber pot? Perhaps a fantastic leaded windowed door, or the pulpit from the Arrowhead Church or the searchlight from the Minto.

We also have one jail, first in the district. Huge hand-hewn logs. The inside is not completed but a terrific amount of work has gone into restoring this, and this is all voluntary. ...

B. came up this Fall and told us we were trespassing!! We have gone ahead anyway, and it should make for an interesting confrontation. So of course we are not quitting and if we go to jail we do hope that it is into our own.

ONE AND A HALF MILLION PAPER CUPS

One peculiar problem arose from the fact that below the Arrow dam site the Columbia River was the source of many individual and community water supplies and that at one stage in the construction of the dam a great deal of silt was being dumped in the river. This of course made the river quite turbid and unusable for domestic purposes. One of Hydro's responses to this was to provide the affected communities with water from wells drilled for that purpose. But as anyone acquainted with the vagaries of wells will appreciate, these provided Hydro's reservoir engineers with many a headache resulting from clogged screens or failing supply, and it was a happy day for Hydro when its need for them ceased.

One unusual variation on this problem arose at some of the many plants of the Consolidated Mining and Smelting Company at Trail. It was found that it would cost a very considerable amount of money to provide a new supply to the drinking fountains in these plants, in which a great deal of water was consumed by the men. Hydro's answer to this was to supply 200 water coolers, which were filled daily at the water treatment plant and taken down to the works, along with one and a half million paper cups, which ministered to the needs of the thirsty for the year during which the river was affected.

THE CARE OF OLD PEOPLE

The special needs of older displaced people presented Hydro with a problem of no little delicacy. As a result of the whole history of the Arrow Lakes region an unusually high proportion of the total population in the smaller communities was over sixty. From the time of the hearings in Ottawa Hydro had committed itself to special care for these people, and as a first step the planning group undertook to identify them and ascertain their special problems and needs. Thus the *Columbia Newsletter* of October 1964 contained a letter and a questionnaire addressed to all residents over sixty, inviting them to complete the questionnaire and mail it back to Hydro. To this invitation some eighty people responded, probably about half of the total number, and most of them indicated a desire for a personal interview. This response was further publicized and most of the interviews were carried out in October by the planning staff.

The end result of the survey was a report dated January 1965, which read substantially as follows:

PROBLEMS

Displacement presents special problems to older people.[5] Some typical problems and their frequency are as follows:

(*a*) their property values may not cover replacement costs – about a quarter of cases;

(*b*) their income and earning powers are low, and they depend on the very low cost of living of their present setting, which cannot easily be duplicated elsewhere – about two-fifths of cases;

(*c*) they suffer from various physical disabilities (chronic illnesses, deafness, blindness, arthritis, partial disablement due to injuries) which make them dependent on other – three-quarters of cases;

(*d*) living in an isolated locality they lack mobility; that is they have no vehicle, no licence or are unable to drive – two-fifths of cases;

(*e*) they often depend on neighbours for such things as telephone, mail, supplies, wood-chopping, company, transport (for example, to doctors) – over half of cases.

We were able to make estimates of the numbers of people who would need help and the kinds of action necessary to help them, as follow:

(*a*) those who need help with shelter: people whose property values and financial resources are believed to be inadequate to replace their present shelter, about 25 cases;

(*b*) those needing relocation advice only, about 25 cases;

(*c*) those not directly affected who need relocation help. This refers to people not necessarily eligible for compensation because they do not own property but rent, at very low rates, accommodation which is to be removed by the flooding; they own property which, although not directly affected, will be

5 An 'older person' was defined as one who was over sixty at the time of the survey, that is, one who would be of pensionable age (sixty-five) when flooding took place in 1969.

rendered virtually untenable or unmarketable by the impact of flooding on the surrounding community; or they own businesses which are affected by the loss of local markets as local populations decline, about ten cases.

PROPOSALS

In the light of our 'fair and generous' principle and our repeated pledges of solicitude for older people, a general policy of assistance going beyond strict compensation and embracing some people not directly affected should be considered. This policy might take several forms:

Direct assistance with housing

For those cases where compensation will simply not permit the purchase of reasonable shelter, and assuming that we do not own a suitable house which might be made available, a cottage of, say, prefabricated cedar construction might be provided on the surrender of their compensation to the Authority; the house to return to the Authority and the compensation to be paid to the owner or his estate when the need for the house is gone. The house would remain Hydro property and the taxes would be paid by Hydro.

Cases indirectly affected[6]

Cases indirectly affected by the removal of the core of their community or the majority of its inhabitants might be treated substantially as if they were directly affected.

Housing projects

No consideration should be given to group-housing projects for older people. There will not be enough people interested to justify this; almost all of the people affected are far too independent for communal living. However, if one or two suitable cases do appear, bound for established communities such as Revelstoke, Nakusp, or Castlegar, we could well contribute appropriately on their behalf to any community project which might be started by local initiative. In passing, the payment of a cash settlement would not necessarily make anyone ineligible for NHA-based low-rent housing. The Central Mortgage and Housing Corporation would evaluate any such payment in terms of its income-producing value and would merely wish to be assured that the person's total monthly income, including this derived income, did not exceed their 'poverty limit' of about $150.00 per month.

6 This is another residual problem that tends to be obscured when the job is defined as 'property acquisition.' Another, already mentioned, was the plight of the renter.

Appraisal priority
Older people have not many years to enjoy their compensation, and their ability to manage the shift to a new location is dwindling. The appraisal programme should therefore give them high priority.

Maintenance of community services
(This proposal does not relate only to older people but is included as a type of special compensation). Since it appears inevitable, even with programming of the removal of houses and of the construction of new communities, that there will be a gradual fading away of affected communities, it is desirable that essential community services should be maintained throughout the transition period. To this end an effort should be made to maintain stores, post offices, etc., until such time as they can properly be allowed to go. This might well involve offering some guarantee of stock valuation and income to proprietors of stores, and assistance in disposing of their assets at reasonable valuations.

Other approaches
It is essential that the Manager of the Land Division retain wide discretion in dealing appropriately with the nuances of individual cases. This study, which confines itself to establishing basic facts and suggesting general policies, does not attempt to cover all possible problems or solutions to them.

Financial Implications
Only proposal number one (direct assistance with housing) appears to have any calculable significance for capital expenditures by the Authority. A rough estimate suggests that, if the conditions suggested are adopted the net additional capital cost to the Authority would not exceed $50,000. In any event if in due course the property later reverted to Hydro and were salable, we should recoup the whole cost. This cannot be a firm estimate, but it does suggest that 'fairness and generosity' to the older people of the Arrow Lakes will not cause a significant burden of cost to the Authority.'

Prior to its consideration by the Columbia projects committee this report had been circulated to the members, who included the representative of the information services division. When the report was broached, the information representative, who had discussed it with those responsible for property acquisition, advised the committee that in his view it would be dangerous for Hydro to distinguish between people on grounds of age, and that anything it committed itself to doing for the older people it might be forced to do for all. He did not suggest that Hydro should do any less for older people than the report recommended, but only that these policies should not be publicized.

Round-the-table discussion resulted in acceptance of this view by the committee. Their judgment was no doubt affected by the tension in the region, for in these early days any stick might well have been used to beat Hydro (or perhaps the analogy of jujitsu would be better, since in that gentle art it is the opponent's own momentum which is used to throw him). While it was possible to wonder if the elephant was being cowed by the mice it was not really possible to cavil at this decision. It was the collective judgment of a group of experienced men who did not propose thereby to do any less than was recommended for the older people. It also resulted in considerable discretion being given to the manager of the land division to implement the proposals of the report as he might see fit, a thoroughly sensible approach reflecting the integrity of the man concerned. But it meant that the Authority could be embarrassed by its earlier public statements, and in that event it would have nothing to fall back on but shopworn assurances of 'fair and generous' dealings and the passage of time to prove it right. What is surprising is that so little was made of it by Hydro's opponents at the time.

CELGAR LIMITED

A unique and momentous problem for Hydro arose from the pervasive presence in the Arrow Lakes of Celgar Limited a subsidiary of the (American) Columbia Cellulose Corporation. In 1955 this company was granted a tree farm licence which is the basis of its integrated forestry operation. In addition to the woods operations based on Nakusp this consisted of a pulp mill and saw mill complex just downstream of the Arrow dam. In 1964 the whole operation was said to employ 1200 men based on the cropping of 900,000 acres of productive forest. Furthermore, much of the land used by the company fronted on the Lakes, focusing on 'dumps' where logs were dumped into the lake for towing down to the mills, and on 'tie-up' areas where logs or booms were tied up pending assembly or transportation.

Thus, seen or unseen, the company was everywhere: as a major land user, which had developed its own system of logging access roads and dumps; as the major lake user, which transported men and logs on the surface of the water; as an important user of water in its pulp mill; and as the economic mainstay of the region. The Arrow Lakes project was therefore of great significance to Celgar and vice versa.

Some of the implications were obvious: destruction of logging roads, dumps and tie-ups; flooding of the company's logging headquarters site at Nakusp; and loss of productive land from the leased area. Some were a little less obvious: the disruption of the pulp mill's water intake by the dam construction; the need for large quantities of logs to pass through the dam (hence the lock in the dam); the need to provide for the passage of logs around the dam site during construction; and one that was perhaps least obvious but most important of all: the possibility that the company's normal production operation might be affected, thus laying Hydro open to claims for production and income losses.

Without embarking here on inappropriate detail it may be said that Hydro's entanglement with Celgar's operations and interests was the source of one of its biggest, most complex, and longest-lasting problems. It necessitated both engineering responses, such as the construction of a completely new water-intake for the pulp mill and money compensation, as well as other types of negotiated settlement. It also necessitated extensive employment by Hydro of consulting forestry experts. It had still not been completely resolved in the fall of 1970.

These then, were some of the peripheral problems facing Hydro, and their very diversity raises questions about the Authority and its capacity to deal with them. What *was* the BC Hydro and Power Authority?

13
The workings of Hydro

Projects such as the Columbia are necessarily carried out by complex organizations, and these in turn reflect the men who staff them. Thus it would be fatuous to describe the Columbia River project without commenting on Hydro and its staff and also on the broader administrative framework of the provincial government, of which Hydro was but a part.

By the time the Columbia River Treaty was ratified by Parliament in 1964, BC Hydro had barely grown into its new name. For only two years before Hydro had not exist as such. Instead the province was served by two major power agencies: the private enterprise BC Electric Company and the provincial government's own creature, the BC Power Commission.

In 1961 Premier Bennett expropriated the BC Electric Company, presumably in order to have full control over all major power developments and markets in the province and thus to be able to bargain authoritatively with Ottawa and the United States.[1] A little later the company bought out the Peace River Power Development Company which was promoting the huge Peace River project. By this time the Power Commission had been working steadily but with very limited funds towards the Columbia project for some years.

Faced with two organizations serving the same basic purpose the Premier, never at a loss, solved this problem of surplus by ordering a shotgun wedding between the two agencies, but not for the reasons traditionally associated with such arrangements, for the two were scarcely on speaking terms. Now

1 And also to save for his province the corporation taxes payable to the national treasury by a private power company but not by a public one.

called the British Columbia Hydro and Power Authority the two partners set up house in 'the BC Electric Building' in Vancouver.

The two subjects of this mandatory alliance were vastly different in history, temper, and complexity. The BC Power Commission was a simple power organization conceived after the war to bring power to the rural parts of the province which had not so far attracted the attention of private enterprise power. But the Commission's short life had not been without trouble: first a physical disaster at one of its plants and then the recalcitrant views of its general manager on provincial policies had brought upon it the attentions of two commissions of inquiry. (The second of these had ironically been headed by Dr Shrum, then a dean at the University of British Columbia, who in 1962 belonged to 'the other side.') As a result the general manager was fired and the commissioners resigned. Thus the Power Commission was an embattled creature which had become something of a trial to its foster parents.

The BC Electric Company was a very different cup of tea. First it had several strings to its bow. It not only produced and distributed electric power but also ran Vancouver's bus system and an industrial railway line, distributed natural gas, and sported an array of subsidiaries which developed industrial land, ran a model farm, and had a finger in the original Peace River power proposal. Its success since the Second World War had been striking and the whole organization was characterized by freewheeling ways and an élan which in some of its senior officers amounted to insufferable arrogance. Under these circumstances its summary expropriation by Premier Bennett and the death at the same time of its president Dr A.E. Grauer were demoralizing blows from which the organization took some time to recover.

As if both partners did not already have a sufficiently troubled past at the time of marriage there was also a legacy of bad feeling between them. In several instances, for example, it seems that BC Electric had its way in terms of new territory against what the Power Commission had felt were valid claims of its own. Such recollections die hard.

To top all this the premier solved another problem by decreeing that the new organization should be headed by *both* Dr Hugh Keenleyside from the Commission and Dr Gordon Shrum from BC Electric, an arrangement which could have stemmed equally easily from a malicious Machiavelli or a playful W.S. Gilbert. To some extent the schizophrenia inherent in this situation was obviated by the fact that each co-chairman retained responsibility for his own power project, Keenleyside for the Columbia and Shrum for the Peace, but shared the responsibility for chairmanship of other elements of the organization. Nevertheless the possibility obviously existed for strain in that two men were expected to supervise the undertaking of two massive works, neither being wholly responsible for the organization which was to carry them out.

Under all these circumstances it is scarcely astonishing that the integration of the two organizations left a certain amount of resentment and hostility between some members at all levels of the two original organizations, and led to the emergence of 'BC Electric' and 'Power Commission' cliques. This in turn led to friction and pettiness between new colleagues. In addition the new organization had its own moments of doubt, as in July 1963 when the courts ruled that the act expropriating the BC Electric Company was invalid, thus placing the new Authority in legal limbo.

Within this organization the two huge power projects, the Peace and the Columbia, were proceeding more or less concurrently between 1964 and 1968. On the engineering side the Columbia project was administered by a group consisting mainly of Power Commission engineers who had been working on the project for some years. Property acquisition and the clearing of the reservoirs were administered by the land division, which was also assigned the task of resettlement planning. Overall, Hydro's organization insofar as it related to the Columbia project is shown on Diagram 9.

It would seem from the many-sided nature of the task on one hand and the diversity of Hydro's organization on the other that a co-ordinating device would be mandatory. And there was such a device in the Columbia projects committee, of which more will be said. There was no such body in the Peace project, and while there may not have been the same need there, since the dam and reservoir were located in uninhabited country, nevertheless the two administrative solutions reflected faithfully the personal approaches of the two co-chairmen. Shrum, an aggressive man with a fantastic capacity for work and decision, was his own team. Keenleyside was always the diplomat: cool, self-contained, tough but humane in outlook, and immensely perceptive of people and situations. His knowledge of the ways of government and politics was profound, and as the leader of the Columbia project he was regarded with respect and deference. The resettlement program was greatly indebted to him for his personal concern and support.

The Columbia project committee was an utter necessity. It was the forum in which the full sweep of the project could be seen by all concerned; and it was the means by which many kinds of experience and viewpoint could be brought to bear on any troublesome point. These two advantages are worth discussing for it was obvious that several members of the committee not only did not accept its value but were clearly, and in private admittedly, unco-operative in the work of the committee. Their view tended to be that the less said about their activities in front of others the better; to do so would

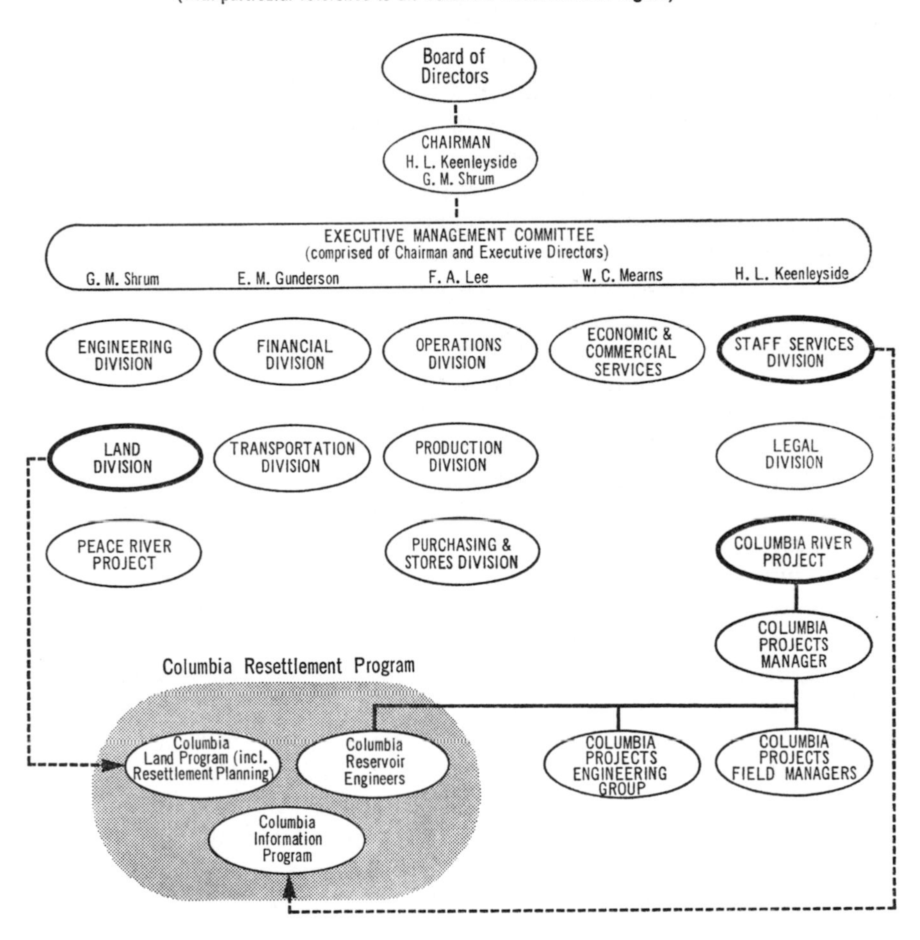

DIAGRAM 9

just invite uninformed comment and trouble, and anything that required policy approval could be straightened out privately with the chairman.

First, the Columbia project was a very complex operation, and while the highly localized task of constructing the dams was underway, the jobs of purchasing properties, disposing of chattels, moving houses, clearing land, building new communities, constructing roads, drilling wells, and many others, were also going on, all in the presence of a partisan and wary populace. This was happening hundreds of miles away in circumstances with which many members of the group were not really familiar, having visited the region infrequently and fleetingly; and it was being administered by them not primarily as members of a Columbia team but as members of Hydro's functional divisions, which sometimes had other responsibilities. Under the circumstances there was the greatest need for regular reporting and full contribution by each member to a common view of the task. By this means overlaps, conflicts, and unappreciated significances became apparent, and all the members inevitably became more fully aware of the contextual significance of their own activities and their implications for others.

Secondly, specific problems often arose on which advice was sought. These were of many kinds: the bids on the contract for the Arrow dam were far above the estimates and it was believed that the crushing penalty for lateness had caused bidders to cover themselves too amply: what should be done? Special policies suggested for displaced old people were believed to contain dangers for the whole property acquisition program. Should humanity or caution prevail? Such questions would have taxed the wisdom of Solomon; solving them was one of the functions of the committee.

The reticence of some of its members did not mean that the committee did not function. It did. However, whether it might have worked better is a valid question. Another is whether this reticence placed a correspondingly greater load on the chairman and the more co-operative members. What was sad, of course, was the cynicism or lack of understanding which stood in the way of full participation by able men.

Since this was the view near the top, where all of one's collaborators could be seen and felt as real people around a common table, it will not be surprising that the problem of separatism extended further down the ladder. In a man's own private office located in his own departmental 'territory' the job tended to become 'my' job, a jurisdiction to be defended jealously rather than a piece of a larger whole to be achieved co-operatively. This attitude was of course reflected in the approach to field matters and field staff.

My own feeling (which must be speculative, for I left Hydro before the actual resettlement program got underway) is that the reservoir program must have suffered from lack of a co-ordinative force at the working level. It has been shown in Diagram 9 that the reservoir program depended on the working of three separate administrative divisions, only one of which had a full-time Columbia responsibility. Two of these reflected the Power Commission–BC Electric schism; their relations were cool rather than cordial, and they had clashed over the allocation of the house-moving responsibility. These groups conferred between themselves, always on a two-way basis rather than three and only when one saw an urgent need to do so. Spontaneous sharing of field intelligence and review of their programs as matters of common interest did not take place (as I know from arranging a few meetings and seeing them wither as the most important 'collaborator' sat through them in sterile silence, like a dutiful, forbearing, submissive wife). It must be wondered whether some of the problems noted by the residents in 1970 and discussed in chapter 14 did not spring from this source.

Apart from the dam construction job, which required and got a site office of appropriate size, the overall question of field organization in the Arrow Lakes was inherently difficult. There were three quite distinct areas to be dealt with, these being strung out along 150 rugged and interrupted miles. Each area required some attention from a civil engineer, several property appraisers, a community planner, and an information officer; some required more than others, and to a different extent from phase to phase of the work. The jobs to be done were relatively small. Under these circumstances it was difficult to know whether or where to set up a Hydro office of any size for coherent operation, some decentralized decision-making, and visible representation of the Authority.

Apart from these difficulties, there were others related to the distance between Vancouver and the Arrow Lakes. This was great enough to be a deterrent to casual travel but not great enough to compel the establishment of a decentralized administrative office. Added to this were other real difficulties, especially for senior officers who had responsibilities other than Columbia affairs. For them there was only one centre, Vancouver, where the whole decision-making apparatus was, complete with colleagues, specialists, services, competitors, and bosses, all the comforts of home and the conveniences and diversions of a metropolitan area. What easier and more logical than to insist that the mountain should come to Mohammed, that the affairs of the Arrow Lakes should be administered from Vancouver?

But there were good reasons why Mohammed should go to the mountain. First, some judgments would be better made in the Arrow Lakes. This applied with particular force to many property appraisal questions, whose variety and nuances were infinite, but which could often be resolved on the site; it also applied to many other areas of concern, such as details of community plans, cemetery undertakings, and minor engineering works. And there were good reasons for as much local decision-making as possible. There was the need to cut down delay – always a source of dissatisfaction for the local people especially on small things in which they could see no real problem; there was the *appearance* of coherence (that is, of seeming to know what they were about) on the part of local staff; and there was the need to deal with people and things where they could be seen, talked with, and judged as they were, not as they might seem through a screen of preconception or misconception in an office in the sky in Vancouver. But desirable as speed, realism, and public image might be, they were not the only things to be achieved. Coherence in the several aspects of the program was also an end to be sought, partly to avoid conflicts and partly to achieve the best possible intelligence operation.

The intelligence function was pervasive and vital. All of Hydro's field men were in day-to-day contact with people whose fate they held, or appeared to hold, in their hands. At any one time the various officers were each liable to see a different cross-section of the region and its problems. Put together, these views could give a reasonably comprehensive view of the scene, but one that could change overnight.

Yet another need was that of supervision of Hydro's field personnel. There were, as there were bound to be, some problems of ethics as well as of personality and behaviour. For example, one man had relatives in one small community in which he was buying properties and although his integrity was known and no one dreamed of charging him with bias, the situation did not go unnoticed. Again, was it proper for a Hydro representative to buy for himself unwanted personal effects from anyone whose property Hydro was acquiring, even at the request of the owner? (Hydro wisely decided it was not.) The truth was that in a situation so complex and so charged with tension there were possibilities of dilemma and embarrassment that demanded great watchfulness on the part of the Authority, watchfulness which could only be exercised through the presence, frequent if not continuous, of senior administrative staff.

These were some of the considerations bearing on the question of a field organization. Whatever the real justifications for setting up a representative field office there were equally real difficulties arising mainly from the distances to be covered and the small and diffuse nature of the tasks. But these were not the crucial difficulties. The ultimate problems were, as they so often are, human. In the first place a decentralized regional office, to have much meaning or effect, would have required a trusted senior man as head. This would have cut across the departmental lines of communication to some extent and was therefore not viewed with conspicuous delight by the Vancouver-based officers concerned. ('I'll be damned if I'll have *my* men reporting to any of *his*.') And clearly it would have interposed another person, and potentially another viewpoint, between superior and subordinate, even if the intervention were nothing more than seeing all the mail and calling occasional staff meetings.

Another real human difficulty was that a live and concerned person would scarcely have had enough to do to maintain his interest and self-respect. Such a lack of challenge in fact had led earlier to the withdrawal for a time of an information officer, and to his subsequent reinstatement when the plot thickened again.

In fact Hydro never established *one* regional office; its three main arms made their own arrangements and reported independently to head office. The result? It worked, of course, but one suspects at some cost. In the early days particularly, before detailed working policies had been evolved, the field men corresponded back and forth with Vancouver, and occasionally reported in person, necessitating three days' absence from the field. This meant delays and sometimes inadequate communication of problems on one hand and policies on the other. More important, it meant that in the early days at least some people in head office had no real feel for the situation and were therefore not in a position to make truly informed decisions. Nor was there anyone at roughly their own level to make independent representations to them. Most important, there was in those days no effective monitoring of the performance of the men in the field, a fault which had tragic results in the case already mentioned, which did not pass unnoticed by the people of the valley. Following that, there was much more direct supervision of field affairs by senior officers.

In addition to these organizational problems, Hydro had other working relationships to create and maintain. These were with the many agencies of government at all levels whose programs were related in some way to the Columbia project. The complexity of these is best described by Diagram 10.

It may be noted in passing that Hydro had no staff trained in city or regional planning or research, despite the fact that many of its operations (power and gas distribution, transit and railway operations, and industrial land assembly) deal with integral parts of the urban web. That this is so is a sad commentary on several things: possibly on the image of the city planning profession as seen by outsiders; possibly on the lack of appreciation of what modern urban research can do; possibly on the distrust which both engineers and businessmen often feel for local government and politics; and possibly most of all on the idea that Hydro could pursue supposedly simple ends, defined in engineering and commercial terms, in isolation from the mêlée of urban growth and government. Needless to say this can result in a single-minded, if not simple-minded, approach to the task which arouses both ire and opposition on the part of municipal officials and distrust on the part of the public. The case of the rail line to the Roberts Bank super-port was a good example.[2]

What expectations did Hydro have of its Columbia planning staff? My

2 In this case Hydro proposed a route which was opposed by the Lower Mainland Regional Planning Board, and after considerable public controversy changed the route.

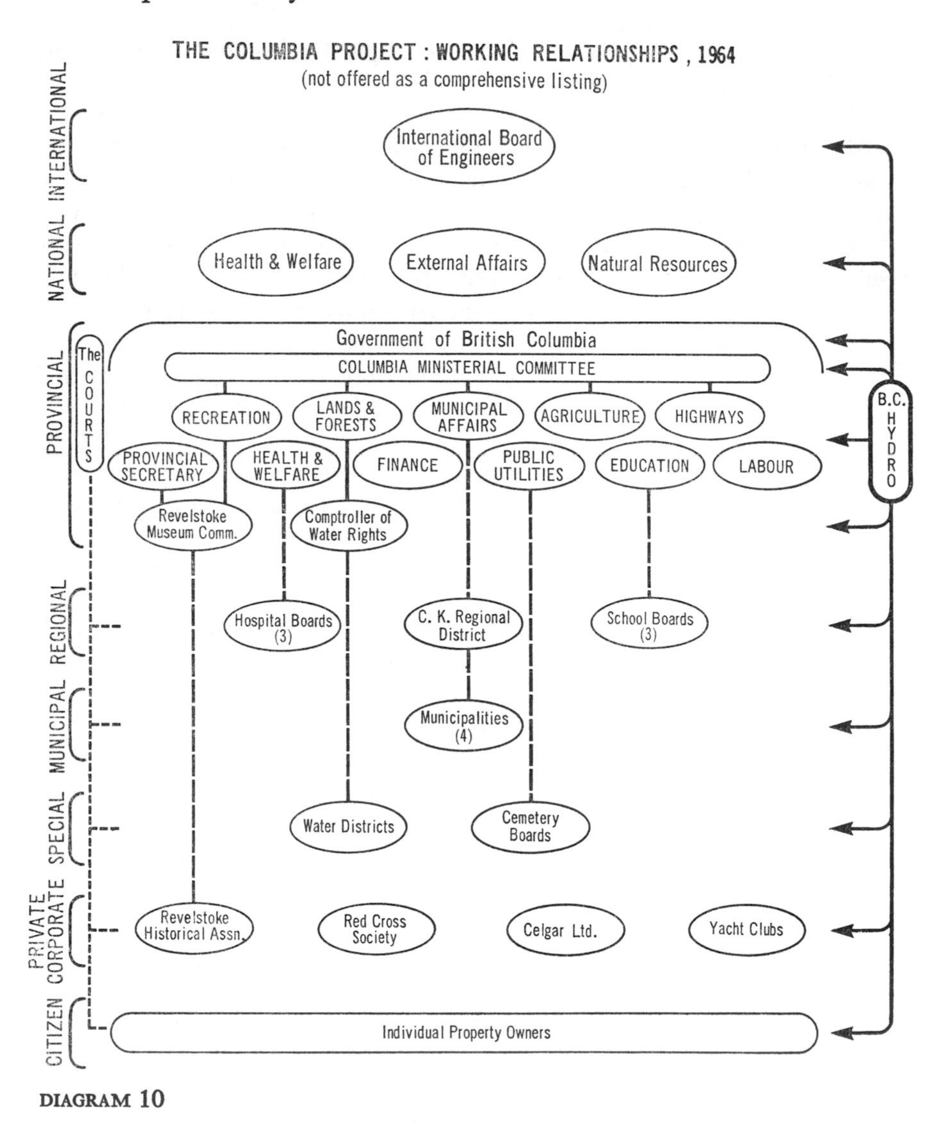

DIAGRAM 10

duties were broadly 'to prepare general plans for the regions and the communities affected ... and action plans and programs to deal with BC Hydro's responsibilities as they may emerge ...' Others would probably have said that I was expected to 'look after the people end of the job.' But at least one senior officer used to delight in saying, possibly not entirely in jest, that he had thought of me as a sort of professional 'firee' – 'you know, the sort of guy they have in big department stores whose job is to get fired when customers complain. So the manager calls him down and fires him, publicly and loudly.' In other words, a latter-day Daniel for the lions of the Lakes. In fact our job, much of which is described in this book, consisted of three main elements: establishing what the Columbia project would do to the Arrow Lakes region, formulating specific plans for resettlement communities, and formulating policies to meet a wide range of problems arising from the project. To the extent that such policy formulation impinged on other people's 'territory' it was not always welcomed with delight. Nevertheless this account shows how often general guidance was given, especially for the broader aspects of the land division's program.[3]

In passing it may be noted that apart from three assistants employed on resettlement surveys in 1965 the planning staff never exceeded three people and its total life span was just over two years. Scarcely a major investment or an unconscionable burden on the Columbia budget.

Before leaving Hydro and its workings it would be wrong not to pay further attention to the subject of personal working philosophies and attitudes. Given the immediate objective of the project, the storage of water, Hydro had a number of specific tasks to undertake. Some of these were disruptive and distasteful to many people who showed their resentment in many ways. In the face of this, each official built up his own attitude to the work depending on his actual experiences and his personal outlook and philosophy. Some retained a sympathetic understanding of the people they dealt with, without forgetting the need to be firm, consistent, and practical in getting their jobs done. Others were not so tough-minded, or perhaps not so understanding. For them the job became primarily one of resisting unreasonable demands, of not being taken for a ride, and their attitude could very easily slip from defensiveness to combativeness. Needless to say, such a reaction simply exacerbated the feelings on the other side.

But the general attitude of Hydro towards its task was very important

3 This footnote will perhaps answer my wife's insistent cry 'For Heaven's sake tell them what *you* did.' Well dear, here are the things which were specifically my staff's doing: The Background Report described in chapter 5, whose overall importance was in my view considerable and which led to many actions; The Broad Brush Plan (chapter 7) and the subsequent new community plans and their discussion with the people in public meetings; the intention surveys which provided the basis for the community plans; the cemetery program (chapter 10); the Clearing Study (chapter 11); and all the many problems discussed in chapter 12 except those of an engineering nature. I like to think that the Background Report and the Old People's Study were two of the more important broadening influences on the compensation program. So there.

and here I speak of the attitude at the top where decisions were made. This was important externally because, in my view, most of the people in the lakes were reasonable in their expectations and it was important not to alienate them in dealing with the 'squeaky wheels' who were not. It was also important internally, in that the lower ranks naturally tended to reflect what they took to be the attitude at the top.

On both fronts the question really became an exercise in communication; externally one of careful choice of public statements, internally one of defining clearly Hydro's stance and its expectations of staff members. My impression is that the Authority did not attend to these needs as carefully as it might. To the extent that this is a valid criticism Hydro failed to do justice to its own philosophies and intentions, for I cannot remember any serious expression of meanness or hostility on the part of its policy-makers.

At this point it is worthwhile to say a little more about the behaviour of 'middle management' and its consequences for jobs such as the Columbia project. I offer these comments not because they emerged from systematic behavioural studies but because my own intuitive observations were beautifully crystallized by a recent study carried out by Derrick Sewell at the University of Victoria [20]. They bear on a problem which seems likely to arise whenever an established organization is given a new task whose nature and scale have not been experienced before by the men who run the functional divisions. Sewell's study reached two very important findings: that professional training predisposes its practitioners to rather narrow views of complex problems, this being in Sewell's study 'environmental quality management' (for example, the engineer is predisposed towards physical works, the public health official towards regulation and education); that seniority in an organization makes men more conservative in their perceptions and behaviour, reflecting primarily the aims and interests of the organization which employs them and the normal state of 'political' equilibrium within it. This may have been the iceberg that barely surfaced in the behaviour of some members of the Columbia projects committee, which apart from the chairman and myself was composed entirely of engineers, lawyers, and financial experts.

The danger to an overall program and the challenge to those who administer its operations are obvious. They may will be greater in Vancouver and Victoria than in most places, for in these lotus-lands the attractions of garden and boat are compelling and often work against the claims of wider professional experience. Hydro filled one gap in its staff competence by hiring a small resettlement planning staff. Nevertheless in some areas, as I saw it, difficulties arose because of the limitations and recalcitrance of officers who had never been exposed on their way up through the ranks to the need to plan and program complex operations. Their tendency was to take umbrage at advice and to limit their activities to what felt they could control safely by themselves.

These observations on organizational behaviour point to two problems of leadership. One is the problem of ensuring that an established organization should, without damaging the morale of existing staff members, acquire the staff capacity to respond to challenges which are new to it in scale and nature. The other is the need to give a sense of direction and coherence to a group of men who may not only be professionally polyglot, but will in most circumstances be engaged in the usual organizational games of pushing, shoving, and one-upmanship. A very heavy responsibility therefore rests on the shoulders of the leader of such projects to bring about discriminating policies while still maintaining harmony within his ranks.

One last question that might well be asked is Hydro's relationship to the provincial government, for example, whether it exercised any degree of independence in its work and whether it received active collaboration from the government and its members. To begin with it will be remembered that there were close working links at the top policy level in that two cabinet ministers, Mr Williston (lands and forests), and Mr Kiernan (recreation and conservation), sat on Hydro's board of directors. These two played an active role in the Authority's affairs and their personal relationships with Hydro's executive officials were friendly. Nor was that the only working connection, for Einaar Gunderson, who was a member of both the board and the executive management committee, carried responsibility for Hydro's financial division. At the same time he had been a long-standing associate of the premier and was known to be one of his most influential advisers. Thus at the top there were close and vital links with the provincial government.

It would be wrong to deduce from this that Hydro always danced to the government's tune. It did in matters of government policy, as it must being a provincial creature. But in the conduct of the Columbia project it showed a degree of independence. For example, R.W. Gross, who carried responsibility for the property acquisition program has stated, privately as well as publicly, that he had never been subjected to political pressure in the conduct of his work. In fact on one occasion in 1966 Hydro, on Gross's advice, rejected a resolution by the provincial legislature recommending that a detailed breakdown of property compensation offers be provided to those affected. Parallel to this the government seems to have played no active role in political representation on behalf of Arrow Lakes citizens who felt aggrieved by Hydro's actions. (Frank Rutter in his 1966 series of articles in the *Vancouver Sun* made this observation three times.) Quite a number of people in the Arrow Lakes expected to be able to muster opposition to

Hydro through political channels and in this they seem to have been largely disappointed.

It may be remarked in passing that while the provincial government avoided any entanglement in Hydro's skirts in the Arrow Lakes, Hydro was not equally able to dissociate itself from the government. Some of the observations made in the 1970 survey made it clear that some people blamed Hydro for matters which were not its doing at all, including, for example, the taking over of the BC Electric Company and the initially inadequate compensation offered to it. And again in 1972 I find people who were displaced from waterfront property blaming Hydro because the department of lands and forest, applying a provincial policy rather rigidly, will not allow them to have Crown-owned waterfront land to replace their Arrow Lakes holdings.

Except in the broad policy sense Hydro was no puppet of the provincial government. This does not mean that it enjoyed the close support at the departmental level which would have made its working life easier, or that it enjoyed the access to the government's councils which a project such as the Columbia really required. The long struggle to bring about the Columbia ministers committee testifies to this. All in all it seems to have been regarded as a step-child rather than a full member of the family.

14
After the flood

In midsummer 1970, with the reservoir almost full, the Arrow Lakes area seemed to be a very different place from the pre-flood region. Its road communications were greatly improved. Nevertheless they fell considerably short of the dream of 1965, for the traveller from Revelstoke south still faced some fifteen miles of logging road in the heart-stopping tradition of British Columbia, and from Nakusp to Castlegar he still clung with trepidation to the bluff face high over Slocan Lake. At Fauquier a ferry much larger than before but not a whit faster shuttled across the lake under the ghostly shadow of the aborted Needles bridge. The proposed road south from the bridge site was only a gleam in a cynical eye. But although its connections to the outside world were still somewhat lacking, the road from Nakusp to Fauquier was vastly improved; it was a dream compared with the rutty, dusty, drunken road of the old days. Furthermore it afforded far better views of the lakes and the mountains than its predecessor.

When the reservoir was full the lake looked more attractive, in a picture-book sense, than before. The shores were cleaner and less littered with forest debris; little beaches seemed to be forming. The lakes themselves were cleaner and much warmer, so that it was no longer a test of manhood to swim in them.

Most noticeable of all to one who knew the old valley was the absence of people. Gone was the long ragged ribbon of orchards, fields, and houses – the humanity of the landscape, evolved over so many years of settlement.

These changes were no improvement to those who loved the comfortable, lived-in quality of the old Arrow Lakes. To them the better roads, appreciated in themselves of course, offered a journey to nowhere: 'We used to be able to call in on half-a-dozen friends between here and Burton, but now ...' To them the richest part of the natural landscape had also gone: the fertile meeting of land and water with its profusion of birds and animals, especially beavers, muskrats, and otters. Gone too was free access to the west bank of the valley with its prized lakes and meadows and practically no people to intrude or to pollute.

Even for the less fastidious the new rose was not without its thorns. One resulted from Hydro's inexplicable failure to stump a couple of areas open to public view near Revelstoke and Burton so that at lower reservoir levels they present a field of tree stumps, an acne on the face of a fair region, and a hazard to the boat-user.

The other thorn was quite unforeseen: the advent of severe dust storms in areas where much cleared land was exposed by the falling water. It is not known whether this was due to the deposition of the river's load of silt or to the blowing-off of the materials of the raw slopes and mud flats. People all along the lake complained bitterly of such storms, especially in springtime when the reservoir was low.

This brings us to the crux of the matter for the future of the Arrow Lakes: the timing of reservoir drawdown. Many people, though not all, believed that when the Arrow reservoir was full the region was generally an improvement over the old days. But when the reservoir was low and stumps and mud flats were exposed, and as long as dust storms continued, all agreed that the Arrow Lakes were far less pleasant than they used to be.[1] This region always was and still is lake-oriented, and to that extent the quality of life is largely bound up with the quality and usability of the lakes. Hydro never undertook to ensure that the reservoir would be full during the whole summer. *The New Outlook* simply said 'normally the reservoir will be full during these (summer) months, unless there has been an exceptionally dry winter.' This implies that if the Arrow reservoir is not full in summertime it will be nature's fault, not Hydro's. It is to be hoped that this will be so, for on it depends much of the quality of life for the people of the region, and also any possibility of developing a dependable tourist trade.

Given this, it is not fanciful to predict that the Arrow Lakes will come into their own again as soon as the reservoir banks settle down and shore land now held by Hydro is made available for settlement. The demand for waterfront land in the southern parts of British Columbia continues to rise

1 To put this situation in perspective, this low-reservoir condition would normally apply only for about six weeks in late spring and a few weeks in late fall. During the winter the lake and its banks are covered in snow; during the summer the reservoir is full and the banks under water.

in response to pressures from the crowded coast, the border states, and the prairie cities, and when better access roads are built and the land is freed, the lakes will be peopled once again. When this happens the Arrow Lakes will still be particularly fortunate in one respect: since the land supply is strictly limited and long stretches of shoreline cannot be settled at all, it will never be overcrowded and should not become polluted. Few areas can say as much.

But these observations were largely those of an outsider. How did the residents of the Arrow Lakes see their valley in 1970? To answer this, surveys were carried out on two groups of people: a few not directly affected by the Columbia project and some actually displaced.

The first group consisted of prominent and active citizens, usually heads of community organizations, in Revelstoke, Nakusp, and Castlegar, together with residents of the undisturbed rural areas in the Central Arrow Lakes. There were thirty-one in all, not nearly enough to give statistically defensible results in any one area.[2] However, they provide a generally credible picture. Here is their message.

The Columbia project had no lasting effect on the economy of any of the areas. Castlegar was affected most, and worst in the sense that the relapse from boom to bust was felt most keenly. Revelstoke felt little effect from the Mica project (eighty miles away), hiring having been done in Vancouver and contractors having dealt with manufacturers and suppliers in distant large cities. In all cases it was realized that in losing population and land local business had lost customers and to that extent the economy was poorer. In all cases too there was belief that tourism will develop when the highway system is completed and when parks and public camp sites are developed.

The changes in the Lakes themselves meant different things to each area. Revelstoke complained of stumps, mud flats, and dust storms, and well it might, for that section of the reservoir is shallowest and most sensitive to change in water level. Castlegar mourned the loss of old established water frontage and noted the absence (at that time) of adequate public parks and campsites to replace it. In Nakusp there were comments on the tidiness and cleanness of the Lakes, and the warmer water was noticed. Here too there was much more concern with the eventual release of waterfront lands, both for local settlement and as the basis of a future boost to the local economy. Control of the old damaging floods was mentioned only in Castlegar.

2 This was a one-page mailed questionnaire, similar in content to the first section of the larger questionnaire described later. Forty were sent out and the response was eighty per cent.

Typically the rural respondents in the Central Area were far more conscious of the effect on the natural environment, and bitter words were written about the lakes, the fish and fishing, ugly mudflats, stumps, and the lack of access to the recreation lands of the west bank.

Limited in reliability as they were, these views are valuable as a prelude to the views of the displaced people who still reside in the Central Arrow Lakes.

To give perspective to resettlement in the Central Area it must also be remembered that more than half of the people displaced (600 out of 1100) in the Ceneral Arrow Lakes left the region entirely. It is believed that many of the older people left because, no longer having family ties, they were conscious of their need for convenient community services, especially medical aid. Sad to say, we know little about all these people, their whereabouts, or their success or failure in resettling. Some, we know, went over the Monashee Mountains into the sunny Okanagan; others went to the cities to be near sons and daughters; still others searched out little communities and valleys in the remote parts of British Columbia. To the extent that we do not know how they fared we do not know the full human impact of the Columbia project.

Secondly, the greatest single body of displaced people who resettled in the Ceneral Arrow Lakes (about fifty families), settled in Nakusp. Apart from a few families who were able to re-establish on higher land on their own properties, all the rest who resettled did so in the three new communities of Burton, Edgewood, and Fauquier. These communities are very different indeed. However, they have one thing in common: each is populated largely by people who previously resided in the same area. In some cases this was obviously because it was convenient to work, but no doubt attachment to the place and community also had a great deal to do with it.

To anyone who knew Burton in the old days, the new community gives the impression that it has merely been moved over a quarter of a mile. It has, superficially at least, the same aura of suspended animation, despite the fact that the houses are much newer and the central core consisting of the community hall, church, and park-playfield is much more coherent than before (Diagram 11). The community sits naturally in its wooded site, an impression which is heightened by the unkempt appearance of the central area. The new community hall is possibly the greatest single improvement in Burton. Compared to its battered and gloomy predecessor, it is spacious, clean, much better for badminton, and provides modern kitchen facilities and offices for the visiting public health nurse.

The most significant change in the Burton area is the great decline in the total population to about one-third of its former size. Some residents feel this loss very keenly. From other points of view, however, Burton has not changed much. It is said that the community (not a score of families in the hamlet itself and a mere handful scattered around it) is split between the adherents of the Recreation Commission and those of the Community Hall Association. No change there. And tiny as it is, and notwithstanding its location on the main highway, Burton boasts three gas stations, two combined with stores.[3] Indeed little has changed.

From Burton to Edgewood is chalk to cheese; not that Edgewood has changed in essence either. It has shrunk greatly in population, but since it has maintained its close connection with the adjacent Inonoaklin Valley (about fifty families) the total population of the wider community has changed relatively little. Physically, however, it has acquired a new lease on life. (Diagram 12)

Like Burton it is set in a background of trees, an immense boon to any community. Unlike Burton it opens out to the lake, which affords a beautiful view through a light screen of birches. Spatially, Edgewood is compact and laid out in a rather informal and pleasant way. The original core area planned by Hydro has provided a framework for an attractive cluster of houses, which present themselves from all angles and give a strong impression of activity and community. Edgewood is well equipped with community facilities: church, school, hall, store (only one, thank heaven), hospital, post office, and credit union, all of which serve the Inonoaklin Valley behind, and in fact would not be possible without its support. The lakeside park is beautifully maintained and affords a striking new site for the old war memorial. One fortunate circumstance is that the store and post office are on the edge of the community, which removes parking, traffic, and gassing-up from the residential clusters. Everything about Edgewood announces that happy and energetic people live here. As one vigorous citizen put it, 'We all pull good together.'

The impression given by Fauquier is different again (Diagram 13). The site is a fine open area with a moderate slope and a magnificent north-west view which all the residents share. But the site is still rather bare. The population of the Needles-Fauquier area has shrunk by almost half, and Fauquier gives the impression of being a new community that has not yet settled down.

THE RESIDENTS SPEAK FOR THEMSELVES

These are only the observations of an outsider. To find out the feelings of the residents I carried out a survey in June 1970 among the relocated families in the Central Arrow Lakes. This was originally intended to be done by

3 The urban reader may well ask how forty to fifty families can support one store, far less two. The answer again lies in the diversified subsistence economy.

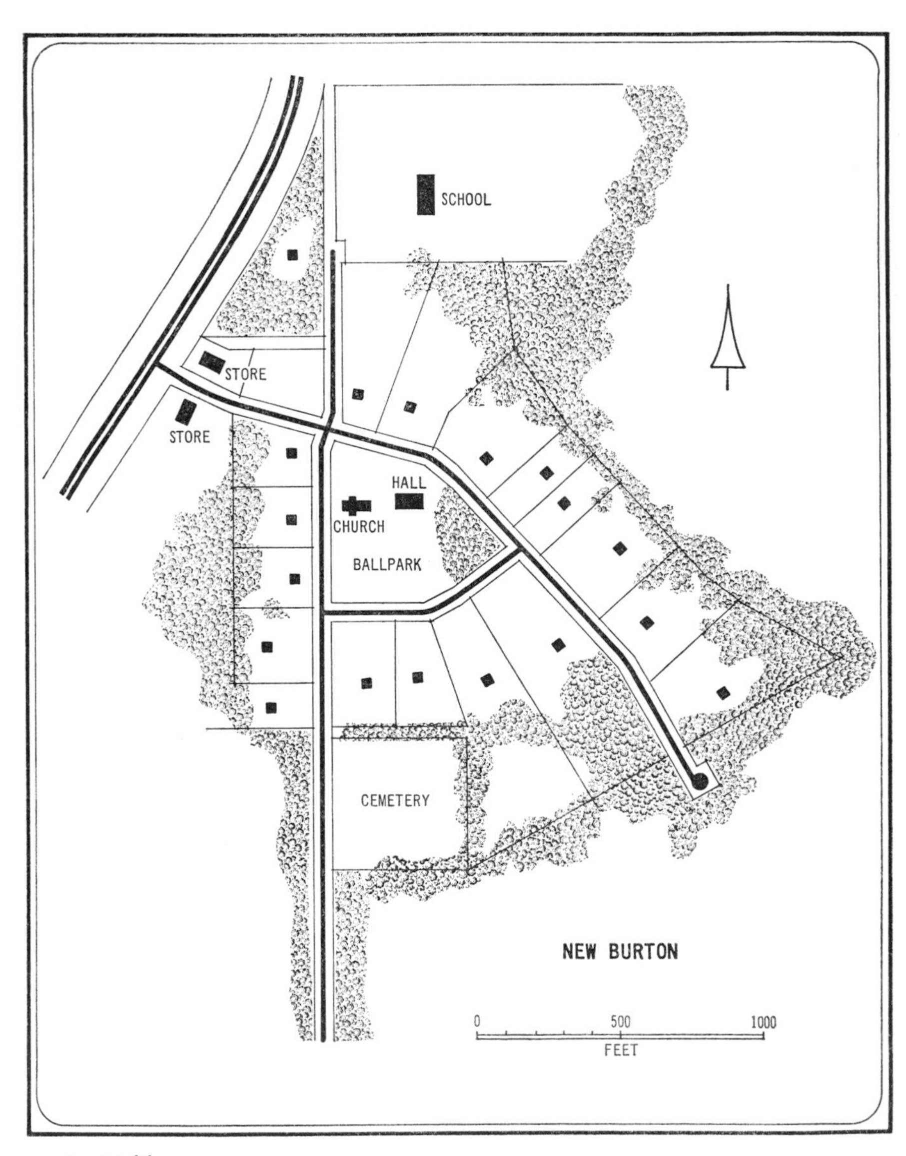
SCHOOL
STORE
STORE
HALL
CHURCH
BALLPARK
CEMETERY
NEW BURTON
0
500
1000
FEET

DIAGRAM 11

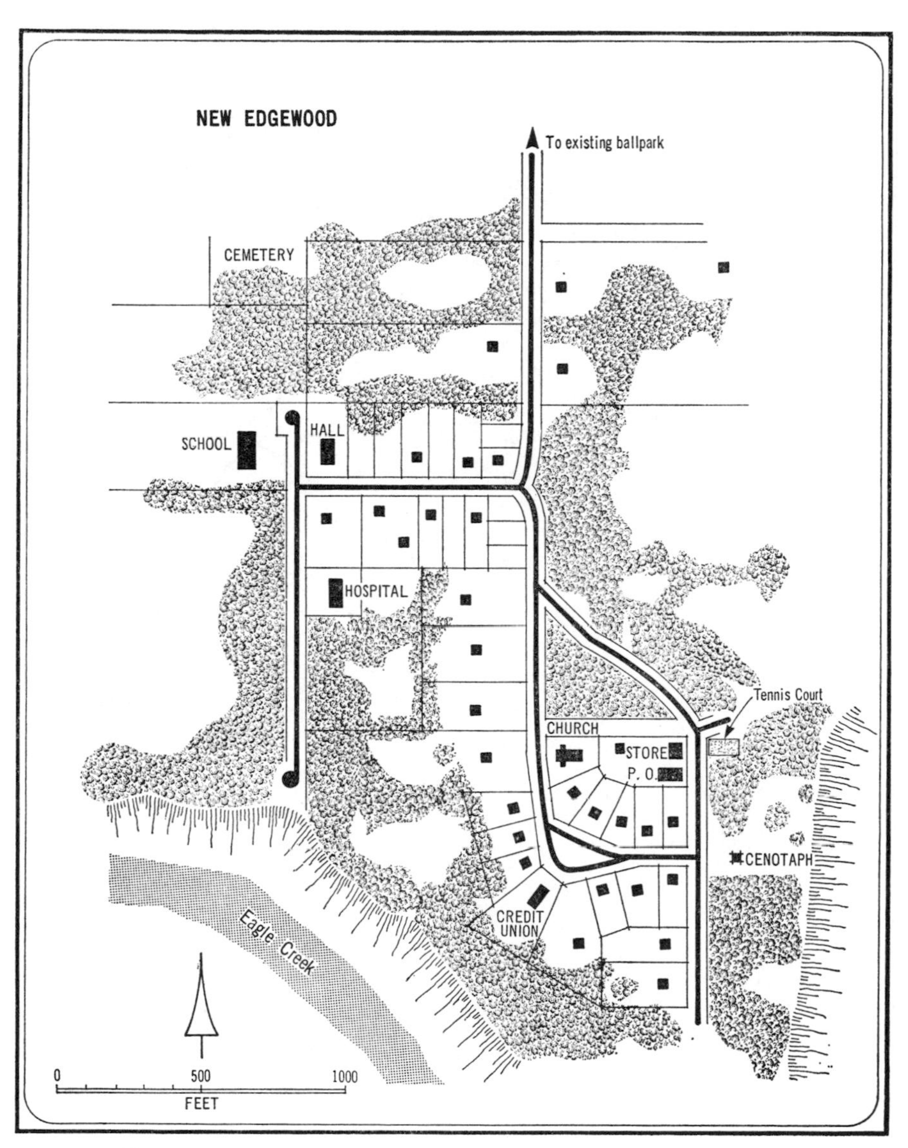
NEW EDGEWOOD
To existing ballpark
CEMETERY
SCHOOL
HALL
HOSPITAL
CHURCH
STORE
P. O.
Tennis Court
CENOTAPH
CREDIT UNION
Eagle Creek
0
500
1000
FEET

DIAGRAM 12

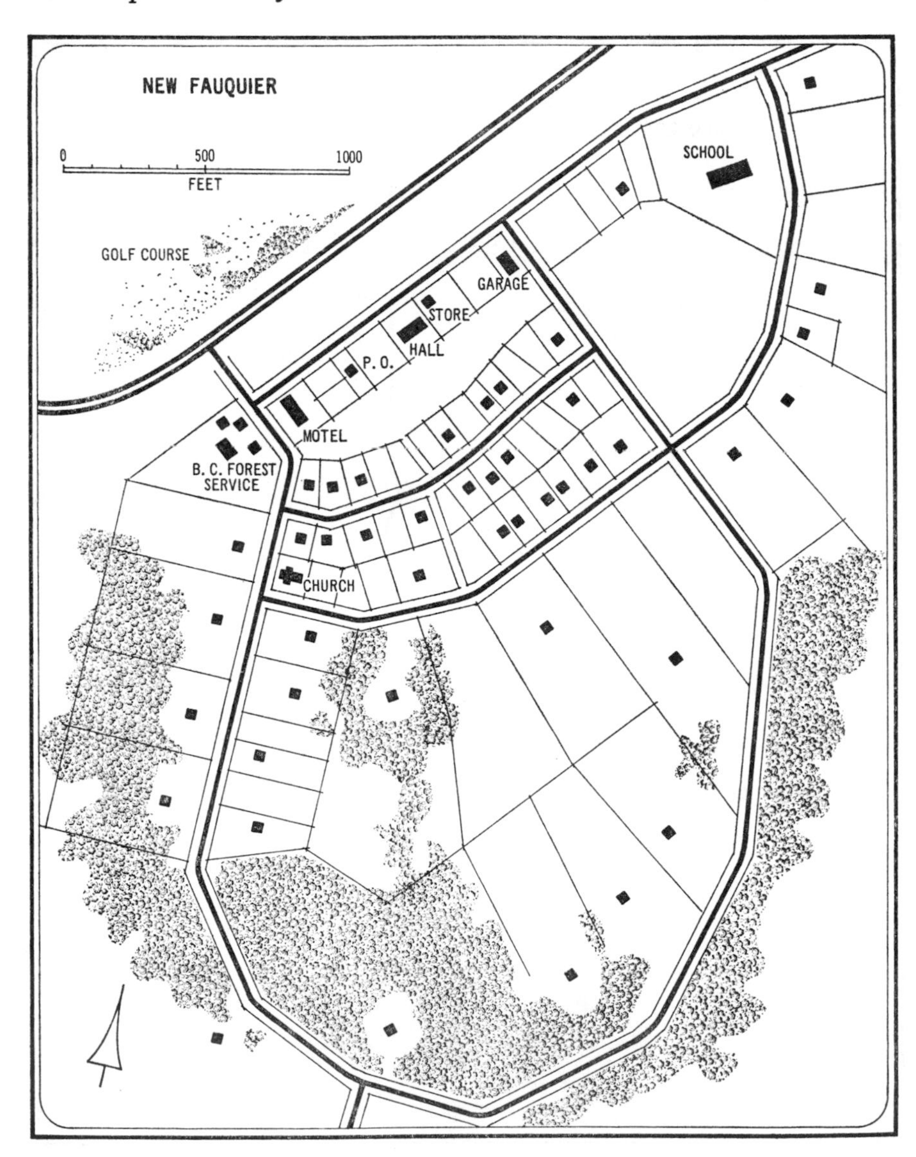

NEW FAUQUIER
0
500
1000
FEET
GOLF COURSE
SCHOOL
GARAGE
STORE
HALL
P.O.
MOTEL
B.C. FOREST SERVICE
CHURCH

DIAGRAM 13

RESIDENTS' FEELINGS ABOUT THEIR COMPENSATION AND ITS FAIRNESS, AND ABOUT THEIR REGION, COMMUNITY AND HOUSES

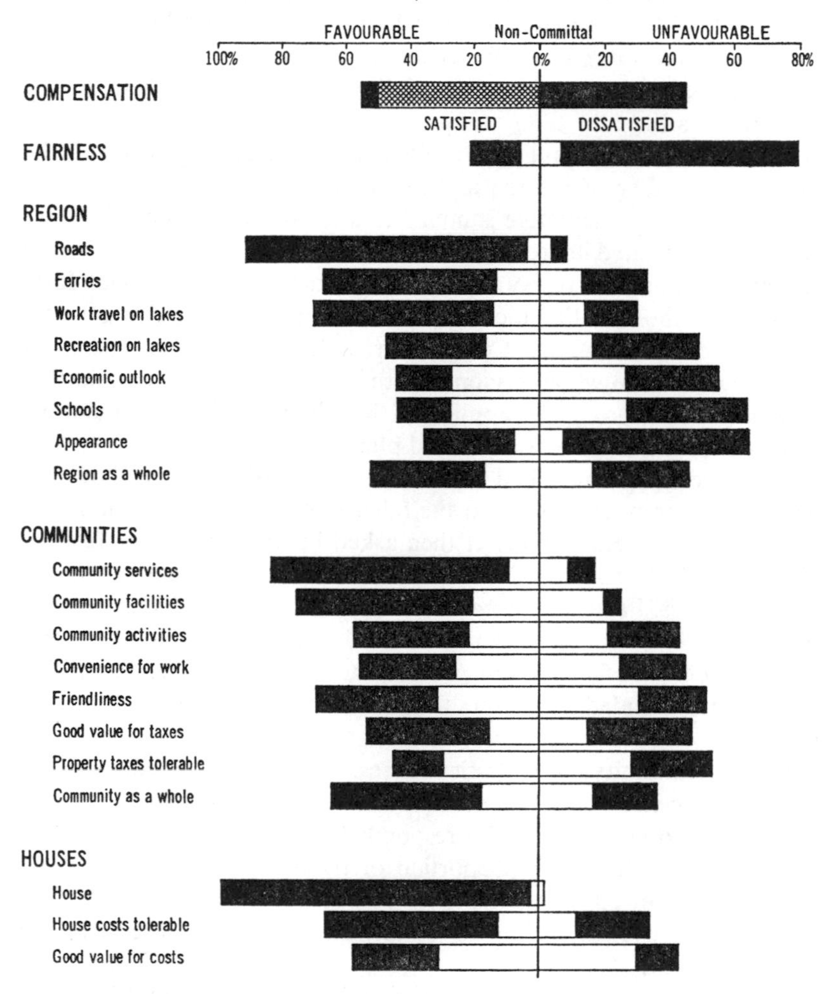

FAVOURABLE/UNFAVOURABLE RATIOS

The above diagram shows percentages without regard for the actual numbers of responses. Below is a comparison of the actual numbers involved in the form of favourable/unfavourable ratios (non-committal responses omitted).

	All	Satisfied	Dissatisfied	Late Returns	Early Returns
Overall	2.1	3.0	1.3	4.6	1.7
Region	1.8	2.3	1.3		
Communities	2.3	4.2	1.1		
Houses	4.7	10.0	2.0		

DIAGRAM 14

personal interviews. But time limitations made this impossible and the questionnaire had to be mailed to every household with an appropriate covering letter. This yielded forty replies out of a hundred cases, a relatively good response to such an approach. The details of this survey and its analysis have been relegated to Appendix 2. What follows is the essence of the survey and its meaning as I see it.

In order not to misinterpret the results it is first necessary to recall the relatively small number of returns and to stress that the response was not a carefully selected representative sample but a self-selecting one. (In other words those who wanted to respond did, and *vice versa*, giving a biased sample.) Furthermore the respondents, though they constitute about forty per cent of those who resettled locally, represent only about twelve per cent of the total displaced from the Central Arrow Lakes and seven per cent of those displaced in the whole region. In other words it *cannot* be said that the results are typical or can be applied to the whole displaced population. Nevertheless they are both interesting and plausible.

Briefly, the survey first asked for the respondents' feelings about the adequacy of their compensation and the fairness of the compensation program as between different people. It then asked in some detail for feelings about the 'new' Central Arrow Lakes area and the resettlement communities and their houses. From the responses two fairly equal but distinct groups of people emerged having somewhat different responses to the questions. These might be described as the *satisfied* and the *dissatisfied*. The dissatisfied were those who responded negatively to both the compensation and fairness questions. They showed a relatively low degree of satisfaction with their region, their community, and their houses. They were predominantly (seventy-five per cent) people who had been born or raised in the Arrow Lakes. The satisfied were those who responded positively to the compensation question, although a high proportion of them also complained about unfairness. They showed a much higher degree of satisfaction with their surroundings. The overall feeling of unfairness was by far the strongest feature of the survey.

The main results in detail are shown graphically in Diagram 14. Suffice it to say at this point that, ignoring non-committal responses ('don't know' or 'not sure'), the overall balance of favourable to unfavourable responses was roughly two to one, but the satisfied showed a ratio of three to one, the dissatisfied a ratio of one to one.

These are not simple or clear findings. They suggest that a good majority were satisfied with their new circumstances. But we might well ask whether it is acceptable that as many as one-third of all responses were unfavourable. In considering this, there are a number of things to be said. First, the responses indicate only the respondents' opinions, not the validity of these opinions. Secondly, there is almost certainly a degree of negative bias in the responses, as suggested by the fact that the early returns were much more negative and aggrieved than those which were obtained by writing a follow-up letter (whose favourable/unfavourable response ratio was more than four to one). Thirdly we have to remember the very significant finding of Lord Taylor's study of English new towns: one-third of the population studied suffered from 'the sub-clinical neurosis syndrome' regardless of their environment, (this syndrome being a constitutional state expressed through anxiety, 'nerves,' undue irritability, depression, or sleeplessness) [24]. If this is so, then a considerable proportion of any population at any time might be expected to react negatively to any added stress in their lives. To put is crudely, if at any time quite a number of people are unhappy because of their wives/husbands, because of boils on their bottoms, or because that's just the way they are, their judgments on *anything* are liable to be jaundiced. There are good reasons, then, for looking critically, even a little sceptically, at these findings, at least in quantitative terms.

One last observation should also be made mainly for the benefit of some residents of the Arrow Lakes who honestly believe that they know their fellows and their values and aspirations. This is simply that the people of the Arrow Lakes are a diverse group of people, and they perceive their environment in many different ways. Are the lakes better or worse than before? The logger who traverses them daily says one thing, the old person who seldom sees them and no longer travels on them says another, the aesthete and the nature-lover yet another. Are the new communities with their relatively small lots anathema to people who 'need lots of space and independence'? Many of them do not agree. Is living in Nakusp a dreadful penance to those who used to enjoy the space and freedom of, say, West Arrow Park? Most old folks at least do not think so. If it comes to that, are the people logical and consistent in their desires? Not necessarily. Some would clearly like to have their cake and eat it too, to have the privacy of West Arrow Park and the range of services in Nakusp.

The two introductory questions were very revealing, especially when taken together. Detailed analysis of the responses on compensation showed first that those who replied 'generous' and those who replied 'reasonable' were in fact both expressing much the same degree of satisfaction. Thus the overall response shows about sixty per cent were satisfied and forty per cent dissatisfied with the amount of their compensation. On the question of 'fairness,' however, ignoring the non-committal responses (which at fifteen per cent were relatively few), there were three times as many clearly dissatisfied as clearly satisfied. This feeling of unfairness not only pervaded those who were not content with their compensation; it also affected half of those who were apparently content with it. This finding fits very well with a statement by D.G. Blair which is quoted in full in the next chapter: 'there remains a rankling sense of injustice long after the event of expropriation and despite reasonably generous settlement' [3]. As will be seen later, this general feeling of injustice found expression in written comments, which offer some suggestions as to its meaning and causes.

The second group of questions dealt with people's feelings about the Central Arrow Lakes, and it elicited the least favourable overall responses, having a favourable/unfavourable ratio of only 1.6 to 1.0. It was answered more precisely, and favourably, on specific and familiar matters (roads and ferries) than on more general ones. The one clearly negative response was on the appearance of the new lakes.[4] However, spontaneous comments were revealing, especially in that almost twice as many mentioned 'newer, brighter communities' as any other matter, postive or negative. These, in order of frequency, were: newer, brighter communities; the loss of friends and neighbours; the loss of farmland, beaches, and the west bank meadows and lakes; improved communications.

The third section dealt with the new communities and showed a generally favourable pattern of response (favourable/unfavourable ratio 2.3 to 1.0). Spontaneous comments by a margin of three to one mentioned the advantages of the new communities. A few in two communities mentioned 'poor community spirit' and 'bickering over compensation.'

The fourth section asked whether people felt that they had made a wise decision in settling in the Arrow Lakes and their new communities. In both cases the response was strongly affirmative. These questions also brought out a few answers of characteristic defiance and humour: 'I still haven't seen any place I like better and anyway, who knows what valley Hydro will spoil next?' And in gratuitous answer to the question 'Where do you wish you had settled,' 'Noah's Ark (drier).'

The responses suggest that there are considerable differences in morale between the new communities. Edgewood emerges as a fiercely proud, coherent, self-conscious, community; it boasts of 'unity in the face of oppression' and feels that it has emerged stronger than ever from its ordeal by water,

4 It should be pointed out that these questions covered matters much beyond Hydro's field of responsibility, for example, schools. In this particular matter much of the negative feeling was recorded by Edgewood people who resented the school board's failure to re-establish the previous two-room 'junior high' school at Needles instead of busing students to the high school at Nakusp.

and 'no thanks to Hydro.'[5] If Edgewood had a coat of arms it would surely show Excalibur brandished above the lake, over a motto reading: *Nemo me impune lacessit*. Burton sounds depressed. Fauquier values its new services and its site, but still sounds somewhat unhappy. The settlers in Nakusp seem to have experienced least upset and to appreciate the services and activities of the larger community, while feeling most the impact of higher taxes.

The fifth section of the survey addressed itself to housing, and shows a very strong expression (favourable/unfavourable ratio 4.5 to 1.0) in favour of all aspects of the program: the moving of old houses (very successful), the improved quality of housing, and a tolerable level of cost increase. Significantly too the weight of opinion says that these extra costs are worthwhile.

The last section asked questions about Hydro's overall performance and the value of the *Columbia Newsletter*, both of which were answered very negatively (favourable/unfavourable ratios of 0.5 to 1.0 and 0.6 to 1.0 respectively). A common view was that the *Newsletter* was 'a propaganda sheet and quite unreliable.'

These were the responses to given questions. However, there were many spontaneous written comments, and while they reinforce the findings of the questionnaire some of them are worth repeating. The most frequent by far was on the question of fairness: twenty-six comments which were unfavourable four to one. Unfairness was attributed variously to appraisers' incompetence or unfamiliarity with the region, to gullibility, to susceptibility to hard bargaining, and to sheer favouritism.[6]

The next group of comments was on the apparent slowness and confusion of Hydro's programs: fourteen comments, all strongly critical. Typical of these were: 'Hydro changed personnel in the Nakusp office too often so you never knew who you were dealing with in regard to property. Each one never seemed to stay long enough to finish a job.' 'they kept people dangling ... asked lots of questions and told you nothing ... the war of nerves should have been scrapped.' The third was on the adequacy of compensation: twelve comments which were unfavourable three to one. The fourth was on the treatment of older people: ten comments which were laudatory two to one. Eight people complained of Hydro's inconsistent and allegedly selective policy on making land available for resettlement. Lastly, and especially in view of the generally critical tone of the written comments and the

5 Bellwether Bill, of course. Who else?

6 One case frequently referred to made it clear either how far word of an 'over-generous' settlement can be spread or alternatively how an already unpopular man can quickly become the object of suspicion and resentment.

widespread expressions of resentment, it should be mentioned that five people spontaneously approved of Hydro's performance in general.

OUT OF THE MOUTHS OF BABES

So far we have considered only the views of adults. But how did the children see their changed environment? Might we not get a more sensitive 'reading' from them? Or will we simply hear the views of parents through the mouths of their children?

The school authorities were asked in 1970 to invite displaced children to write an essay on the Arrow Lakes. It was late in the school year and only a few did. The only thing they had in common was in the main a preoccupation with the visible and usable things that furnish their world. Apart from that they exhibited much the same range of views as their elders, and the same range of sensitivity to the atmosphere of their communities.

Three of these compositions are quoted. They were not chosen for their verdicts but for their content and, as far as could be judged, their authenticity.

EDGEWOOD

In 1966 Hydro came to visit us. They explained that we had to move to higher ground because the United States needed water and that a dam was being built to store this water. They offered to purchase our homes and property which would be flooded. Edgewood at this time was a completely settled town. Suddenly the people were always busy and were unable to go out and have a good time. All the serenity was lost and because of this lost serenity, many disagreements were started with Hydro. The people moved and the water began to rise.[7]

In old Edgewood we had a weekly show, which was soon stopped because of the sudden interest in television. In new Edgewood we have a tennis court, which just about makes up for the shows. We have paved roads, while down in the old town we had dirt roads. We have new beaches and picnic tables. Down in the old town we had a hardware store. In new Edgewood, everyone was given a chance to start a new life. Those who wanted to move could move. By the Hydro buying our land we were offered a choice.

I have lived in Edgewood all my life. I liked old Edgewood better than new Edgewood because in old Edgewood we were able to live as friends and neighbours. New Edgewood is still a confused town. But before old Edgewood became settled it was probably confused too. Old Edgewood to me was home.
Brian Bargery

7 Is this the King James version showing through or just the natural simplicity of a child who has not learned to complicate language?

FAUQUIER: NEW ARROW LAKES DEVELOPMENT

In Needles the old townsite I lived in we had no paved or systematized roads – all we had was criss-crossing dirt roads. In the way of houses they were mostly pretty old ones. In the way of community buildings we had an old wooden store that was high off of the ground, a small post office the size of a bathroom and it was always dusty. We had no church except one old abandoned one next to our community hall which was ready to fall in anytime. We did have a garage but it was old and dusty, and one old hotel. There was only a 6–10 school.

In the new Fauquier townsite where I live now we have paved streets with cement sidewalks. Our houses are all bright and modern. Our community buildings now consist of a new generously windowed store, a bright clean post office, two convenient churches, a new modern community hall, a new gas station, a modern hotel with kitchen units, there is a ranch style cafe a little way out with horses. We also have a 1–7 school.

In the way of the appearance of the community we have seeded with lawn and planted with trees boulevards and a park, there is a beach and campgrounds under way, a golf course is under way.

The new community is much better than the old. Another thing is that before we only had an old cable-run ferry; we now has a free floating one with washrooms and heated waiting rooms. It is worth almost 1,000,000.

Debbie Schmidt

BURTON, BEFORE AND AFTER

The new communities are well planned. However, at Burton the New Park is so small that you can not play baseball on it. The old park you could camp, set up tents and still have enough room for a baseball diamond, and a tennis court. Also the old Burton Park was the most beautiful on the lakes.

Burton has a nice new Hall but the upkeep on it is so high for the people left in Burton that no club can afford to hire it. At least the old hall could be used for basketball and there was always something going on in it. The new one stands months at a time with no use.

Old Burton used to have a hotel and pub which drew people from up and down the lakes. Many tourists would stop and sometimes stay for a week or so in the lovely and peaceful place.

The view from the new community hall is lovely in July and August. However when its low, all there is is an ugly mud flat field of stumps. This is a sad thing to look at because we still remember the lush green valley we had.

What I miss the most is the beautiful sandy beaches and riding trails that there used to be.

I wish everything was the same as it was before.

Darwin Buerge, Grade 7

One last remark on the survey. The ground swell of resentment was clear; but in a number of cases these feelings crested up in cries of grief which no humane society could possibly ignore. These came from two groups of about half-a-dozen people in all who expressed their feelings in spontaneous comment. The first consisted of people who had owned and made a living from working farms or gardens. All felt badly used and harboured deep resentments. One expressed himself with savage irony, distorting every survey question and hurling it back like a boomerang. The other vented his feelings with searing simplicity: 'I feel for Hydro anger, frustration and hatred.'

The second group, represented by two older ladies, expressed very clearly the bewilderment and anguish of people torn out of the landscape and the communities they loved. Listen to a lady of sixty-five who has lived for forty years in the Arrow Lakes: 'We had a three bedroom home, large kitchen and bathroom – no running water, a large sitting room facing the Arrow Lakes, a beautiful sandy beach just outside the fence, fruit trees, a cow and chickens, a large garden. We pumped water from the Lake and could grow anything. We had to get an electric stove, fencing, etc., as we had a wood stove before and got our wood free off my son's place, so our little bit over was spent fixing and getting for this one. I don't like it here, but where could we go? My income is very small. I say, dam the dam, let's go home where we were happy.'[8]

Listen also to a lady of fifty who has lived all her life in the Lakes: 'We moved in August 1968 and I am still not squared around so to say – the yard requires more lawn to be seeded – fence to put up. I am doing most of the work myself ... that was a tough job salvaging [materials from the old house]. I often wish we hadn't as it was tough work on my husband as when we quit salvaging as our time was up he took seriously ill ... He died less than a year after we moved. In some ways it hurt him to move as he loved the old place, in fact he was bitter about it all – but I had made up my mind seeing it had to be I would make the best of it which I am still doing and hope to do.'

Several other people spoke in similar terms of spouses who have died since moving, and it may be salutary for us to reflect that some people may have been *killed* by their expulsion. To mention this possibility is not to

8 I am reminded of that agonized soliloquy in *The Grapes of Wrath*: 'How'll it be not to know what land's outside the door? How if you wake up in the night and know – and know the willow tree's not there? Can you live without the willow tree? Well, no, you can't. The willow tree is you' [22, p. 120]. This is not writer's licence. I knew one man in Renata who felt exactly this way about his cherished ginko tree.

impute callousness to Hydro, which demonstrated its concern in many ways, but to mark the fact that forced removal of people from a familiar environment is an inescapably brutal act which should in no way be glossed over.

In summary what do all these measurements convey? Despite their variety and limitations they do present a reasonably coherent picture of the way in which the respondents saw their environment in 1970. These perceptions, however, varied widely depending on the interests and predilections of the viewer and, on whether he had been born and raised in the Arrow Lakes. They saw the region as both worse and better as a result of the Columbia project. One man put it in a nutshell: 'Roads and towns better, lakes spoiled.' Another in turn got right to the heart of the latter: 'There is all the difference in the world between a lake and a reservoir.' The new townsites and houses were greatly appreciated, and although both cost more to maintain they were not regarded as a serious burden. But here too approval is tinged with nostalgia and regret. 'It may be a better place to live because it is newer ... but I personally am not as happy. It just isn't the peaceful, quiet, little place it used to be. It changed too suddenly and too fast, I guess.'

The compensation program left much dissatisfaction behind it, more on grounds of believed inequity and poor execution than of inadequate compensation. Corresponding to this, Hydro's overall performance drew much criticism, mainly because of apparent lack of coherence and direction. Although many regret the passing of the old communities and old friendships, the people who are left do not regret staying in the region. Despite the admirable fortitude and resilience of many individuals, the strains of being uprooted and putting down new roots were severe, especially for older people.

But without any disrespect to the survey respondents and without any attempt to discredit their views the question also arises of how we are to *interpret* those responses. They could be read as meaning that Hydro did a rather poor job on the Columbia project. Nevertheless, of the things that Hydro could do something about (new communities and houses for example) there is general approval. And there are few regrets over staying. My own feeling, after much agonizing, is that in most respects the survey records not a poor performance but an inevitable situation, one in which a 'good' performance was virtually impossible under the ground rules of the day. I suggest that it represents the feelings of a group of people who are not necessarily representative, who have recently emerged from a traumatic experience. To echo D.G. Blair's comment, their sense of outrage lingers on and continues to find expression against Hydro as the agent of change. Nevertheless, however we interpret the survey, there are questions begging to be examined, especially the over-riding question of the compensation program, and to these we now turn.

15
Fair and generous?

The evidence suggests that the whole Arrow Lakes program as seen by the people affected was over-shadowed by the question of compensation. A number of the displaced people have said that their compensation was far from generous. Their feeling is a fact. What is also a fact is Hydro's feeling to the contrary. The Authority always accepted the inevitability of some error but is convinced of the generosity of its compensation program in general. Is there any way of adjudicating between these opposite views? Short of a study by a royal commission, no. For such evidence as there is does not present a clear picture.

First we must return to the theme that the 1970 survey elicited the views of only a very small and possibly unrepresentative group of people who resettled in the Central Area. We know nothing of the views and experiences of the other seventy-five per cent. It may be that their feelings would be little different. However it is also possible that many of them were glad (to use the water comptroller's inelegant phrase) 'to get the hell out' of the Arrow Lakes and into other areas offering wider economic and social opportunities, particularly the chance to earn more money in an increasingly cash-oriented society. In this context of uncertainty the analysis that follows is focused perforce on the relatively small number of cases which were the subject of expropriation proceedings, and while the ultimate conclusions about compensation *processes* are fundamentally important, they should be viewed in light of that uncertainty and of the limited field to which they apply. They do not provide anyone with a stick for measuring Hydro's overall performance on compensation, far less for beating the Authority with. Now on to the evidence, such as it is.

On one hand Hydro's expropriation rate of about six per cent (78 cases out of 1280 ownerships) was consistent with recent experience in the United States.[1] Along with this was the experience of the Royal Canadian Legion in Nakusp which established a committee with a budget of $10,000 to take up the legal cudgels on behalf of any legionnaires who felt aggrieved. This committee found it necessary to act in only two cases, a rate of two and a half per cent. There is also, for what it is worth, some local opinion on the subject. In May 1966 the *Vancouver Sun* reported Carl Dumont, then a village councillor in Nakusp, saying, 'A lot of the people scream about the poor deal they're getting, but round at the back door they brag about how much money they got.' In 1972 Donald Waterfield, a highly critical observer of the scene and no apologist for Hydro, wrote, 'Inevitably in so many awards there must be some peculiar ones. My impression now is that, with a few exceptions, all the small people were well paid. But the middling ones had to fight for what they got.' He has also said, 'Hydro leaned over backwards to be generous in most cases.'

On the other hand study of those cases which went as far as expropriation proceedings throws another light on the situation. There were sixty-four cases for which specific and clear records were available.[2] Of these, twenty-three were cases which for one reason or another did not result in a valuator's judgment. Presumably, this means that expropriation was nominal rather than real and further negotiation took place which resulted in voluntary agreement. This could perhaps be described as 'negotiation by expropriation.' The results are interesting. One-third (eight) of these cases were settled at Hydro's original offer. Two-thirds (fifteen) were settled at a higher value than the Hydro offer, but the range of the increase was quite narrow, the median being ten per cent, the maximum thirty per cent. One can only speculate that while naïve and diffident property owners withdrew from the apparently uneven contest at this point, the tougher and the worldly-wise went on to do battle, realizing that Hydro would not wish to go to court either, except as a matter of principle.[3]

This leaves us with forty-one cases which did go through the process of arbitration by a valuator. These too give interesting results. In twenty-five per cent (ten), the valuator's award was virtually the same as Hydro's

1 These are Hydro's figures, although as will be clear later, not all of these cases went through the process of expropriation.

2 Hydro describes seventy-eight cases as 'expropriation cases' but in a number of these the records open to me in 1972 were incomplete.

3 It need scarcely be said that the property owners were a varied group in their ability to negotiate, from the completely incompetent and the naive, to the shrewdies, toughies, and outright opportunists.

offer (specifically, not more than ten per cent different). In the other seventy-five per cent (thirty-one), the valuator awarded a significantly higher value than Hydro's offer, the average (median) being twenty to twenty-five per cent higher. Eight of this latter group then went to appeal. In six of these the court upheld or bettered the valuator's award; in the remaining two the court somewhat reduced the valuator's offer.[4]

The image that emerges from these figures is not one of generosity. But, granting that, there are many reasons for refraining from sweeping conclusions on the basis of these figures. There is no logic which would enable us to generalize from these 60 cases to the whole compensation program of 1300 cases. There were the inevitable impasse cases, many of them involving larger holdings and presumably the livelihoods of their owners; and there is no yardstick by which we can say that the valuators were right and Hydro wrong. But in spite of these caveats the impression that emerges is not one of generosity and we should now ask why.

In passing we might well ask what 'generosity' might mean. Funk and Wagnall's *Standard College Dictionary*, Canadian Edition (1963), offers some useful synonyms, particularly 'liberality' and 'the quality of being free of pettiness.' Clearly it is not a precise or definitive term and in fact it seems clearest when used comparatively, that is, meaning generous rather than mean, or perhaps meaning more ample than a strict legalistic assessment or one based on the competition of the market place would support. Certainly if it does not mean going beyond what would be required by routine, 'neutral,' or competitive measures it has little meaning in this context.

First, it is necessary to look at the implications of the task for the two parties, Hydro and the property owners, for the task had entirely different meanings for the two. Hydro's operational interest was in acquiring land and buildings, people being merely complicating circumstances. In words, its task was property acquisition, which necessitated compensation and sometimes expropriation.[5] For the property owners the essence of the situation

4 It may be mentioned in passing that on the average (median) in these forty-one cases the owner was asking for eighty per cent more than Hydro's offer, some for hundreds per cent more. It will thus be seen that the valuators' awards were on the average considerably closer to Hydro's offers than to the owner's demands. C'est la guerre.

5 It may be recalled from chapter 9 that pin-pointing property acquisition as the task obscured the plight of one sector of the Arrow Lakes society, those who had lived in rented houses, many of them for many years. In this context, they had no legal existence and therefore no right in law to consideration by Hydro, although Hydro did in fact make land and salvaged houses available to at least some of them. This highlights very clearly the importance of the words we use. Once chosen, they shape both our thoughts and our actions, for better or for worse.

was in a very real sense the uprooting, the forced tearing apart from friends, community, and landscape, and the actual obliteration of much of that landscape. Moreover, its timing was not in their control but in Hydro's. And lastly, in 1964 Hydro was not an unknown quantity, but the executor of a widely-resented political decision, a party to apparently sham public hearings, the big-city corporation from far across the mountains, and the enunciator of an ambiguous compensation policy – fair and generous but also tough.

Under these unhappy circumstances people could be expected to react in accordance with their own personalities and sense of security. (A man with a large bank balance or one who has successfully wrested a living from the woods can be expected to face displacement with some equanimity.) Nevertheless, certain patterns of response to displacement could be anticipated. D. Gordon Blair, former member of parliament for Grenville-Carleton, has written on the workings of the former Expropriation Act of Canada and his comments could probably be applied to any forced taking:

> The power of the state to expropriate property of a citizen is one of the greatest and certainly the most terrifying it possesses. The sense of outrage which it creates in the person expropriated is almost indescribable, as I can say after some experience in dealing with ordinary people whose property has been taken away from them ... there remains a rankling sense of injustice long after the event of expropriation, and despite reasonably generous settlement ... A person who has had his property taken from him can, perhaps, never be fully compensated for ... the sense of outrage he invariably feels [3].

These are the observations of an experienced barrister. Other evidence is now available. Experiments in psychology have shown that people tend to like what is familiar to them regardless of others' views, and one psychologist writes of

> the strong attachment for their wretched environment shown even by those who live in the slums – an affection for locale that causes them to experience the pangs of genuine grief over a lost home, when they are relocated ... The chief component of this virtually omnipresent attitude of retrospective devotion to scenes and abodes of the past is undoubtedly a longing for the remembered security of early days. However hazardous life may seem to the elders, and however miserable the conditions of existence may be, the four walls of home still mean food and shelter to the very young, and the familiar sights of the neighborhood give assurance to small adventurers that they have not lost their way into a world they can not cope with ... The more we change the world around us, the less we leave of stimuli likely to restore the feeling of security so easily gained

when we were very young and so terribly hard to develop under different circumstances later in life [19, p. 44].

And a recent writer goes so far as to say, '... the surest way to induce pathological responses in people through environmental manipulation is to force their move from a neighbourhood which is congruent with their life-style ...' [16, p. 166].

All of these observations were echoed by the finding of the 1970 survey in the Arrow Lakes. The Arrow Lakes was no ordinary setting and many of its residents were deeply attached to it. The people surveyed in 1970 had lived in the area for thirty-one years on the average, and their average age was fifty-three. These facts are significant in the light of Lord Taylor's dictum: 'Full satisfaction with environment is a product of time. It takes time to establish strong roots, as well as the branches of social intercourse. The longer one lives in any community, the greater appears to be the degree of satisfaction' [24, p. 174].

In view of all this evidence it would have been a miracle if the Arrow Lakes displacement program had not been troubled, for pain and grief were inherent in it. 'Even in ordinary circumstances,' an experienced American property manager has written, 'who is there among us who does not buy a house and wonder between the signing of the contract and the closing of the transaction whether he paid more than he should? In the same way those who sell to the Government may be left with a gnawing feeling that they should have received more.' It is well to remember these things and their implications of deep feelings and irrational behaviour in considering now the ways in which Hydro went about its task, and in particular what it said as well as what it did.

Perhaps we may start by assuming that ideally what is sought is replacement. If that were possible questions of value and fairness would never arise. But strict replacement is usually not possible, so that value is used instead as a measure of what existed. But the establishment of value is a very difficult and a subjective process. First, many intangibles cannot easily be given dollar values, and in the Arrow Lakes intangibles bulked very large indeed. How do you compensate for 'independence, privacy, the ripple of water on the lake and the colt in the far pasture' (to use Tom Hazlitt's sensitive words of 1964)? In circumstances like these, to rely on market value as the basis for compensation, as Hydro said it did, was to depend on a very blunt tool. In a populous area the market-value approach may work tolerably well because reasonable fascimiles of house and lot can usually be obtained. But in other circumstances dollars may be only a small part of the problem; the other part is not resolved by arguing that it is difficult to measure, which is tantamount to saying that what cannot be measured in dollars does not exist.

Secondly, even tangibles can be attributed incredibly different values by apparently competent appraisers. In fact the officer responsible for property acquisition on the Columbia project admitted that Hydro's offers were based largely on opinion, an honest if not reassuring admission. Even of the densely settled situation in Southern Ontario a royal commission report said, 'where sales are scarce a range of fifteen [percentage] points on either side [of the average] may be the best that can be expected' [17, p. 247].

Thirdly, the compensation bases acknowledged by Hydro were either deeply suspect in the eyes of the residents or simply not understood. 'Market value' was more than suspect to people who knew that there had been no real property market in their area for years. They not only attributed this fact to the long gestation period of the Columbia project; they also believed that the situation so created was now being used against them. In addition the concept of 'market value' was clearly not understood, or simply not accepted as valid, by those who complained that Hydro paid only fifty dollars per acre for land already cleared although it cost it five hundred dollars per acre to have forested land cleared anew. (Perhaps there was more truth than humour in one of the project's classic stories about the Scandinavian who was being told what he would be recompensed for: his house, his barn, his fences, his well, his ... 'Ja ja,' he broke in, 'but vat about my compensation?')

Of course market value did not comprise the whole of the compensation normally given. Allowances were made for disturbance and moving costs as well. Even so the question may well be asked: does market value plus disturbance plus moving equal generosity? A good case can be made for judging that it perhaps equals justice in an eye-for-an-eye sense, but not generosity. For one thing, several people surveyed in 1970 mentioned the amount of work involved in putting down roots again, in adjusting to a new house, fixing it to their special needs, breaking new soil, building paths and walks, and so on. Everyone who regards his home as reasonably permanent will sympathize. If this is what a disturbance allowance covers then it is in no sense a bonus but an acknowledgement of a very real expenditure of time and energy. Similarly a moving allowance is intended to cover real expenses. If these things are true the displaced person is receiving only the bare equivalent of property value plus real expenses and is being allowed nothing to recompense him for the distress of being uprooted against his will. This is surely the only point at which one can honestly begin to talk of generosity. To prate of it before then is hypocrisy.

If this were all that could be said, each authority would have to decide what, if anything, it meant by generosity over and above market value plus disturbance plus moving allowance. Ten per cent? Twenty? Fifty? What is inflicted human distress worth?

In addition to the elusive question of value and its relationship to the equally elusive question of loss or injury, there was also the matter of equity, to which Hydro had pledged itself. In the circumstances of the Arrow Lakes, where communities were small and their inhabitants visible, it could be expected that settlements, real or rumoured, would be the subject of close comparison by neighbours, and it would be surprising if doubt, jealousy, and avarice were not sometimes aroused. But apart from such inherent hazards, any compensation program would be in trouble which did not use a stable yardstick, and it was here that Hydro seems to have run into most trouble. The most practical way of showing compassion was to use an elastic yardstick to over-value poor properties in order that their owners would have enough capital to acquire another property. As Hazlitt's articles showed, Hydro's officials did not conceal their use of this approach. The 1970 survey gave ample evidence of the results. However well-intentioned, distortions of value were bound to cause resentment. Thus the rose of compassion concealed the thorn of inequity or, if you will, the elastic yardstick snapped back.

But it was not only over compensation and inequity that Hydro incurred the odium of the Arrow Lakes people. Two complaints were made about time. First, it was said that the whole process took far too long and that it was disorganized. Communities withered slowly as the people dribbled away, family by family, leaving the survivors desolate and distraught. It takes little imagination to understand that situation. What is more serious, inasmuch as it implies a deliberate strategy, is the charge that if people proved obdurate, or if their cases were genuinely difficult, Hydro dropped their cases for a time, presumably in order to make progress through easier cases. I do not believe that this was ever a deliberate strategy, but it is the kind of decision that an official, frustrated in his efforts to make progress and convinced of the rightness of his case, can very easily make, with or without rationalization.

What comes through clearly is the general feeling that Hydro was unthinking or autocratic, favouring its own administrative convenience over people's feelings and needs. It made an ostensibly immutable offer based on its concept of value and generosity; but it refused to show the basis of its offer. Nevertheless it required the owner to demonstrate that something of value had been overlooked; and it clearly carried the bigger stick in the event of court proceedings. If justice was being done, it was not *seen* to be done.

Could anything have been done to obviate these complaints? Hindsight and freedom from responsibility make some solutions apparent, if not necessarily practicable:

1 Perhaps Hydro should not have used an elastic yardstick. But did it not do so for a praiseworthy purpose – succour of the needy? In this sense the Authority was in a cleft stick: to be fair (that is, not to discriminate) was to injure those in need; to be mindful of them was to give them partial that is, unfair) treatment. The irony of this situation was well expressed by two people in the 1970 survey. One woman, no friend of Hydro's, wrote, 'I think the general treatment of old people and those who were really badly off was good on the whole.' On the other hand the feelings of the others were well put by an older lady who wrote, 'Those who had nothing (a decent home) were far better compensated in comparison to those who had carved their homes by hard work out of the bush. We started out in the depression and had no money, and worked our fingers to the bone grubbing stumps, clearing and seeding. Those Johnny-come-lately's who bought up land for a song that pioneers had cleared were better compensated than we were.' Clearly there was only one solution: to be strictly impartial but to raise the compensation base to a level at which the poorest would have enough money to resettle themselves with; that is, to overvalue *all* the properties.
2 No judgment can be made here of the generosity of the compensation program. However, a note can be added on perspective. If it is assumed that an increase of twenty-five per cent on all payments would have constituted generosity and that property acquisition cost 20 million dollars out of a total Columbia project cost of 565 million dollars, the cost of the program would have been increased by only one per cent.[6] What is inflicted human misery worth?
3 Was the compensation program too slow? Perhaps a more useful question would be: Could it have been speeded up without other kinds of damage to its objectives? For one thing, if the program had been completed in three years instead of four, the pressure on the real estate market in the various resettlement areas (for example, the Okanagan and Slocan valleys) would have been one-third more intense than it was and prices correspondingly higher. For another, Hydro would have required more time to prepare for its task than it was given, for one of the keys to a successful program is meticulous preparation of property maps, title

6 The Toronto *Globe and Mail* on 28 October 1972 quoted Premier Barrett as giving the estimated cost of the three Columbia water storage projects at 565.1 million dollars.

deeds, surveys of reception areas, etc. Another would have been the employment of more field representatives, at a time when suitable men were very scarce. It is one thing to speed up a program, another to do it without loss of the care and accuracy essential to satisfactory results. As an experienced Ontario government official wrote, 'Relocation problems increase in some cases in direct relationship to the shortening of the time allotted for acquisition.' Nevertheless there were good counter-reasons for establishing speed as an important objective: the people to be uprooted were entitled to speedy release from a very trying situation; from Hydro's own point of view an unsettled man, in any sense of the word, was likely to be irritable, susceptible to rumour, and potentially hostile; the project period being one of rapidly rising costs, Hydro would have had less to pay for properties and would have been free of the necessity of keeping up and seeming to keep up with inflated costs; and lastly, with more people in possession of capital more would have been able to make firm decisions about resettlement, thus giving the Authority a better base on which to plan its new communities.

4 In a sense the charge of autocratic behaviour is the most important of all because it seems to have coloured the image of the whole program and may well have given rise to all the other charges, right or wrong. And in terms of public impression there was no real difference between being autocratic and seeming to be autocratic. The problem was that Hydro seems to have failed to run what one American authority described as 'a clean-cut acquisition program ... one which everyone can understand and which leaves no room for anyone to doubt the intentions and integrity of the land acquisition organization.'[7]

In discussing these charges it should first be mentioned that in 1964 the legislation empowering Hydro to acquire property was completely unhelpful as to *how* the task should be done. Hydro's power to expropriate property is contained in the *British Columbia Hydro and Power Authority Act, 1964* [4]. It is tempting to say that this is an indecently business-like act, to the extent that there is no statement of purpose for the Authority, only a bald list of twenty-five powers it may wield. This lack of ceremony or need to explain itself extends to the section on powers of expropriation. It first empowers the Authority 'to pay compensation ... in an amount to be agreed upon;' that is, by negotiation with the owner. Failing agreement, the Lieutenant-Governor-in-Council may appoint a valuator who shall 'fix the compensation.' Either party may appeal the award to the supreme court and again to the court of appeal. Behind this act is the Lands Clauses Act of

7 About which Hydro says, 'There ain't no such animal.'

British Columbia with its concept of 'value to the owner,' that is, 'the particular value (excluding sentimental value) of the land to its owner which value it may or may not have to any other person' [10, p. 9]. It would seem from this that there would be no barrier inherent in the law to humane and sensitive compensation to property owners.

The person whose property is to be taken and whose livelihood, habitat, and serenity may thus be destroyed appears in the Hydro Act as a disembodied legal entity who is given no special privileges and no protection against costs in his struggle with the Authority: 'The costs of the parties to the appeal are in the discretion of the judge.' Of this sort of situation the Honourable J.V. Clyne in the royal commission report on expropriation wrote, 'If the City of Vancouver feels that the costs involved in a disputed compensation case are excessive, there is all the more reason that small landowners should be apprehensive in agreeing to submit their cases to arbitration.' [10, p. 8].

On the Columbia River the actual conduct of the compensation program was left to the discretion of the manager of the land division under the general supervision of the chairman and the executive management committee. But in assessing the significance of such discretionary powers it is well to consider the forces operating on the servants of a public corporation responsible for spending public funds under these circumstances. For one thing there was no specific legal basis for generosity and no definition of it. Nowhere did the law say: Thou shalt be generous; that is, thou shalt act as follows. For another, the officers of an agency not only owe loyalty to it but they inevitably personify that loyalty in the face of external pressures. And these pressures are frequently exerted not in ways to which a man can react rationally and dispassionately but in ways which arouse both his personal and professional pride. The behaviour of *some* of the people affected – their avarice, combativeness, malice, and opportunism – make impartial behaviour on the agency's side highly unlikely. The compensation administrator is hard pressed to be Solomon without also aspiring to be blind Justice herself.

Those in this position did not necessarily view the situation in this way, but one cannot but be sceptical about the objectivity of any Hydro employee of many years standing who could impute motives to himself and to his opponents with the Olympian assurance of the following memorandum:

A property owner who is given a detailed breakdown is going to gloss over those items on which he is satisfied, or may even be more than satisfied, and seize on any items on which he thinks he can make a convincing argument for an increase. Our object, of course, is to be fair and consistent with everyone. The property owner's objective is generally to get the best settlement he can and if he can beat out his neighbours that is part of the game.

I wince at such innocent arrogance because I know that some of the Arrow Lakes residents were gentle people, not competitive in the sense which is taken for granted in urban life, who awaited the approach of Hydro's representatives with passive expectations of fairness. And I remember well the comment in 1970 of one old man, whom I had known as a serene man in 1965, who said, flaring up in sudden resentment, 'They wouldn't find me so easy to get on with next time.'

Another example of the ambivalence of Hydro's situation lay in a remark which one often heard: 'We could very easily make good fellows of ourselves by being free with the public's money,' a valid comment but one which immediately raised the inevitable question when placed against the word 'generosity.'

There is something fundamentally absurd in this situation. In a field of valuation which is characterized by opinion rather than by science, two parties with widely different interests and views of value are brought together in the hope that they will agree. One of them may be dealing with his livelihood, his accumulated wealth, and his social being, and he may well be both unrealistic and unreasonable. But his position and interests are reasonably clear. His opponent on the other hand is in a most ambiguous position. As a public employee spending public money he must dispense it in a way that cannot possibly be attacked as irresponsible or profligate; yet at the same time he is enjoined to be generous. And while he may be subject to furious and emotional behaviour which calls into question his very humanity, he is also expected to be fair. Under such circumstances it would be very surprising if many an impasse were not reached.

Another gap yawned beneath the two parties in that, if either were dissatisfied with the valuator's award and went to the courts to appeal, the property owner ran the risk of incurring the costs of the action. Such risks were inconsequential to Hydro, but as the royal commission on expropriation pointed out, they might be a serious deterrent to an individual property owner.

These comments are not intended as an attack on the integrity or competence of Hydro personnel. They are intended only to highlight the hazards in a situation where two opposing parties may hold, honestly and with complete conviction, two widely different views of value; where men can very easily delude themselves about their own motives; and where the risks involved in pursuing a judgment in the courts are by no means equally felt by the litigants. In my view the significance of the expropriation statistics set out earlier is not that Hydro was miserly but that it was cautious, in accordance with its bureaucratic role.[8] And it was probably quite unrealistic to expect it to act in any other way, for to the extent that 'generosity' meant the exercise of a very sensitive kind of discretion it should not be expected of a bureaucracy as such.

Hydro's leadership was not blind to the issue, for it was presumably this concern which prompted Dr Keenleyside to arrange for the appointment of an ombudsman. But events showed that this was not enough, possibly because it was still regarded as a Hydro ploy, possibly also because it was a step which was available only *after* the normal negotiation process had been completed and which did not mitigate the process itself. Under these circumstances Hydro might have requested the provincial government to appoint a compensation commission for the Columbia project, or it might have used more broadly a 'board of evaluators' which it was already empowered to establish by the Hydro Act [4, section 25/1].[9] This board could have investigated the unusual situation in the Arrow Lakes, held hearings if necessary and recommended to Hydro the principles to be followed in compensating the displaced people. This would have removed from Hydro's neck the millstone it assumed in trying to be both judge and jury. It might also have removed from the people's necks the millstone of suspicion and resentment which many of them carry to this day.

In view of the overall expropriation record cited earlier it might be thought that those who finished up with more money than they had originally been offered would be skipping their way happily to the bank. Consider then the views of Mr C, a successful farmer and a man of education and proven courage, not given to complaint or self-pity. He ran into double trouble. Hydro took most of his farm, finally paying thirty-five per cent more than it had first offered him. Then the department of highways took another piece of his land, and on being taken to court was ordered to pay him 140 per cent *more* than its original offer. He writes:

> property owners are afraid of the powerful legal apparatus that Hydro or Highways can bring to bear against them. If no agreement can be reached on compensation the property owner should not be afraid to go to litigation for fear of being unable to pay the legal costs. The expropriation authority wields a most

8 I do not, of course, use the word 'bureaucratic' in any 'loaded' or pejorative sense, but merely in reference to large governmental bodies and their staffs.

9 I put this proposal in 1964 to the officer in charge, who rejected it, pointing out that it might embarrass Hydro since most of its field staff were not professionally qualified appraisers. Once more, echoes of Sewell's findings.

> unfair advantage. I myself had to be prepared to pay out $10,000 in legal and appraisal costs to take my case to court; but, the risk is very serious and extremely worrying. It took four and a half years of constant battle before we got a settlement, and at one time we were expropriated. I happened to have an excellent lawyer but without him I would have lost my shirt; as it was, I nearly lost my sanity ...

And, significantly, he writes, 'Four years ago I might have started a new farm; today I doubt if I could.' On the Columbia project Hydro acted in the spirit of its times as expressed in the legislation of British Columbia, which remains unchanged today. But while the sort of thing described here can still take place in British Columbia a new concern has been manifested by the Canadian parliament and the Ontario legislature, which have both enacted new legislation in the field of expropriation. The federal act embodies a completely new approach to the rights of the citizen [5]. According to D. Gordon Blair, 'The purpose of the new Act ... is to give the citizen a better break in expropriation proceedings ... It equalizes the power of the citizen with the state' [3]. The act has several salient features:

1 Adequate notice of intention to expropriate must be served, and if objections are registered a hearing must be held, *not* by a public servant. The minister responsible must give to any objector a copy of the hearing officer's report as well as reasons for disregarding objections.

2 If voluntary agreement on price cannot be reached, either party may require the other to enter into formal negotiation. The Crown is required to pay to the owner any legal, appraisal, or other costs reasonably incurred in asserting his claim. Even if negotiation fails the owner may take the case to the Exchequer Court, with some assistance, if his claim was not unreasonable, against the hazard of costs.

3 The owner is entitled to the higher of two values reached by different valuation methods described in the Act.

4 When the value payable under the general rule is not enough to enable an owner to relocate in premises reasonably equivalent to his old residence an additional allowance is to be added to enable him to do this.

The Ontario Act also breaks new ground in terms of humanitarianism [20]. In several sections it makes provision for special circumstances in the determination of compensation. More specifically, it authorizes the Land Compensation Board (appointed by the cabinet) to award, on application, 'such additional amount of compensation as, in the opinion of the Board, is necessary to enable the owner to relocate his residence in accommodation that is at least equivalent to the accommodation expropriated'; it requires the expropriating authority to 'serve a copy of the (mandatory) appraisal report upon the owner at the time the offer is made'; and it also gives reasonable assurance to anyone appealing an offer that his costs of appeal will be met.

No one will deny the absolute necessity for government to have the power to expropriate private property. Equally no one can deny that its excercise can inflict grievous injury. It is the duty of a civilized society to see to it that its concern and compassion are spelled out in legislation. Law, as an instrument of social purpose and social conscience, must keep up with the times. In that respect, British Columbia has some catching up to do.[10]

But before we leave this crucial subject a final word is in order, one which reminds us yet again of the importance of the way in which we define our responsibilities and the words we use for that purpose. Earlier in this chapter Hydro's operational interest was defined as property acquisition, the term insisted on by those concerned with it. But this was not only a limited and limiting definition but a misleading one insofar as it encouraged Hydro to think only about property and its owners (hence the renter problem, for example). In fact the focus was on *people* and their many needs, hence the new communities, the conservation of houses, and many other facets of the resettlement program. But the true dilemma facing displaced people has never been defined, nor has the real purpose of compensation in the broadest social sense.

Just as every family's life is a complex of ties, activities, and responsibilities, so displacement shatters that complex and requires it to be reconstituted. In other words, the members are required to abandon a long-evolved and shaken-down way of life, re-examine its many elements and consciously put them back together again in ways that seem to fit their new situation best. A large part of the problem frequently lies in the fact that they may not know the area into which they think they would like to move, and the range and nature of its opportunities. In the face of this they have to weigh and decide a number of inter-related questions peculiar to their own circum-

10 This again brings to mind the report of the BC royal commission on expropriation [10] and it may be pointed out that this report has not *one* word to say about the human and emotional aspects of involuntary displacement. When British Columbia does turn its attention to new expropriation legislation I trust that the strictly human viewpoint will take its place beside that of legal process. Law will be a chilling thing if it does not. The need was well stated in the Toronto *Globe and Mail*, 2 June 1972, by Justice Bora Laskin of the Supreme Court of Canada: 'The law is not a still pool merely to be tended and occasionally skimmed of accumulated debris, rather it should be looked upon as a running stream, carrying society's hopes, and reflecting all its values, and hence requiring a constant attention to its tributaries, the social and other sciences, to see that they feed in sustaining elements.'

stances: Can Dad get a job? Can he change that job if he doesn't like it? Can we get a place where we can grow fruit, cut wood, and graze a cow? Can we afford a house? Will we have to fix it up much? What will the taxes be? What and where are the schools and colleges? Are there doctors, dentists, and hospitals within reach? Is there a supermarket? Are the people friendly and do we have any kin nearby?

These may be vexing questions, especially in the absence of firm facts, but no outsider can resolve them. Nevertheless a humane taking authority will ask itself not 'How can we acquire the necessary land?' but 'How can we best enable these people, whom we are displacing for the public good, to get established again with maximum efficiency and least stress for them?' Viewed as a partial but important answer to this question, compensation becomes much more than a pound of flesh required by law and measured on the scales of the property market; it becomes a tool by which the dispossessed can solve the taking authority's problem by looking after themselves. There is a good deal of sense then, in the policy of one US agency which directs its property manager 'to appraise land and make offers at a price to encourage voluntary conveyance' however arguable this idea may be in legal terms and whatever its limitations in relation to the inevitable scalper. Compensation in this sense becomes the means which imposes on the dispossessed the least constraints as they grapple with their problems, which only they can resolve wholly. This was very clearly and cogently expressed in a letter to me in 1964 by Mr C, whose trials and tribulations were noted earlier. I cannot think of a better reminder to any agency charged with such a vexing task:

> individuals are better at solving problems by themselves rather than by direction from outside. I am quite sure in my own mind that this moral holds good with regard to most of problems of resettlement and relocation; if Hydro officials at the top can be persuaded to really live up to their avowed intentions to give 'fair and generous' compensation then I think that the individuals will effectively solve their personal problems themselves, which is surely what you want. If on the other hand, the valuers are directed to be penny-pinching and to hold down every valuation to the barest minimum then I am sure that many extra problems will be landed in the Hydro's lap, and there will be lots of frustration and ill feeling for a long time to come.

16
A well-behaved chapter

A well-behaved book, it has been said, should not raise more questions, or at least not many more, than it hopes to answer. What then can we learn from the Columbia River experience?

CONCEPT

Probably the most fundamental lesson the Columbia experience offers is the crucial need, from the beginning, for an adequate definition of the job to be done. This is the starting point from which good and evil flow; for then the die is cast for the myriad decisions, programs, and processes which follow. Yet fundamental as it is (and basic to the idea of professionalism, which is meaningless if it does not involve personal judgment of the nature of the problem to be tackled), this point is seldom given adequate attention in the planning process.

Essentially the task is one of problem formulation, and it has attracted the attention of many inquiring minds. Albert Einstein has said, 'The formulation of a problem is often more essential than its solution, which may be merely a matter of mathematical or experimental skill.' Long before Einstein, John Stuart Mill had said, 'The next thing to having a problem solved is to have it well raised.' But the question has probably been most vividly stated in our day by the philosopher Alan Watts: 'The question "What shall we do about it?" is only asked by those who do not understand the problem. If a problem can be solved at all, to understand it and to know what to do about it are the same thing. On the other hand, doing something about a problem which you do not understand is like trying to clear away darkness by thrusting it aside with your own hands. When light is brought, the darkness vanishes at once' [28, p. 75].

Application of this point of view to the Columbia takes us back over a quarter of a century; for the start of the Columbia scheme was not inauspicious judging by one of the earliest documents, the *Columbia River Reference.* This said, 'It is desired that the [International Joint] Commission shall determine whether ... further development of the water resources of the [Columbia] river basin would be practicable and in the public interest ... having in mind (*a*) domestic water supply and sanitation, (*b*) navigation, (c) efficient development of water power, (*d*) the control of floods, (*e*) the needs of irrigation, (f) reclamation of wet lands, (*g*) *conservation of fish and wildlife* and (*h*)*other beneficial purposes.*' At least it recognized the existence of fish and wildlife and left a useful loophole for 'other beneficial purposes' [6, p. 21].

By the time the Treaty was drafted, however, Canada's prime objectives were spelled out very tersely in Article II: '(1) Canada shall provide in the Columbia River Basin in Canada 15,500,000 acre-feet of storage usable for improving the flow of the Columbia River. (2) In order to provide this storage, Canada shall construct dams (*a*) on the Columbia River near Mica Creek ... (*b*) near the outlet of Arrow Lakes ... and (*c*) on one or more tributaries of the Kootenay River ... near Duncan Lake' [6, pp. 117, 118]. Such language is proper to an international treaty which binds its signatories to specific undertakings. But it is less than adequate as an overall directive for the actual carrying out of such a project.

At this point we might look for a statement of purpose and policy from the BC Government to its civil service which would recognize the complexities of the task and provide some flesh for the bare bones of the Treaty. Of course there was none, or Hydro would not have been scrambling to obtain the co-operation of provincial departments in 1965. The Columbia project in 1964 bore all the marks of an engineering project dedicated exclusively to the narrow purposes of the Treaty.

This was not the fault of the Authority but of the BC Government, through its many actions or non-actions. For one thing the government kept a tight grip on the project through the comptroller of water rights, who can be regarded as the main mouthpiece of whatever policies the government had. For another it had carefully excluded matters such as fish, wildlife, and parks from the earlier planning of the project.

The only broadening influences discernible were those laid down by the comptroller in his water licence issued in April 1962, a full year after the original signing of the treaty. These were scarcely inspiring:

l The licensee shall clear the reservoir in the manner and to the extent as directed by the Comptroller.

m The licensee shall provide public access to the reservoir area as may be directed by the Comptroller.

n The licensee shall make available an amount not to exceed $5,000 per annum to the Department of Recreation and Conservation in each of the years 1962 and 1963 to conduct a study on such remedial measures as may be necessary for the protection of fisheries and wildlife.

o The licensee shall undertake such remedial measures for the protection of fisheries and wildlife as the Comptroller may direct following receipt of the aforesaid report.

r The licensee shall provide such facilities over or through any structure for the general handling of forest products and general water transport as may be directed by the Comptroller.

It is scarcely credible that, in the middle of the twentieth century and thirty years after TVA had shown the way, this document should be expected to provide the added sweep, not to mention funds, necessary to allow the Treaty's skeletal provisions to cope with the complexities of the task, or that this should be the vehicle chosen for that purpose by the BC government. Here was an international project worth hundreds of millions of dollars, which flooded a major valley and displaced 2000 people. Yet all the concerns of Her Majesty's government in British Columbia seem to have been expressed in terms of acre-feet through a routine water licence.

What is equally incredible is that the whole subject should never have been presented to the BC legislature. Randolph Harding, MP for Kootenay West and the opposition member of the legislative assembly for the Arrow Lakes area, has written to me:

The BC House did not have a detailed examination of the treaty. This examination was done at the Federal level, since it came under Federal jurisdiction. I can recall our group requesting a similar inquiry in BC. It was rejected on jurisdictional grounds. Since we had no specific legislation to discuss in the legislature, the opportunities for dealing with the matter were somewhat limited. The members were able to make speeches on the topic during the Throne debate and the budget debate. During the estimates, we were in a position to question the Premier or the Minister of Lands and Forests on those aspects of the project which came under their respective departments. As I recall, the government never allowed the topic to go before any of the House Committees, as it felt that the questioning in the legislature under estimates was sufficient.

Thus, whatever the justification – lack of prime jurisdiction or the expediting of an admittedly cumbersome trilateral negotiation – the Columbia scheme was never presented or examined formally in its home province. Instead, information and plans had to be wormed out of the un-forthcoming provincial government by the opposition, using whatever routine channels for questions that the legislative session might provide.

This stratagem may well have saved the provincial government (ill-prepared as it was on various aspects of the project) a considerable amount of embarrassment; but it certainly did not help the project and the people in the Arrow Lakes that the legislators who knew the Columbia region best were given no opportunity to study the scheme. Thus, missing from the treaty and its subsequent operational documents are a concept commensurate with the scale and scope of the task, and a statement of concept. A concept was needed as a means of defining and harmonizing all the elements of the task, a statement as notice to all concerned of what was to be done and how it was to be done. Someone of statesmanlike cast of thought, the BC equivalent of President Roosevelt or Senator George Norris (the father of TVA), should have drafted the equivalent of a manifesto, a call to arms, reading as follows:

The Government of British Columbia, having undertaken to provide water storage in the Columbia basin according to the provisions of the Columbia River Treaty, resolves that this shall be done in such a way as to promote the optimum development of the human and natural resources of the basin and thus to maximize its contribution to the wealth and well-being of the people of this province. To this end it directs that the Columbia River project shall be governed by the following principles:

1 People who are unavoidably displaced by the project and those whose livelihood is demonstrably affected shall be generously compensated in recognition of the injury inflicted on them for the public good. The principles and bases of compensation shall be determined, subject only to approval by the minister of finance, by a special Columbia compensation commission, which shall also sit as a board of appeal.
2 The British Columbia Hydro and Power Authority shall assist in the resettlement of displaced people and shall where necessary undertake the construction of new communities, serviced and equipped to standards appropriate to their size and circumstances. Displaced people may purchase lots in these communities at prices comparable with the price of lots in their existing communities. The Authority shall be responsible for the maintenance of such communities for a period of three years after the date on which the respective dams become operational.
3 The Authority shall take appropriate steps to answer the special needs of the

old, the sick, and the handicapped, and shall make appropriate arrangements to this end with the department of health and welfare.

4 The Authority shall compensate, or assist in the rehabilitation of, any community or settlement which has been adversely affected by the Columbia project, whether through a municipality, a school district, a regional district or any other properly constituted local authority.

5 The Authority shall clear the reservoir areas prior to flooding to standards compatible with the anticipated accessibility and use of each reservoir.

6 The Authority, in co-operation with the BC department of recreation and conservation, shall survey the recreational resources of the Columbia region and prepare plans, short and long term, for the realization of these resources in accordance with public need. It shall undertake a program of development at least sufficient to replace recreational resources and developments destroyed by flooding. In this context 'recreational developments' shall include parks, camp sites, scenic viewpoints, historical and archaeological exhibitions, natural phenomena such as hot springs, and programs to preserve and develop fish and wildlife resources.

7 The Authority, in co-operation with the BC department of highways, shall plan and construct a system of roads appropriately connected to the provincial highway network, capable of serving the everyday needs of the people of the Columbia region and the anticipated needs of tourists and visitors.

8 The departments of agriculture, mines, lands, and forests, and industry, trade, and development shall prepare surveys of the economic resources and potential of the Columbia region and shall assist local groups, organizations, and individuals with their plans to develop such resources.

9 The Authority, in consultation with other provincial departments, shall prepare a plan for the ultimate disposition of any lands acquired in the course of the Columbia River project which may be surplus to the requirements of the project. First priority in the disposition of such lands shall normally be given to the owners of lakefront property who were dispossessed by the project.

10 The Authority shall make arrangements whereby the actual effects of its works on the people and communities affected may be studied, giving particular attention to the adequacy of property compensation. The results of these studies shall be tabled in the legislature of British Columbia.

11 The Authority shall carry out all its responsibilities under the Columbia River treaty in such a way as to enhance the well-being of the people and communities in the Columbia region and thus the common good of the people of British Columbia.

Any development of the nature and scale of the Columbia River project has many ramifications. It also generates an immense amount of opportunity.

But to deal with its ramifications and to grasp its opportunities we must first see the enterprise in all its diversity. Given an adequate concept there still exists the task of enunciating it and thus giving understanding and guidance to all concerned, enlisting their co-operation, and if possible, motivating them to strive towards a truly inspiring ideal. But in British Columbia Jove thundered not.

By today's standards the governing concepts behind the Columbia River project were inadequate. Before we cast the first stone, however, we should remember that in the 1950s and 1960s words such as ecology were to be found only in dictionaries and textbooks, not in the public vocabulary. And, although there were people in the ranks of the BC civil service who were devoted to environmental causes, as there were people in the Hydro organization concerned about the human implications of the project, both were subject to restrictions which were not of their own choosing.

Here the Social Credit government of British Columbia was clearly at fault. It had in its employ dedicated men trained in recreation and wildlife management, for example. Yet these groups were so starved of support that a report written in 1961 said, 'The Parks Branch of the BC Department of Recreation is grossly understaffed. It contains on the technical side only five people, who are expected to do justice to the planning of parks and campsites for a province which is bigger than Washington, Oregon and California combined and three times as big as legendary Texas [15, p. 45].

This soft-headed, short-sighted attitude was all the more culpable since it was only necessary to look south of the border to see what the Americans had long since done in assessing their own resources. As early as 1947 the US department of the interior had produced a monumental report entitled *The Columbia River: Our Rivers, Total Use for Greater Wealth.* This studied the American basin in considerable detail, including recreation, fish and wildlife, and transportation. There can be no excuse for BC's failure to know its own resources and its own interests, given such warning. A few less miles of blacktop would have paid for all the studies required.

TIME TO PLAN

Another of the outstanding lessons of the Columbia project, at least for the non-engineering works, is the absolute necessity of time to plan. Many of Hydro's difficulties and much of the odium which it incurred arose not from its indifference, irresponsibility, or dishonesty (as it must have seemed to the people of the Lakes) but from sheer unpreparedness. Examples are plentiful, and many of them were accentuated by the Authority's creditable efforts to keep the people informed through the *Columbia Newsletter*. Many promises were made in good faith but simply could not be implemented: supplying waterfront land for resettlement, building Needles bridge, developing parks and campsites. All of these things were based on tentative evidence or on ill-founded assurances which later examination proved false. Thus is a reputation created.

Many delays were also attributable to lack of preparation: the early lack of knowledge about slipping banks and the safety of townsites, and the long-delayed, ill-fated process of consultation with the government. This again seems to have been the fault not of Hydro but of the Bennett government, which kept rigid control over Columbia expenditures right up to the time of ratification of the Treaty.[1] Even in these days of surveys by satellite time is essential and any agency which embarks on extensive developments without adequate data and forethought will certainly pay a price in other ways as it stumbles through its task.

WORKING MECHANISMS

It will be obvious from what has been said that a project such as the Columbia River scheme cannot properly be the preserve of any ordinary functional agency of government. Its effects are too pervasive for that. One of Hydro's greatest handicaps was that circumstances required it to operate so much on its own, a situation which was exacerbated by its semi-autonomous status as a Crown corporation. What is required in such circumstances is a mechanism capable of integrating the work of many departments. At the same time many of the problems involved can only be resolved through top level policies and extensive departmental contributions, which thus require the active involvement of the ministers concerned.

All this points to the need for a cabinet committee such as the Columbia ministers committee. But such a committee is essentially a policy-making body and requires the staff support of the line departments. In other words, the ministerial committee needs to be mirrored by a comparable working committee at a lower level. Nobody with any knowledge of either human nature or bureaucratic behaviour will imagine that such arrangements of themselves provide a key to harmony. As Sewell's study confirms, it is hard to get men to see what they have not been accustomed to see, or to act as they do not wish to act. In spite of this there is no real substitute, in any complex task, for bringing together those whose contribution to the whole job is essential.

1 This same point is mentioned by Paddy Sherman in *Bennett* [21, p. 242].

ON UNDERSTANDING PEOPLE

Several comments emerging from the 1970 surveys suggested that Hydro's resettlement planners did not understand the people for whom they were planning, despite the many attempts the field staff made to get to know them and their needs. I believe nevertheless that *under the conditions prevailing when the resettlement intention surveys were carried out* the resettlement plans were sound. The events and non-events which worked against Fauquier and to some extent for Edgewood were not of Hydro's doing. In any case people's minds were not nearly as clear in 1965 and 1966 as some hindsighted folk would have us believe today. There were many voices in the valley in the early years and there are many today.

Nevertheless it is possible that we did not set about understanding the people as well as we might. Perhaps the obvious external features were misleading: they were Canadians, were they not, sharing our own conventions of language, religion, and technology? The real difficulties were not at all obvious. First, most of us were essentially urban people with middle-class ideas about 'proper' dress, 'adequate' housing, and tidy serviced communities. The people of the Lakes did not share these values, yet some of them were sensitive about the differences and quick to feel that they were regarded as Canadian hillbillies. As one man said, 'We resent being talked down to as a lot of backward peasants.' Ironically, many believed themselves to have the better of the comparison: 'Who wants a mortgaged house in a stifling suburb in a stinking city? We have everything here that you want and don't have.'

Secondly, we did not come to them simply as people in our own human right, no matter how well intentioned, but also as representatives of 'the enemy.' In other words every personal contact, of which there were thousands in the course of the work, was an ambiguous one in which friend/enemy images could be reversed by a look, a gesture, a word. Here were all the raw materials of confused, confusing, frustrating, and potentially cynical behaviour.

In such a situation the attitude of each field representative is important. Jim Lotz has put the situation very well in his book *The People Outside*: 'Personality is important in that he has to be neither an authoritarian personality nor a "bleeding heart" (although he must have genuine empathy with "outsiders"). He must have a considerable capacity for handling ambiguity, for keeping his cool, and understanding how a complex situation can be handled ... The people on the fringe are usually friendly – but suspicious. They too live in a world of ambiguities – is a newcomer someone who can help them, or will he make life more difficult? What power does each new person who arrives to "help" really have?' [14, p. 32].

Does this imply that every Hydro representative, especially those with the prickly task of negotiation, would have had to be a paragon of compassion, objectivity, and firmness? It does. It also points out that it is impossible for a program of this kind to be completely trouble free. There just are not enough saints to go around.

Thirdly, I question whether many of those working in the Hydro organization, preoccupied as they were with carrying out their own demanding tasks, really understood the full scope of the Arrow Lakes situation as the people *felt* it. Few confirmed urbanites could be expected to grasp how fully the way of life being disrupted was based on the land, its fruits (timber, water, pasture, animals, etc.), and its aesthetic qualities, or how strong were the personal and social ties of long-established people and communities, with their traditions of practical neighbourliness. It we accept the psychological view that two fundamentals for emotional health are a sense of identity and a sense of security, and if we understand how closely these factors are related to the landscape itself in rural, wilderness regions like the Arrow Lakes, then we may begin to appreciate the nature of the shock involved for many people when they are removed from such a landscape against their will. But beyond this basic fact few Hydro officials, many of whom were new to the Columbia scheme or to the Hydro organization, could be expected to understand the significance for the inhabitants' morale of the long, painful, gestation period of the Columbia project, the ostensibly sham hearings, and the apparent unpreparedness of the Authority. Few could understand the effects of the fragmented program in the Arrow Lakes, the absence of a responsible, empowered spokesman, and the feeling that the whole business was a puppet show with all the strings in Vancouver. Perhaps most of all few could appreciate the feeling of *powerlessness* which many people must have felt in the face of a remote and mighty opponent armed with all the legal and financial powers of government.

As I see it now there must have been tremendous psychological pressures, of which we were only dimly aware, weighing on the inhabitants, causing confusion and anxiety, and inviting highly emotional reactions from them. Blair's term 'sense of outrage' seems a most fitting one under these circumstances, and it seems to me that resentment and aggrieved behaviour should have been expected as a matter of course. The question remains to be asked: what might Hydro have done to understand the human situation better and to direct its operations more wisely? As to resettlement planning, I would not change the approach one iota. I can see no better, more humane or more constructive way than to meet the people face-to-face, eyeball-to-eyeball if need be, where one can see and be seen in open discussion, see the light and feel the heat. It is the risky and unpredictable way, which is not for autocrats or zealots, and it may appear at first blush to raise more problems than it solves. But it is the only way for anyone who wishes to *respond* to a situation rather than to prejudge it, and its human values, therapeutic and stimulative, are immense.

Even so, could we have done better? Perhaps. We might have used a social scientist as a consultant – if a paragon of insight and pragmatic philosophy could have been found – for two main purposes: first to observe the social scene more systematically and direct the resettlement surveys with more rigour; and secondly, to report his findings to a wider audience within the Authority, for I do not believe that there was enough understanding of the human situation among the many Hydro officers concerned.[2] He could have reported direct to the chairman, who might have organized seminars for senior staff members at which informal presentations and open discussion could take place.

The essence of such an arrangement would have been objectivity, and to this end it would have been essential to have as advisor an outside consultant, not an insider subject to all the usual forces of peer competition, rank-pulling, and sycophancy. It might be said that no regular Hydro employee could possibly have a totally objective view since it was a two-sided situation and he would be on one side. In such circumstances an independent observer could ask the key question which a Hydro employee would be less likely to ask: *Who* are the problem? Are they? Or possibly are we too?

THE VULNERABLE ONES

It can scarcely be said too often that forced displacement from a familiar environment is a harsh and shocking experience for many of its victims, which even the balm of time may never heal. A development authority which does not understand this and prepare its staff for the kinds of behaviour it will meet in the field must be judged seriously culpable.

The Columbia experience suggests that two groups of people will always be particularly vulnerable in the face of displacement: first, people who have made a satisfactory living from working the land; second, those who have grown up or lived long in the area and have become part of it. It is doubtful

2 It has been pointed out to me that 1964 was 'pre-history' as far as social science in Canada was concerned, and that there were only a handful of suitable PHDS in the country at that time.

if such people can ever be fully compensated, and they deserve the most sympathetic consideration from the development authority.

EXPROPRIATION LEGISLATION

Judging from the Columbia experience there is much to be gained by setting down some basic considerations regarding compensation to displaced people. These basics as I see them, are:

1. The taking party must be regarded at all times as an *interested* party, so that while open negotiation with the property owner should be the first step, it should be made crystal clear that the taker has no advantage, legal or psychological, over the owner, however poor he may be.
2. The processes of arbitration and appeal should be open to the property owner without risk (unless a higher appeal is adjudged frivolous by the court), and should be *seen* to be so. It should be incumbent on the taking agency to inform the owner in clear, non-technical language of the process and his rights within it.
3. It *must* be accepted that the displaced person is liable to suffer real, personal, and possibly irremediable injury, especially if he is deprived of the comfort and support of longstanding community ties. This has nothing to do with property, which should be substantially replaced without question. It recognizes injury of a purely personal kind, which only a legalistic or callous society will brush aside either because it cannot conveniently be measured or because it may not be felt by *all* concerned.
4. If this is accepted there should be no *moral* difficulty involved in the idea of 'generosity.' (I suspect that the difficulties facing legal and administrative officials are, first, they do not accept the existence of real injury which warrants compensation, and second, they think that nobody should get anything 'for nothing' at the expense of the public purse.) Given this basic acceptance the *amount* of compensation should present no great difficulty, for it will inevitably be a matter for arbitrary decision: twenty-five per cent? fifty per cent? flat rate? geared to length of residence? It should not be beyond the wisdom of our legislators to make humane and generous rules.
5. Mechanisms and procedures should be laid down (for example, the establishment of advisory boards) to govern situations such as the Arrow Lakes and many rural areas where normal market mechanisms may not be functioning, or where special circumstances should be taken into account in determining the basis of compensation.

Where a province has adopted legislation similar to the expropriation acts of Canada and Ontario the property owner need have little fear. Where this is not so, however, it is tempting to conclude that the property owner should fight expropriation as a matter of course. The observations in this book on bureaucratic behaviour suggest that he would be naive if he did not; Hydro's expropriation record suggests that he would probably profit financially if he did. But this overlooks the emotional cost to ordinary people who entrust their fortunes to the complex and slow-moving processes of the law. As one woman who had been through the appeal process wrote in 1970, 'I see now why people accepted poor settlements rather than go to court.' Life is too short and too precious for that sort of purgatory to be acceptable. The only fair approach lies in humane provincial legislation.

FIELD ORGANIZATION

The evidence and arguments already presented suggest that Hydro should have established an integrated field office, headed by a senior officer, in the Central Arrow Lakes. Among other things a senior field officer could have acted as a local lightning rod. The 1970 responses showed some of the local frustrations that built up in the absence of a focal figure. Trying as his task would be, his function might have been a constructive and humane one. Speaking generally, however, whenever many men are carrying out touchy operations and whenever there is a complex human situation to be interpreted and monitored there will be a need for responsible, on-the-spot representation of the development agency.

COMMUNITY RESPONSE

One of the fascinating aspects of the Arrow Lakes experience was the way in which the several communities responded to the challenge of the project. In trying to analyse why the communities responded as they did we should first recognize that the challenge was not the kind of crisis which would normally stir the region to arms. It was a largely invisible, attenuated problem lacking martyrs to avenge or barricades to man. Furthermore the problem had potential for dividing people as much as uniting them, for each compensation case was a private matter invested not only with hope and fear but also with the raw materials of envy and suspicion. In this sense the threat seemed more like infiltration in the dusk than a frontal attack in daylight, and the response was more like the defense of individual homes than of a common fortress. Under these circumstances too there was no possibility of a *relative deprivation mechanism*, the psychological mechanism by which the victims of disaster are stirred to help others visibly worse off than themselves.

There may have been still other reasons why a united response was not forthcoming. The old communities were not united, being given to parochial attitudes, and Nakusp, the main centre of population, was little affected and remained aloof. Outside of Edgewood the only concerted action seems to have been taken by the Royal Canadian Legion in Nakusp. The Chamber of Commerce, which in pre-project days had provided a focus for some of the more experienced and better educated people in the area, seems to have played no significant part once the Treaty had been ratified.

The exception to the rule was Edgewood, which demonstrated its unity from beginning to end. This was evident not only in the constant activity of the New Edgewood development committee but in the actions of community figures such as Ernest Donselaar and institutions such as the Women's Institute, both from the Inonoaklin Valley beyond. What were the keys? Mainly, one suspects, that Edgewood suffered little loss of population and remained a coherent community throughout; that it had one or two accepted leaders; and that it had in Bellwether Bill Haggart an articulate man of endless energy and some knowledge of political processes. Edgewood had the human resources and social mechanisms essential to survival, and survive it did.

ON COMMUNICATION

Hydro went to considerable trouble to communicate with the people of the Arrow Lakes. There was nothing mandatory about the publication of the *Property Owners Guide* or the *Columbia Newsletter* nor was Hydro compelled to explain itself in public. These things it did because it thought it should. Nevertheless the evidence of 1970 suggests that these efforts were not appreciated, and it is worthwhile to speculate on the reasons for this.

To begin with, whatever it might *say* Hydro was *doing* various things which precluded acceptance of formal messages of reassurance. As long as the conduct of the property acquisition program aroused uncertainty and resentment and as long as resettlement preparations seemed slow, Hydro's actions would speak louder than its words. In addition as long as plans were changed and assurances withdrawn (on the bridge and road issues, on the availability of waterfront land, on freedom to continue living in purchased houses) Hydro's credibility would remain low, whether or not it was responsible for these failures. It may also be wondered if Hydro's image could be very favourable as long as its program seemed to lack order and as long as it lacked a figurehead in the Arrow Lakes and therefore seemed to be controlled from 'back there' in Vancouver. Under such handicaps Hydro's 'public relations,' the phrase most often used in 1970, could scarcely be good.

Sometimes too, little things transmitted their own unspoken message. Dress in the Arrow Lakes was informal, to say the least. The tie was literally a mark of urbanity ('only teachers 'n preachers wear ties.')[3] Legalistic language in Hydro's letters carried its own message, as did egocentric epistles of notice to vacate a home ending, 'we trust you will understand our position in this matter'! So did the occasional unctuous phrase in the *Columbia Newsletter*, taking pains to point out 'another example of our concern for the well-being of the people of the Arrow Lakes,' and liable to be interpreted, 'the lady doth protest too much.'

The moral is that a program has its silent language as well as its spoken one, and a formal communication or PR program that does not respond to the real needs of the situation as the people see them will be regarded as a mere cosmetic designed to put a fair face on a dark reality.

THE HOMING INSTINCT

In the Arrow Lakes almost all of the people who stayed in the region settled as close as possible to their old communities. Only those whose previous areas were totally unavailable chose to settle in other communities. Arguments in favour of more convenient sites and better-serviced communities seem to have borne little weight against the counter-attractions of a familiar environment. We do not know, by the way, whether people proposing to resettle knew, when they made their decisions, how many members of the old communities were also proposing to resettle. It seems likely however, that they had some idea and that it was the pull of the social as well as the physical environment that drew them. It goes without saying too, that such resettlement was usually based on continued convenience for work.

ON PLANNING FOR RESETTLEMENT

From the resettlement operations some useful lessons can be deduced. However, one thing should first be underlined: timely and adequate compensation is a prerequisite to the individual's ability to resettle. If compensation is adequate in terms of current building costs, people will have the power to resettle; if it is timely in relation to the planning of new townsites, they will be able to make their intentions known and it will thus afford a firm base for replanning. On the other hand if people do not have money in time, they will not *feel* able to make firm decisions and the foundation of resettlement plans will be unreliable.

3 It is interesting that one of the sketches in *The Property Owner's Guide* shows two people, resident and appraiser, both wearing suits and ties – a dead give-a-way of its origin.

In the case of those who prefer to settle in rural areas there are other prerequisites: building land, power, and water. Power and water, it is true, are not absolute preconditions, but in today's world they are almost so. By the same token the success of new communities will depend primarily on these same factors, which are not only compelling in themselves but are also visible proof that the resettling authority is in earnest.

Once people start settling in communities, however, the need for communal services may arise even before the total population is adequate to support them. The resettling authority, if it is concerned about the long-run success of its plans, may have to consider constructing and leasing commercial buildings or providing temporary buildings. This has the effect of compelling the authority to assume a stake in the success of the venture and giving it an incentive to conduct it in the most efficient way. Also it requires the authority to involve other agencies (the telephone company, school board, post office, for example) at an early stage in the process.

Another point may well be introduced here: the desirability of requiring the developing authority to act *in loco parentis* for some time after the physical completion of the community skeleton. Justification for this can be found in the complaint made by a number of people, all fairly well on in years, about the unappreciated amount of work involved not only in settling into a new home but also in literally breaking new ground, in building walls, and in coping with a new soil, a new micro-climate and new pests. It might also be found in some cases, as it was in Fauquier, that for reasons of personality, origin, and ambitions, not to mention disappointment and unease about the community's prospects, the new mix of people takes some time to settle down to an effective communal life. The case of Edgewood could undoubtedly be cited to support the contrary argument that 'sweet are the uses of adversity,' but it has already been pointed out that in terms of both leadership and solidarity Edgewood had a head start. Each situation provides its own case, but it may take quite some time to build up a sense of community and the head of steam necessary to run a community effectively.[4] In this sense Hydro acted with commendable understanding in continuing to operate the services and utilities in its new communities for as long as two years after the communities were finished.

Lastly, one observation may be made by comparing Edgewood and Fau-

4 This may have been the reason for one small difficulty between Hydro and Fauquier at one time. Hydro provided a certain amount of planting in the centre of the town, which for some reason was not maintained (each side gives a different reason). Apart from the fact that *public* planting and its maintenance does not seem to occur in very small communities, the residents of Fauquier may simply have not been ready for it physically or psychologically.

quier regarding space and the psychology of growth. The core of Edgewood is a tight, 'busy' cluster of houses which gives an immediate impression of human activity and community. But Fauquier has too much bare space, at its front-door-cum-centre, and the impression is one of emptiness and lack of activity. Where settlements are small, and clustering is natural and desirable, the *appearance* of clustering is itself an asset. In fairness to Hydro it should be added that the Fauquier layout is another victim of the bridge debacle, having been conceived in the days when the community was confidently expected to be bigger than it is. But whatever the reason, the lesson is there to be learned.

RESETTLEMENT RESEARCH

Experiment in social science is often beset with special difficulties. The physical scientist can create the necessary test conditions in his laboratory as and when he wishes. The social scientist on the other hand cannot order the social conditions he wants, control the variables, or sometimes even identify the forces at play in his study community. In matters of profound social concern, particularly matters of stress and crisis, he must seize whatever opportunities are thrown up by the times, and opportunities of any scale are relatively rare.

In this sense it is regrettable that no social research was done on the Columbia project, and that no provision was made for follow-up surveys. Nothing is known about two-thirds of the victims of the Arrow project; no one knows where they are, far less how they fared. Has government and society become so indifferent to the fate of those whose lives it disrupts? Or is British Columbia so poor that its agencies are not allowed such luxuries?

Whatever the reason it should not happen again. It should be understood as part of the initial concept that the social and human consequences will be determined. This implies not only that funds will be made available but that social surveys will be carried out from the early stages of project investigation. This would not only let us know what we have done to our fellow men; it would also give us the information we need to deal effectively next time with social problems at the time they arise. This research should have many facets.[5] We should know how people are (did grief take a toll?), where

5 I do not wish to labour the point here, but it seems to me that there is another field of research, not obvious or so immediately useful as the above, which social science should tackle. This approach would study situations such as the Arrow Lakes during the Columbia period as 'disasters' and seek to analyse the inhabitants' behaviour under stress. It is my feeling that for some at least the disorienting and anxiety-creating effects of displacement must have resembled, on a different time-

they are, whether they chose well, whether they got jobs. We should also know whether their compensation sufficed, how their new homes and circumstances compare with the old, whether the move involved new and tolerable costs, whether the disturbance allowance was absorbed by unforeseen costs of resettlement. Not to know these things is to be cavalier about peoples lives.

scale, those studied by Allen Barton in *Communities in Disaster* [2]. If this sort of research did nothing else it would help to sensitize development agencies to the deeper human implications of their programs and perhaps help them to deal with these implications more sensitively.

Epilogue

I have made no effort here to conceal my views or sympathies at various points. Sometimes they favoured the Authority which employed me, sometimes the people of the Arrow Lakes with whom, and for whom I worked. Certainly my position did not relieve me of bias, but it did offer me considerable insight into both sides of a complex situation.

Nevertheless writing this book, with all the judgments of fact and significance which it entailed, has been at times a vexing task. It is hard to justify the fact that some people were grievously hurt by arguing that bureaucracies are hard to handle and that politics is a hazardous business. Perhaps only a very small percentage of those affected were really hard done by but when their words scream at you from the pages of a questionnaire and their faces loom before you as you write, it is hard to look in Olympian fashion at the whole program and judge it well done. I do not know, nor does anyone else, how the majority of those displaced by the Columbia project fared. I can only hope that they did not suffer too much stress, and that at least some benefitted in the long run.

This book has recorded many examples of Hydro's good will and practical concern. The 1970 survey suggests that Hydro's rehabilitative works, particularly the new communities, have been as successful as they could be under the circumstances, and we need not doubt that in the course of time they too will become familiar and comfortable to their inhabitants. If Hydro failed to do justice to its own ideals, I believe it was either the result of human frailty in bureaucratic circumstances (and who will cast the first stone?) or of circumstances beyond its control. And in that connection the former Social Credit government of British Columbia has much to answer for.

But that is not the point of this book. The point is that Canada's appetite for energy and water remains unsated. There may well be more Columbia projects. And in urban regions also public projects such as metropolitan airports and transportation corridors grow ever larger in scale and impact. With such prospects before us the question now is: have we learned from the Columbia experience? Only fools insist on learning all their lessons anew, and we have no right to foolishness when there are lives at stake – the lives of the people in the way.

APPENDIXES

1
The Property Owners' Guide (September 1964)

PURPOSE OF THIS BOOKLET

Now that the Columbia River Treaty between Canada and the United States has become a reality, BC Hydro must concentrate on two things: (1) completing the three Treaty dams in BC on schedule; and (2) helping the individuals and communities affected by the projects to become resettled.

The purpose of this booklet is to tell you in general terms how we plan to purchase property required for these projects. It will not answer all of your questions because each purchase of land will require special negotiations with the individual property owner, but it does explain the principles and procedures which will govern our dealings with you.

We are confident that, as a result of the Treaty works, the Columbia Region will become richer, more stable and more accessible. Nevertheless, we realize that the owners of property to be affected by the Columbia projects are deeply concerned. For you it will mean dislocation and change. Some of you may be pleased to sell your properties to us because it suits your plans to move elsewhere. Some of you, understandably, would prefer to stay where you are and have no desire to sell. We cannot avoid the impact the development will have on your lives, but it is our intention to assist you as far as we can to ensure that the changes will take place as smoothly as possible.

THE LAND WE WILL NEED

Lands will be purchased for construction of three storage dams, as follows:
Mica – located ninety-two miles north of Revelstoke;
Arrow – located five miles west of Castlegar;
Duncan – located twenty-five miles north of Kaslo.

Land also will be purchased adjacent to these damsites for work camps, construction areas and access roads. In addition, the properties upstream from each dam which will be affected by the filling of the reservoirs will also be purchased. In some areas, the new reservoirs will flood existing highways, railroads and other facilities. As a result, land on higher ground will be purchased wherever relocation of these facilities is necessary.

Some of the land needed belongs to the Crown and will be obtained from the provincial government. Other land necessary for the Treaty projects belongs to organizations and private individuals. Some of it may belong to you.

Land survey still under way

A careful survey of all the areas concerned has been under way for some time to determine exactly which properties will be required for the three Treaty dams and the associated works. The survey markers you may have seen in your area are part of this large and important job.

As the work proceeds, the detailed land requirements for each project become known. The description of each parcel of land is checked and the owner identified. One of our land representatives then calls on the owner and requests his permission to go on the property to make a detailed inspection. This will be the beginning of our negotiation with you for the purchase of your property.

Appraising the value of your property

Appraisal is the procedure used to estimate the value of your property in dollars. It is a complicated process and involves a thorough study of many factors.

Information must be assembled about all the things affecting real estate prices in the areas concerned. For example, it is necessary to determine the availability of, and demand for, the various types of land involved; also the volume and frequency of land sales must be considered, together with the prices at which various types of land have been sold during the past few years, or are currently listed for sale. In this connection, because the areas involved have been under the shadow of the Columbia Treaty in recent years, we realize that the normal buying and selling of real estate may have slowed down with an adverse effect on property values. We have therefore gone beyond the areas directly affected by the Treaty projects and have studied other comparable parts of the Province.

Our study also includes an examination of physical and topographic features, ownership patterns, available services and markets, land utilization, land management and farming practices, crop varieties and yields and other economic factors which tend to establish local real estate price levels.

HOW WE ARRIVE AT THE SUM WE OFFER YOU

Using our background studies as a base, an experienced land representative will make a detailed inspection of your property. He will then send a written report to our Land Division. His report will outline the circumstances surrounding your occupancy of the property and will contain a recommendation as to a fair purchase price. This report will be thoroughly checked by skilled staff in the Land Division and then our land representative will be instructed to make you an offer.

This offer will be based on a generous interpretation of the appraised value of your land. It is our policy to try to obtain land not at the lowest possible price but at a fair price. In most instances, it will include an extra allowance to compensate for disturbance and moving expenses.

Negotiations – everyone treated the same

Generally, you will receive our purchase offer from the same land representative who inspected your property. If the offer is acceptable, you will be asked to sign a written offer of sale, which will in turn be accepted by us. This will be followed by the completion of formal sale documents.

If discussions between our land representative and yourself show that some element of value was overlooked or that we erred in some other way in arriving at our valuation, the error will be corrected and a revised purchase offer will be made. Apart from this, no changes will be made to our original offers. This means there will be no bargaining or price-trading. We know that it is difficult to fix the value of property precisely and that there is often room for differences of opinion. We believe, however, that by adopting a generous approach to property appraisal this problem will be overcome. If bargaining were permitted, then inevitably the hard bargainers would get more than the easy bargainers and this would be unfair.

A sample property purchase

The following is an imaginary example of a property purchase. In this example it is assumed that the full value of settlement agreed to by the property owner is $16,000 and that this value is made up of the following items:

House value	$10,000
Other improvements (landscaping, well, septic tank, driveway, fencing, etc.)	3 000
Value of land	2 000
Disturbance and moving expenses	1 000
Total	$16,000

Suppose that a house-moving company has estimated the cost of moving this house to a new location above the flood level, setting it on a proper foundation and providing all services, to be $5000. If we bought this property outright we could move the house to a new location and sell it. Since the house is worth $10,000 but would cost $5000 to move, we could presumably salvage $5000 after moving and selling it. To do so, however, we would have to spend more money on administrative costs, on supervising moving, and in looking after the house until it was sold. By this time, the net salvage value we would obtain might only be about $2500.

With this in mind, we would be prepared to pay the owner either $16,000 for the outright purchase of everything or $13,500 ($16,000 minus $2500) if he wishes to remove the house and any other improvements such as fencing that he wishes to take. If he decided to accept the offer, we would then pay him $13,500 and it would be his responsibility to remove the house.

Would it be to his advantage to do so?

From the figures we have assumed, it would cost $5000 to move the house and another $3000 to establish fencing, landscaping, driveway, well, septic tank, etc. In addition the owner would have to pay, say, $2000 to buy a new property. Thus, the move would cost the owner a total of about $10,000. Since, in this example, he has received $13,500 as his settlement payment, he would have $3500 left over to compensate him for inconvenience and disturbance, for the trouble and expense involved in acquiring a new home site, for supervising the movement of his home. In addition, if his original property were in one of the flood areas where we do not require the property at an early date, he would be able to live rent and tax-free on his property for up to four years, and would have received our payment in advance.

Sometimes we need only part of a property

When a property will be substantially but not entirely flooded, the complete property will normally be purchased. However, when only part of a property will be flooded and a substantial portion remains above the flood level, we may buy only the land below the flood level.

In these circumstances, our purchase offer will take into account not only the value of the land to be flooded but also the cost of moving any buildings or other improvements on that land to a location above the flood level. The settlement also will include, where appropriate, an allowance for any reduction in value of the remaining portion of the property resulting from the partial sale. For example, flooding may so disturb an economic farming unit that the remaining acreage may be insufficient to justify the full use of remaining buildings or improvements. In such a case, the settlement would provide compensation for this situation. This is just one example of how the principle could apply. Each transaction will be dealt with on the basis of its own circumstances.

No deals at excessive prices

From time to time, a property owner demands an excessive price for his property – sometimes as much as ten times what the property is worth. Some people feel that Hydro should meet these excessive demands and pay the owner the amount he asks. This is unrealistic for two reasons. In the first place, Hydro has a responsibility to ensure that public money is spent properly and wisely. Secondly, fairness demands that we deal with all property owners on an equal basis. To meet one owner's excessive demand would be unfair to other owners who settled on a reasonable basis.

Expropriation – only when necessary

The Columbia Treaty requires us to complete construction of the three storage dams and associated works in accordance with a rigid time schedule. If we fail to meet the schedule, BC Hydro will have to pay penalties to the United States. That is why it is essential that each part of our work be completed on time.

There may be a few occasions when we are unable to reach a settlement with property owners before the property is required. If this should happen, we will be obliged to commence expropriation proceedings.

Expropriation will take place in one of two ways – under the Water Act or under the BC Hydro and Power Authority Act. In each instance, we are required to serve notice of expropriation on the property owner and state our readiness to pay compensation or state the amount of our offer.

Direct discussions between the property owner and ourselves may continue. If agreement is reached, the purchase is completed and the matter ends there. If no agreement is reached within a reasonable time, the matter is referred to arbitration or to a valuator appointed to determine the value of the property.

We will send full details of expropriation proceedings under the two Acts to any property owner desiring them. If you wish to obtain this information, please write to the Manager, Land Division, BC Hydro, 970 Burrard Street, Vancouver 1.

WHEN IT WILL BE TIME TO MOVE

We realize you want to know when your property will be purchased and when it will be necessary for you to move.

Construction areas first. The land required for construction purposes is now being purchased and we will need possession of it within the next few months. In general, these are the lands on which the storage dams will be built and the immediate areas around the damsites which are required for working space. It is also necessary for us to purchase at this stage some additional land for road relocation which must be completed before construction can begin at the damsites.

Other land required for the Treaty projects is in the areas which will be affected by the reservoirs, but it will not be necessary for us to take possession of this land for some time. In the Arrow reservoir area, this land will be required for storage of water by the spring of 1969; in the Duncan reservoir area by the spring of 1968; and in the Mica reservoir area by the spring of 1973.

Six months in advance of these dates, we will require complete possession of the properties affected. This is necessary to allow time to remove any buildings, fences, etc., remaining in the reservoir areas.

Some owners need to make an early sale. We are giving purchase priority not only to land we require for construction purposes but also to properties whose owners have urgent need to reach an early settlement with us. Property owners in this group who have health, family or business reasons which compel them to move quickly should contact our land representative or information officer in the area or write directly to: Land Division, BC Hydro, 970 Burrard Street, Vancouver 1. We will do our best to ensure that all such property owners receive prompt attention.

Some property owners have suggested that if they ask for early settlement they may receive less favourable treatment than others who are able to remain on their property until the last moment. This is not so. Whether your property is purchased now or later, exactly the same procedures will be employed to appraise its value and to arrive at the price you will be offered for it.

In most instances, we expect to buy your property in the normal way. When the documents transferring title to BC Hydro have been registered in the Land Registry office, you will receive payment for your property. Then, you will vacate the property unless you have decided to retain possession of it under one of the schemes outlined on the following pages.

You may wish to keep your home

In general, we do not want houses on our hands or the direct responsibility for moving them. Also we recognize that homes and other improvements may be worth more to the owners than to us. Because of this, we are prepared to purchase most properties for their fair value less the salvage value of the home and improvements. The owner would then be free to remove the home and other improvements for his own use. This may be done at any time before we need possession of the property. In addition, the owner may, if he wishes, remain on the property during the period between its sale to BC Hydro and the date we require possession, and may continue to live in his home without payment of rent or taxes. (This right applies only to the owner and may not be assigned to any other party without the written consent of BC Hydro – normally this consent will be given if the new occupant gives BC Hydro a written undertaking to abide by the terms of the original agreement.) However, during this period, we will retain the right to use the property other than the home for any purposes connected with the projects, such as clearing operations.

There may in certain cases be some interference with the normal means of access to a property. Risks related to this problem must be assumed by the property owner who remains on his land after we have purchased it. However, this situation is likely to arise only in isolated cases.

Not all homes suitable for moving

The property purchase example on page 185 considers the possibility of moving a house from one location to another. Of course, not all homes are suitable for moving. Firstly, the house itself must be of solid construction and in good condition before moving it can be considered. Secondly, it is reasonable to consider moving homes only if they have a value greater than the cost of moving them. It will be possible to move homes only in areas where house-moving machinery can operate.

We are now undertaking a detailed study of house moving and we will inform you of our findings as soon as they are available.

We may have some homes to sell

During our land purchase activities, we expect to obtain a limited number of good houses which are not wanted by their original owners. In this event, we will consider moving these houses to higher ground and then selling them to other property owners whose homes cannot be moved.

ESTABLISHING NEW COMMUNITIES

Studies are being undertaken of the need to establish new communities to replace communities which will be flooded. These studies will be discussed openly with representatives of the communities affected so that you may have a chance to express your views and wishes with all the facts in front of you.

Compensating communities

We will relocate, replace or otherwise provide compensation for all community properties affected by flooding. These properties will include churches, halls, schools, water systems, parks, cemeteries, etc. Where any existing communities wish to relocate, we will assist them in financing, purchasing, laying-out and servicing their new locations.

Housing for senior citizens

We are now undertaking a study of the needs of older people in the reservoir areas – some of whom may find it difficult to re-establish themselves. In particular we are considering the possibility that special housing projects, designed to meet the needs of older people, might be undertaken in suitable areas in co-operation with the community concerned.

Relocation assistance for farm owners

A number of farms will be affected by reservoir flooding. Owners of these farms who wish to locate new farms can obtain assistance in doing so from the Provincial Department of Agriculture.

Waterfront property

Arrangements have been made with the Provincial Department of Lands, Forests and Water Resources so that owners of waterfront property to be purchased for the Treaty projects may buy Crown-owned water frontage in the area or elsewhere in the province. Where such an owner requests it, we will purchase new waterfront property from the Crown and then convey it to him. The cost of the purchase will then be deducted from the settlement payment made to the owner. It would be up to the owner to select the tract of Crown land he wants, identify it on a plan and then forward the plan to us so we can make application to the Crown.

Possible land development

If it appears necessary to facilitate relocation and resettlement, we may purchase and develop suitable land for sale at reasonable prices to property owners who are being displaced.

CO-OPERATION NEEDED

This booklet has outlined our land purchase procedures, and has provided information on housing and community affairs. This information is of a general nature since we know that each property purchased will be different from all others. In practice, we shall deal with each property owner on an individual basis and shall give due consideration to the age, health, circumstances and desires of each person concerned. Similarly, we shall give detailed attention to the unique problems of each individual community.

It is obvious that careful consideration must be given to each situation to ensure fair treatment for everyone and that our assessment of all pertinent factors must not be rushed.

We have engaged skilled professional people with wide experience in these matters and they are now working on your and our problems. As their studies are completed, their findings will be made known in order that you may consider and discuss these vitally important matters and make your personal and community plans on a solid basis.

Obviously, these things cannot be done in a one-sided way either by you or by us. We at BC Hydro are pledged to give you sympathetic treatment, fair compensation and such reasonable assistance as you may need to relocate yourselves. From you we ask understanding of the magnitude and complexity of our task, and co-operation in achieving it.

2
The 1970 Survey

The survey was directed only to displaced people who had resettled in the Central Arrow Lakes. It was carried out in June 1970 using the questionnaire reproduced on pages 193–5. This questionnaire with a covering letter was distributed through the boxes in the post offices in Burton, Edgewood, and Fauquier, and also to known resettlers in Nakusp, whose names had been obtained through the Nakusp municipal hall.

Forty personal responses were received which were distributed as shown in Table 4. This return represented about ten per cent of all the households displaced in the Central Arrow Lakes and about six per cent of all the households displaced by the project.

CHARACTERISTICS OF RESPONDENTS

Of the forty respondents, seven were wives whose husbands also reported. Twenty males and twenty females replied; there was no discernible difference in their responses. The average age was fifty-three, with a range from thirty-three to eighty-eight.

The average length of residence in the Arrow Lakes was thirty-one years, with a range from ten to sixty years. Of the forty total, seventeen had been born in the region or had moved in by the age of twelve. These 'natives' showed the lowest satisfaction ratio of all, 1.7 to 1.0.

Ten people responded to a follow-up letter sent out two months after the distribution of the original questionnaires. They showed the highest satisfaction ratio of all, 4.6 to 1.0.

More than half of the male respondents were in some way dependent

TABLE 4

	Individual replies	Household replies	Relocated households replying	Percentage of households replying
Burton	10	7	18	39
Edgewood	7	6	27	22
Fauquier	13	11	40	28
Nakusp	10	9	50	18
TOTAL	40	33	135	24

on logging, the rest being in service jobs or retired. The women were all housewives; only four listed other jobs as well.

RESPONSES

Twenty-two of the forty were 'satisfied' (with their compensation), including the respondents who replied 'all right' as well as 'adequate'; eighteen were 'dissatisfied' (that is, compensation described as 'inadequate').

As to fairness, six said the compensation was 'fair'; five said 'don't know'; the rest (twenty-nine) said 'unfair.'

Ten said their appraiser's attitude towards them had been 'helpful'; twenty, 'all right,' and ten 'not helpful.' These responses showed little relationship to the responses on compensation and fairness.

The composition of the responses on the main (largely environmental) questions is shown on Diagram 14 (page 137), which also shows, through the satisfaction ratio, the difference between the 'satisfied' and 'dissatisfied' groups.

The several communities showed quite different satisfaction ratios – Burton, 1.2; Fauquier, 3.3; Edgewood, 1.9; and Nakusp, 2.6. These are, of course, statistically quite unreliable and certain distorting factors are obvious, such as the presence of two deeply embittered expropriated families (yielding three responses) in Burton. My own explanations for them would be as follows: Burton is too small and is possibly still troubled by schisms; Fauquier is happy with the community despite strains and uncertainties; Edgewood is still resentful; the Nakusp group, which contained a high proportion of older people, are quite happy with Nakusp as a familiar and better-serviced community.

It should be said that the satisfaction ratio was based only on responses to questions three (the region), five (communities), and six (houses), and attempts to measure environmental satisfactions generally.

The spontaneous comments were very revealing. They confirmed and strengthened the statistical results; they also revealed factors not set out in the questionnaire, principally the reasons for dissatisfactions.

The fundamental hypothesis was that compensation would be the governing factor. This seems to have been borne out despite the fact that 'unfairness' (a sense of outrage and resentment) was an even stronger factor and one that pervaded all other categories, including the 'satisfied.'

It goes without saying that the survey should have been carried out by interview, as was originally intended. This would have yielded valuable data on the personality, present situation, and 'Columbia experience' of the respondents as well as more of the reasons and feelings behind the responses.

COLUMBIA RIVER: RESETTLEMENT SURVEY

Please check the appropriate word in each case. There is an extra sheet at the back for additional comments.

1 *Personal*

Your name (if you wish) Mr Mrs Miss
Age
Sex
Occupation
How many children are living at home?
They attend: high school secondary school no school
How many years have you lived in the Central Arrow Lakes?
Present community: Edgewood Burton Fauquier Nakusp
Former community

2 *Compensation*

1 / Do you think the compensation you got from BC Hydro was
generous reasonable too little

2 / Do you think that Hydro treated people fairly? (i.e. everyone more or less alike) fairly don't know unfairly

3 / What was the Hydro appraisers' attitude towards you?
helpful all right not helpful

4 / If you have any other comments to make on compensation please write them in the space at the back.

3 *The Nakusp-Edgewood area*

1 / Do you think the Nakusp-Edgewood area is a better or worse place to live as a result of the Columbia Project? better same worse

2 / Please give your reasons

3 / How do you now feel about the Nakusp-Edgewood Area in regard to:
economic outlook? better same worse
roads? better same worse

ferries?	better	same	worse
recreation on the Lakes?	better	same	worse
the appearance of the Lakes?	better	same	worse
work travel on the Lakes?	better	same	worse
schools?	better	same	worse
convenience for travel to places outside the area (e.g. Vernon, Nelson)?	better	same	worse

4 *Your resettlement decision*

1 / Do you think you made a wise decision in staying in the central Arrow Lakes Area? yes not sure no
2 / If not, why not?
3 / Do you think you made a wise decision in settling in your present community? yes not sure no
4 / If not, why not?
5 / If not, where do you wish you had settled?
6 / Why?
7 / (To be answered only by those who made their decision *before* the Needles Bridge was cancelled)
Would you have chosen another community if you had known the bridge was not going to be built? yes not sure no
(To be answered only by those who made their decision *after* the Needles Bridge was cancelled)
Would you have chosen another community if the bridge had gone ahead? yes not sure no
8 / If yes, which community?
Burton Edgewood Fauquier Nakusp

5 *Your present community*

1 / Is your present community a better or worse place to live in than your old one? better same worse
2 / Please give your reasons.
3 / How do you feel about your present community in regard to:

friendliness?	better	same	worse
community activities?	better	same	worse
convenience for work?	better	same	worse
community facilities? (hall, store, post office, etc.)	better	same	worse
community services? (power, telephone, paving, lights, fire equipment)	better	same	worse

property taxes? (i.e. for water, sewer, street lighting, etc., but not for billed utilities such as telephone, power) higher same lower
if property taxes are higher, how serious is this for you? serious tolerable not serious
Do you think you get good value for your property taxes? yes not sure no

6 *Your present house*

1 / Do you live in an older house which was moved from one of the old communities? yes no
2 / If yes to question (1), do you feel that it was moved and relocated in a satisfactory way? yes no
3 / If yes to question (1) why did you choose an old, moved house?
4 / If no to question (1) is your new house better than the previous one? better same worse
5 / Please give your reasons.
6 / Do you own or rent your present house? own rent
7 / Did you own or rent your former house? owned rented
8 / Did you *have* to get a mortgage in order to get your present house? yes no
9 / Did you have a mortgage on your previous house? yes no
10 / Does your present house cost you more per month? (mortgage payments, insurance, maintenance) more same less
11 / If it is more costly, how serious is this for you? serious tolerable not serious
12 / Do you think you get good value for your money? yes not sure no

7 *Hydro performance on resettlement*

1 / How do you think BC Hydro did the resettlement job? well not sure badly
2 / Were the *Columbia Newsletters* helpful in any way? yes not sure no
3 / In your opinion, what aspects of the resettlement job were *badly* handled?
4 / In your opinion, what aspects of the resettlement job were *well* handled?
5 / Have you any additional comments on Hydro's replanning and resettlement program?

References

1 *Arrow Lakes News*, Nakusp

2 BARTON, ALLEN H. *Communities in Disaster*. Garden City, NY: Doubleday, 1969

3 BLAIR, D. GORDON 'The Canadian Expropriation Act' in *The Appraisal Institute Magazine*, Summer 1970

4 BRITISH COLUMBIA *British Columbia Hydro and Power Authority Act, 1964*. Victoria: Statutes of British Columbia

5 CANADA *The Expropriation Act*, Revised Statutes of Canada 1970, chap. 16 (1st Supp.)

6 CANADA Departments of External Affairs and Northern Affairs and National Resources *The Columbia River Treaty and Protocol*. Ottawa: April 1964

7 CANADA House of Commons, *Debates*, Volume VIII, 1964

8 CANADA House of Commons, Standing Committee on External Affairs, *Minutes of Proceedings and Evidence No 2*, April 7, 1964

9 *Castlegar News*

10 CLYNE, J.V. *The Report of the British Columbia Royal Commission on Expropriation, 1961–63*. Victoria, 1964

11 DAVIES, JON GOWER *The Evangelistic Bureaucrat*. London: Tavistock Publications; Toronto: Methuen Publications, 1972

12 DYKE, PRINCE 'Subsistence Production in the Household Economy of Rural Newfoundland' in SKOLNIK, M.L. ed. *Viewpoints on Communities in Crisis*. St John's, Nfld: Institute of Social and Economic Research, Memorial University, 1968

13 INTERNATIONAL COLUMBIA RIVER ENGINEERING BOARD *Water Resources of the Columbia River Basin* (a report to the International Joint Commission). Ottawa: March 1959

14 LOTZ, JIM *The People Outside*. Ottawa: The Canadian Research Centre for Anthropology, Saint Paul University, 1971
15 LOWER MAINLAND REGIONAL PLANNING BOARD *Land for Leisure*. New Westminster: 1961
16 MICHELSON, W.H. *Man and his Urban Environment*. Don Mills: Addison-Wesley, 1970
17 ONTARIO COMMITTEE ON TAXATION *Report*. Toronto: 1967
18 ONTARIO *The Expropriation Act, 1968–1969*, Statutes of Ontario, 1968–69, chap. 36
19 PARR, A.E. 'Psychological Aspects of Urbanology' in *The Journal of Social Issues* XXII, No 4, October 1966
20 SEWELL, W.R.D. 'Environmental Perceptions and Attitudes of Engineers and Public Health Officials' in *Environment and Behaviour* 3, no 1, March 1971
21 SHERMAN, PADDY *Bennett*. Vancouver: Paddy Sherman, 1969
22 STEINBECK, JOHN *Grapes of Wrath*. New York: Viking Press, 1965
23 SWETTENHAM, JOHN *McNaughton, Volume 3, 1944–1966*. Toronto: Ryerson Press, 1969
24 TAYLOR, LORD and CHAVE, SIDNEY *Mental Health and Environment*. London: Longman, 1964
25 *Vancouver Province*
26 WARKENTIN, MARY and ROHN, ROSE *The Story of Renata*. Vancouver: British Columbia Hydro and Power Authority, 1965
27 WATERFIELD, DONALD *Continental Waterboy*. Toronto: Clarke Irwin, 1970
28 WATTS, ALAN *The Wisdom of Insecurity*. New York: Vintage Books, 1951

Index